PRESCHOOL

The **IDEA MAGAZINE FOR TEACHERS**®

MAILBOX®

2010–2011 YEARBOOK

The Education Center, Inc.
Greensboro, North Carolina

The Mailbox® 2010–2011 Preschool Yearbook

Managing Editor, *The Mailbox* Magazine: Kimberly A. Brugger

Editorial Team: Becky S. Andrews, Diane Badden, Kimberley Bruck, Karen A. Brudnak, Pam Crane, Chris Curry, Pierce Foster, Tazmen Hansen, Marsha Heim, Lori Z. Henry, Troy Lawrence, Kitty Lowrance, Brenda Fay, Tina Petersen, Gary Phillips (COVER ARTIST), Mark Rainey, Greg D. Rieves, Hope Rodgers, Rebecca Saunders, Donna K. Teal, Rachael Traylor, Sharon M. Tresino, Zane Williard

ISBN 978-1-61276-138-1
ISSN 1088-5536

©2011 The Education Center, Inc., PO Box 9753, Greensboro, NC 27429-0753

Printed in the United States of America.

The Mailbox® Yearbook
P.O. Box 6189
Harlan, IA 51593-1689

Look for *The Mailbox® 2011–2012 Preschool Yearbook* in the summer of 2012. The Education Center, Inc., is the publisher of *The Mailbox®*, *Teacher's Helper®*, and *Learning®* magazines, as well as other fine products. Look for these wherever quality teacher materials are sold, call 1-866-477-4273, or visit www.themailbox.com.

HPS 232523

Contents

Literacy Units

Math Units

Thematic Units

Arts & Crafts for Little Hands

Arts & Crafts for Little Hands

Process Art

Yarn Designs

This simple process art develops fine-motor skills and results in a lovely piece of artwork! Play a recording of upbeat music. Then use a pair of tongs to dip a length of yarn in a shallow container of paint and "dance" the yarn across a sheet of paper. Continue with other lengths of yarn and colors of paint until a desired effect is achieved.

Joyce Wilson
Fellowship Friends Preschool
Trophy Club, TX

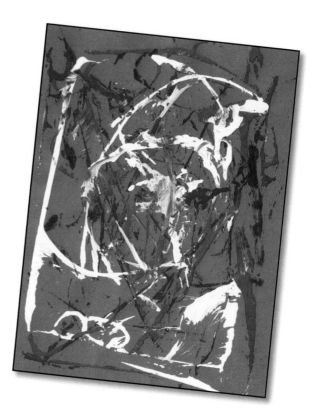

Apple Tree

Draw a tree trunk on a sheet of paper. Dip a leaf-shaped cookie cutter in green paint; then repeatedly press the cookie cutter on the paper above the trunk, adding more paint to the cookie cutter as needed. Repeat the process until the tree has plenty of leaves; then glue red construction paper circles (apples) to the project.

Deborah Garmon
Groton, CT

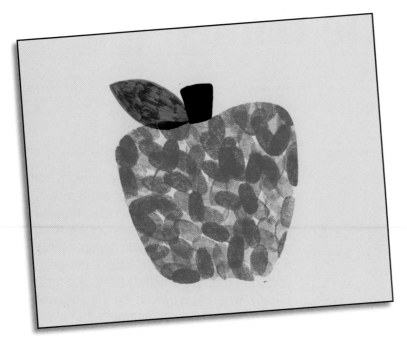

Inside or Out

Tape a stencil to a sheet of white construction paper. Press your fingertips on a stamp pad and then on the paper inside the stencil. Repeat the process to fill in the area. Remove the stencil and use markers to add details to the project. To do a reverse project, attach a shape cutout to a sheet of paper and then fill the paper with fingerprints around the shape.

Janet Boyce
Cokato, MN

Dandy Dinosaur

Make an enlarged construction paper copy of the dinosaur pattern on page 19. Dip a crumpled paper lunch bag in a shallow container of paint and then press it on the dinosaur. Repeat the process until you are satisfied with your work. When the paint is dry, cut out the pattern (with help as needed). Then glue triangle cutouts labeled with the letters of your name to the dinosaur's back.

adapted from an idea by Jennifer Nguyen
SENDCAA Head Start
West Fargo, ND

Arts & Crafts for Little Hands

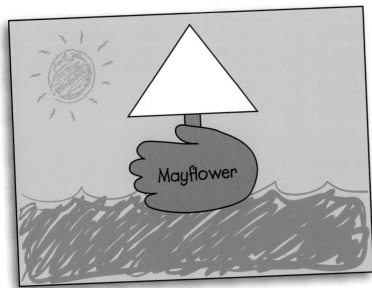

The *Mayflower*

To make this Thanksgiving artwork, paint the palm and fingers of your hand brown. Then, keeping your fingers close together, press your hand horizontally onto a sheet of light blue paper to make a ship. Glue a paper rectangle (mast) above the ship and then glue a triangle (sail) to the mast. Finally, write "Mayflower" on the ship and add additional details as desired.

Jaclyn Bussian
YMCA of Dodge County
Beaver Dam, WI

Fabulous Frank

This one-of-a-kind creature is sure to spice up your Halloween decor! To make one, paint your toes black and the rest of your foot green and then press your foot onto a sheet of construction paper. When the paint is dry, trim around the footprint; then cut features from paper scraps, as shown, and glue them in place.

Terrific Turkey

Cut a V shape in the center of a paper plate and bend it forward to make a beak. Next, paint the beak yellow and the middle of the plate brown. Use a thick brush to paint feathers around the edge of the plate. Glue white construction paper circles above the beak and then attach jumbo wiggle eyes to the circles. Finally, glue a red construction paper wattle to the project as shown.

Jerelyn Tice
Noah's Ark Nursery School
Quarryville, PA

Sweet Scarecrow

To make this adorable craft, color an enlarged copy of the patterns on page 20. Then cut out the patterns. Tear colorful paper scraps and glue them to the shirt and pants. Glue a trimmed headshot photo to the top of the shirt; then glue the hat to the photo. To complete the scarecrow, glue yellow crinkle shreds near the hands and feet so they resemble straw.

Linda and Jodi Remington
Busy Day Child Care
Okemos, MI

Arts & Crafts for Little Hands

Splendid Snowballs!

This process art is fun to create and gives the artist a gross-motor workout! Partially fill the foot of a knee-high stocking with uncooked rice or dry beans; then tie a knot in the stocking just above the filling. To make a print, hold the loose end of the stocking and dip the stuffed end in a shallow container of white paint. Gently bounce the stocking on a sheet of paper to make snowball-like prints. Then sprinkle glitter on the wet paint. For added fun, fill the toe of a stocking with bells instead!

Judy Clark
Vista Colina Child Development Program
Phoenix, AZ

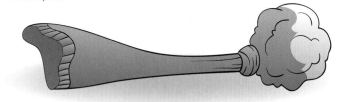

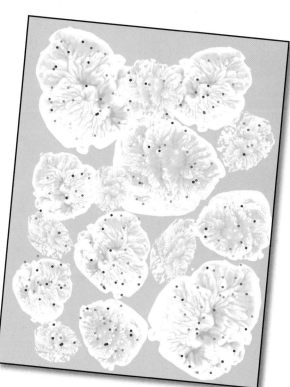

Candy Cane Stripes

This candy cane is simple to make and smells good too! Add peppermint extract to two different-color shallow containers of paint. Then grip a candy cane by the crook and dip the straight edge in the paint. Press the candy cane onto a candy cane cutout to make a stripe. Repeat the process, alternating paint colors until the cutout is covered with peppermint-scented stripes. Sweet! 💻

Joanna Mcfadden
Liberty Christian Preschool
Huntington Beach, CA

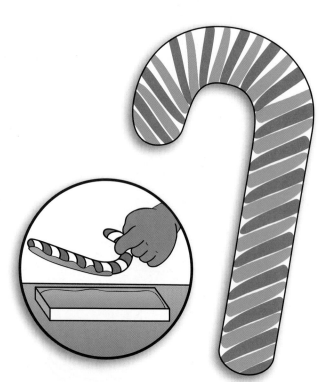

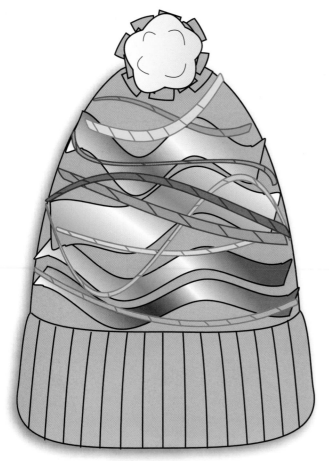

Cozy Winter Hat

Glue lengths of colorful ribbon and yarn to a simple hat cutout (enlarge the pattern on page 108). Then attach a white cotton ball to the top of the hat. When the glue is dry, trim the ends of the ribbon and yarn so they are flush with the cutout. These adorable and vibrant hats look lovely on a bulletin board or display! 🖥

Shining Star!

To make a personalized Star of David ornament, glue three craft sticks together to form a triangle. Make a second triangle and then glue the triangles together as shown. When the glue is dry, paint the star blue and decorate it with glitter. To complete the project, glue a head shot photo to the center of the ornament and add a ribbon for hanging.

Michelle Fernandez
Buckeye Elementary School Lower Campus
Buckeye, AZ

Arts & Crafts for Little Hands

> I'm a little groundhog.
> Small and round.
> I sleep in a burrow
> Deep in the ground.
> I look to find my shadow
> On Groundhog Day
> To tell if spring
> Is on its way!

Groundhog's Burrow

To make this adorable craft, glue a manila burrow-shaped cutout to a sheet of brown paper. Next, dip a potato half in a mixture of brown and gray paint and press it onto the burrow to make a groundhog's body; then draw face and body details. To complete the project, add green Spanish moss and a copy of the poem shown.

Linda Brooks
Safe & Sound Child Development Center
Butler, NJ

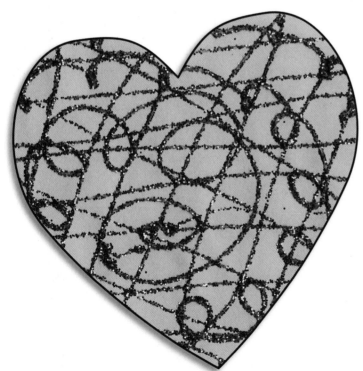

Process Art

Valentine Design

To make this dazzling artwork, place a construction paper heart in a plastic tub. Use a squeeze bottle of glue to drizzle glue designs onto the heart, making sure to gently apply pressure to the bottle while squeezing. When the design is complete, sprinkle glitter onto the wet glue and then shake off any excess glitter. How pretty! 🖥

Janet Boyce
Cokato, MN

Spicy Shamrock

To make a shamrock, glue together three white construction paper hearts and a green paper stem as shown (or enlarge the shamrock on page 48). Place the shamrock on a sheet of waxed paper. Brush a thick layer of green-tinted glue onto the shamrock and then sprinkle green spices—such as oregano, parsley, basil, and mint—onto the glue. When the project is dry, remove it from the waxed paper. These scented shamrocks make a delightfully aromatic display! 🖥️

Suzanne Foote
East Ithaca Preschool
Ithaca, NY

I would eat them when it's sunny.
I would share them with a bunny!
Kari

Green Eggs

Follow up a read-aloud of Dr. Seuss's *Green Eggs and Ham* with this fun project! Add a small amount of green paint to a mixture of shaving cream and white glue. Then spread the mixture over a large fried egg cutout. Press a large green pom-pom (egg yolk) onto the egg. If desired, dictate onto a blank card how you would or would not eat this cuisine and then press the card on the mixture.

Amy Krall
Bible Fellowship Church Preschool
Ventura, CA

Arts & Crafts for Little Hands

Cracked Egg

This process art results in a one-of-a-kind egg! Use a white crayon to draw jagged lines on a white paper egg cutout, making sure to press down hard when drawing. Then paint the entire egg with watercolors. The crayon resists the watercolors, revealing a cracked design! 🖥

adapted from an idea by Diane Dean
Bright Beginnings Christian Center
Goldsboro, NC

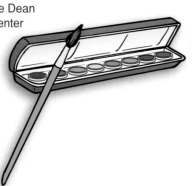

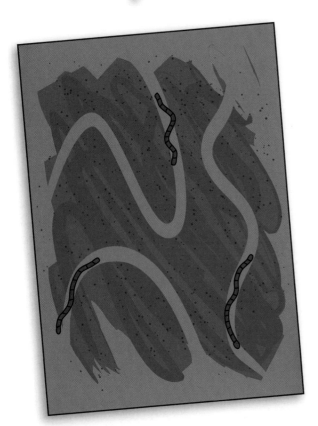

Worm Tunnels

Fingerpaint a sheet of brown construction paper with a mixture of brown paint and flour (soil). When you are finished painting, drag your fingertip through the soil to create worm tunnels. Then glue pieces of brown or pink yarn to the project so they resemble worms crawling through tunnels.

Carissa Dwyer
Discovery Kids Preschool
Maple Plain, MN

Process Art

Paint, Spray, Rotate

This abstract art is fun to make and gives the artist a fine-motor workout! Protect the area you're working at with newspapers or a vinyl tablecloth. Paint a design on a large sheet of paper using a thick layer of tempera paint. Then, while the paint is still wet, spray it with water. (Use a setting on your spray bottle that's between a mist and a squirt.) Rotate the paper and spray the paint again. Repeat until you are satisfied with your work. If desired, mount your masterpiece on contrasting paper. Magnificent!

Danielle Lockwood
Colchester, CT

Editor's Tip:
This is a great activity to do outside on a nice spring day!

Adorable Duck

To make this cute craft, glue (or tape) the ends of a 2" x 9" yellow paper strip to form a circle (body). Repeat with a 1½" x 7" yellow paper strip (head). Then attach the head to the body. Glue two hole-punch dots (eyes), an orange paper triangle (beak), and a yellow feather (tail) in place. Then glue the resulting duck to a pond-shaped cutout.

Emily Gary
St. Anne's Child Care Center and Preschool
New Iberia, LA

Arts & Crafts for Little Hands

Interesting Insects

Reuse old magazines to make these unique insects! Cut from colorful magazine pages three shapes to represent the head, thorax, and abdomen. Also cut six legs and two antennae. Glue the cutouts to a sheet of green construction paper as shown.

Mary Ann Sarmiento
Young Child Academy
Seattle, WA

 **Super Sand Castle**

Draw a castle on a sheet of cardboard. Trace the castle with white glue and then sprinkle sand on the glue. When the glue is dry, shake the excess sand from the cardboard. What a fun and simple summer project!

Beth Knuth
St. Philips Preschool
Rudolph, WI

The Perfect Pop

This adorable keepsake is just perfect for Father's Day! Tape two jumbo craft sticks to a large, white tagboard ice pop cutout. Paint the front of the ice pop with tinted glue; then press a signed copy of the poem shown onto the wet glue. To complete the craft, sprinkle sugar-free powdered drink mix around the poem. The lucky recipient is sure to feel special when he receives this sweet gift! 🖥️

Ellen Butts
Making Friends Preschool
Truro, Nova Scotia, Canada

Process Art

A Lawn Full of Dandelions

Use Mother Nature to help create this lovely dandelion artwork! Gather a few dandelions. Dip a dandelion in yellow paint and gently press it on a sheet of paper several times, adding more paint to the flower as needed. Pull several cotton balls to give them an uneven look. Then glue the cotton balls to the page so they resemble dandelions gone to seed.

Amber Dingman, Play 'n' Learn Family Child Care and
    Preschool, Sterling, MI
Jane Mandia, Little Friends Preschool, Marlboro, NY

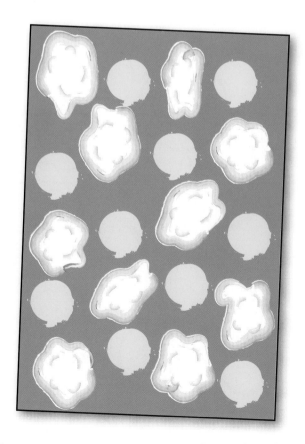

Fireworks Fountain

This three-dimensional art makes a fabulous Fourth of July centerpiece. Paint a small cardboard tube and a five-inch cardboard square with patriotic colors of paint. When the paint is dry, attach craft items—such as curly ribbon, glitter pipe cleaners, and tinsel—to one end of the tube to represent fireworks. Then glue the opposite end of the tube to the square.

Keely Saunders
Bonney Lake ECEAP
Bonney Lake, WA

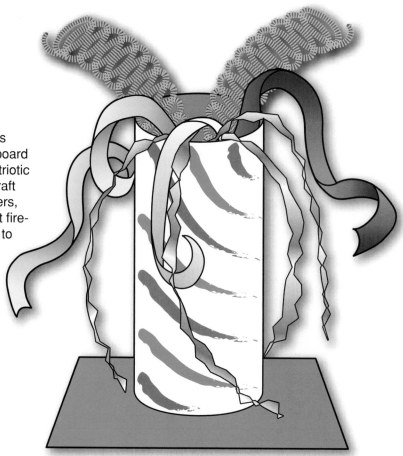

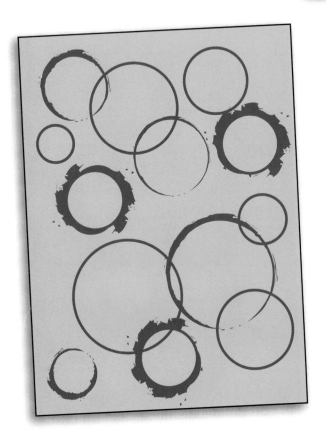

Poppin' Bubbles!

Mix separate containers of paint with generous amounts of dish soap. Place a variety of small, circular cups and containers nearby. A child dips the rim of the cup into the mixture and then makes prints on a sheet of paper. On occasion, the dish soap causes bubbles that pop on the paper. What a fun piece of process art!

Amber Dingman
Play 'n' Learn Family Child Care and Preschool
Sterling, MI

TEC41050

BUSY HANDS

Busy Hands

Fine-Motor Explorations for the Season

PERFECT PATTERN

Attach different-colored sticky notes to a tabletop to begin an *AB* pattern. Provide a supply of corresponding colored sticky notes. A student copies and extends the pattern by attaching sticky notes to the table below the pattern.

Beth Deki
Carebear Preschool
Chandler, AZ

SIMPLE SEASONAL MATS

Provide a supply of seasonal vinyl placemats along with colorful spring-style clothespins. A youngster clips clothespins to the seasonal mat. Refresh this fine-motor area by changing the mats for each season.

Romy Deegan
Newman Catholic Schools at St. Mark Parish
Preschool
Wausau, WI

PEEKABOO!

Attach photos of students to a table or wall; then place a sticky note over each photo. A youngster chooses a sticky note and says, "Peekaboo! Who are you?" Then she lifts the note and identifies the classmate in the picture.

Tricia Brown, Bowling Green, KY

SCHOOL TOOLS

Trace a variety of school-related items—such as a pair of scissors, a ruler, a glue bottle, a roll of tape, and a block—onto a large sheet of paper. Store the items in a container. A student removes each item from the container and places it atop the appropriate outline.

Tricia Brown

KIDDIE BANK

Cover two or three plastic lidded containers with different-colored paper and cut a slit in each lid so it resembles a coin bank. Provide a supply of corresponding colored tagboard circles (coins) for each container. A child takes a coin from the collection and slides it through the slit in the matching bank.

Marie E. Cecchini, West Dundee, IL

Busy Hands

Fine-Motor Explorations for the Season

PUMPKIN PATCH!

Decorate a length of green bulletin board paper with vines and leaves. If desired, add some not-so-scary critters. Then laminate the bulletin board paper and place it at a table along with orange play dough. Encourage youngsters to make large and small pumpkins and place them in the patch. 💻

MONSTER HAIR

Gather lengths of green and purple yarn and place the lengths in a tub along with several pairs of scissors. Have students cut the yarn into small pieces. After each child has an opportunity to give her fine-motor skills a workout, encourage youngsters to draw some friendly monsters and then use the yarn pieces for hair!

SPECTACULAR SPIDERS

Draw vertical lines (spiderweb threads) on a large sheet of paper. Provide stamp pads and markers. A child presses his fingertip on a stamp pad and then onto the end of a thread to make a spider's body. Then he draws eight legs to complete the spider. Youngsters continue until every thread has a spider.

COLORFUL FALL COLLAGE

Attach a sheet of light-colored bulletin board paper to a tabletop. Provide paint-brushes, a collection of leaves, and fall-colored paints. Each student paints a section of the paper and then glues leaves to the paint.

Becky Owen, North Spencer Head Start Dale, IN

GLUE

PUMPKIN SNIP

Provide a container of orange square cutouts, scissors, and a marker or crayon. Youngsters cut the corners from the squares to make pumpkins. Then they draw a face on each pumpkin to make a jack-o'-lantern. If desired, have each student attach his jack-o'-lanterns above a fence displayed on a wall. Too cute!

Mary Ellen Moore, Miller Elementary, Canton, MI

See page 35 for a **reproducible activity** that targets fine-motor skills.

Busy Hands

Fine-Motor Explorations for the Season

HANDMADE GIFT WRAP

Place at a table a cardboard box (gift), holiday-related gift wrap scraps, and bows. Each youngster visits the table and cuts or tears the paper scraps and glues the scraps to the gift. Then students decorate the gift with bows.

Mary Robles
Little Acorns Preschool
Milwaukie, OR

SORTING SNOWBALLS

Fill a tub with medium and large white pompoms (snowballs) and provide a pair of tongs. Also attach snowball cutouts to two containers as shown. Explain that the snowballs are very cold and so students must use tongs to pick them up and sort them into the containers.

Heather Cohen
Sunlight Christian Academy
Port St. Lucie, FL

STAINED GLASS SNOWFLAKE

Cut out an oversize snowflake. Press the snowflake onto the sticky side of a sheet of clear self-adhesive paper. Provide colorful tissue paper scraps and scissors. Students cut or tear the scraps and press them onto the sticky paper in the snowflake design. When the project is complete, trim any excess adhesive paper from the snowflake's edges. Then flip the snowflake over and display it on a wall.

Kelii Krueger, New Adventure Learning Center, Brevard, NC

ANIMALS IN WINTER

Fill your sensory table with small evergreen branches, pine needles, pinecones, medium-size rocks, small red pom-poms (berries), cotton batting (snow), and plastic forest animals. Youngsters visit the table and manipulate the props to engage in pretend winter animal play.

Kimberly Kratochvil
Mountainland Head Start
Provo, UT

CANDY CANE GOLF

Cut a large hole in a gift-wrapped box and place the box on the floor. A child uses a large decorative candy cane (the kind used for an outdoor holiday display) to tap a ball into the box!

Holly Verhoef
Hackmann Early Childhood & Family Education Center
St. Charles, MO

Busy Hands

Fine-Motor Explorations for the Season

HEART RUBBINGS

Attach heart-shaped paper doilies to a tabletop. Provide newsprint paper and unwrapped crayons. A child places a sheet of paper atop a doily. Then she rubs the side of a crayon over the paper. She continues to make rubbings until the paper is filled with lacy hearts.

COLORFUL RAINBOW

Place on the floor a large rainbow cutout like the one shown. A child finds items in the room that correspond to each color of the rainbow. Then he places each item on the appropriate arc.

SUPERSIZE LION

Place a large lion face drawing at a table. Provide a supply of yellow, orange, and brown paper strips; an unsharpened pencil; and glue. A student wraps a strip around the pencil and then carefully slides the pencil out. Then she glues the resulting curly strip to the lion. Youngsters continue until the lion has a full curly mane. 🖳

FIELD OF SHAMROCKS

Attach a sheet of light-color bulletin board paper to tabletop. Set out green stamp pads and markers. A child presses a fingertip on the stamp pad and then on the paper three times to make a cluster of prints (shamrock). Then he draws a stem on each shamrock. Students continue the activity to create a field of shamrocks.

FIND THE LEPRECHAUNS

Hide around the classroom several leprechaun cutouts (patterns on page 109). Also provide a black plastic pot. A child searches for the leprechauns and places each one she finds in the pot. After she has collected all the leprechauns, she does an Irish jig! What fun! 🖳

See page 37 for a **reproducible activity** that targets fine-motor skills.

Busy Hands

Fine-Motor Explorations for the Season

ideas contributed by Roxanne LaBell Dearman
Western NC Early Intervention Program for Children Who Are Deaf or Hard of Hearing, Charlotte, NC

PLANTING BULBS

Partially fill a large plastic tub (or your sand table) with potting soil. Provide medium or large flower bulbs, a small plastic shovel, and an empty watering can. A child digs a hole in the soil, places a bulb in the hole, and then covers it with dirt. He continues until all the bulbs are planted; then he pretends to water his makeshift garden.

FIND THE EGGS!

Gather several old children's magazines and make Easter egg cutouts trimmed from sticky notes. (Make sure each egg has some stickiness!) Then attach the Easter egg cutouts on several pages of the magazines. Place the magazines in a center along with a sheet of paper. Youngsters search through the magazines. Whenever they find an egg, they remove it and attach it to the paper.

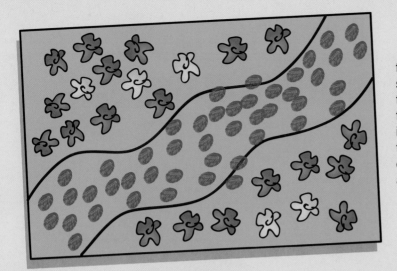

RABBIT TRACKS

Tape green bulletin board paper to a tabletop; then draw a path across the paper. Provide a shallow container of brown paint along with tissue paper squares (for making grass and flowers) and glue. Each child dips two fingertips in the paint and then "hops" them along the path to make bunny pawprints. Then youngsters glue crumpled tissue paper around the path to create a meadow.

IT'S RAINING!

Poke holes in several margarine tubs, varying the number and size of the holes in each tub; then float them in your water table. A youngster scoops up water with a tub and then watches the faux raindrops fall. She continues with other tubs, observing and comparing the rainfalls. For added fun, provide a child-size raincoat and hat!

See page 38 for a **reproducible activity** that targets fine-motor skills.

EARTH-FRIENDLY LACING

To celebrate Earth Day, reuse recyclable items! Remove the front panel from several different food boxes. Punch holes along the edges of the panel; then attach a length of ribbon or yarn to a hole. A student laces the ribbon around the panel.

Tracy Moore,
Bright Beginnings Methodist Preschool,
Warwick, NY

Fine-Motor Explorations for the Season

ideas contributed by Tricia Kylene Brown, Bowling Green, KY

FROZEN TREATS

Fill a cooler with small sections cut from foam pool noodles. Also provide several paint stirring sticks. A child slides noodle sections onto a stick to create a unique frozen treat. What fun!

NO-SAND SAND CASTLES!

Gather a collection of seashells and plastic ocean animals. Place the props in your block center. A child uses the blocks to build a sand castle and decorates it with seashells. Then she uses the ocean animals to engage in pretend play!

SPARKLING SUNSHINE

Place at a table a large poster board sun cutout. Provide yellow-tinted pasta and a shallow container of glue. Each youngster dips pasta in the glue and then attaches the pasta to the sun. When the project is complete, drizzle glue onto the sun and shake gold glitter over the glue.

FRESHLY SQUEEZED LEMONADE

Transform your sensory table into a lemonade stand. Provide yellow play dough, disposable cups, and a plastic bowl and pitcher. A student rolls play dough into lemon shapes and puts them in the bowl. After making several lemons, she squeezes them over the pitcher and then pretends to pour herself a cup of freshly squeezed lemonade.

TAKING A TRIP

Provide a suitcase along with an assortment of summer clothing and summer-related items, such as sunglasses and flip-flops. A youngster unfastens the suitcase and packs it with clothing and other desired items. Then he refastens the suitcase and pretends he's taking a trip. When he is finished, he undoes the fastener and unpacks the suitcase.

Sweet Snack

©The Mailbox® · TEC41050 · Aug./Sept. 2010

Note to the teacher: Have each child color a copy of this page (leaving the fruit of each apple uncolored). Then have her crumple and glue red, yellow, or green tissue paper squares to the apples.

Colorful Cornucopia!

©The Mailbox® • TEC41051 • Oct./Nov. 2010

Note to the teacher: Have each child color the page as desired. Then have her crumple squares of tissue paper, dip them in a shallow pan of glue, and press them on the cornucopia.

Giant Snowball!

Note to the teacher: Have each child trace the snowball on a copy of this page. Then encourage him to tear white facial tissue and glue it to the snowball.

Peeking at a Pot o' Gold

©The Mailbox® • TEC41053 • Feb./Mar. 2011

Note to the teacher: Have each child trace the lines on a copy of this page. Then have her color the page. If desired, invite her to glue torn cotton balls on the cloud and gold glitter on the coins.

High in the Sky!

Note to the teacher: Have each child trace the kite and then color the page. Then have her tear cotton balls and glue them to the cloud. To complete the page, have her glue a length of ribbon to the bottom of the kite so the resulting tail dangles off the page.

CIRCLE TIME

Circle Time

Where Is Worm?

Give each student a construction paper apple. Have him hold his apple in one hand. Then lead youngsters in performing the action song shown, checking to see that they are wiggling their fingers *above* their apples. Repeat the song, replacing the underlined word with other positional words, such as *beside, below, behind, in front of,* and *on.* 🖥

(sung to the tune of "Where Is Thumbkin?")

Where is Worm? Where is Worm?	*Hide hand without the apple behind back.*
Here I am! Here I am!	*Reveal hand and wiggle index finger.*
I'm [above] the apple.	*Wiggle finger [above] the apple.*
I'm [above] the apple.	*Wiggle finger [above] the apple.*
Munch, munch, crunch!	*Move hand so it resembles a mouth.*
Munch, munch, crunch!	*Move hand so it resembles a mouth.*

Chris Stacy
Arrowood Preschool
Xenia, OH

Jump, class, jump!

Jump, Class, Jump!

Write on separate cards the names of several gross-motor movements, such as *jump, hop, stomp, march,* and *crawl.* Display a card and read the word aloud. Then lead youngsters in chanting, "[Jump], class, [jump]!" while you encourage youngsters to perform the named movement. After a few moments, direct students to stop. Then continue in the same way with each remaining card.

Debra Nichols, Jack and Jill Early Learning Center
Norcross, GA

jump

Hi, Brian!

Introduce Yourself

Walk in a circle with your youngsters as you lead them in singing a song or reciting a popular rhyme. When the song or rhyme is finished, prompt students to stand still. Then gesture to the child on your right and say, "This is my friend [child's name]." Encourage the other youngsters to say, "Hi, [child's name]!" Then prompt the named child to gesture to the classmate on his right and repeat the process. Continue in the same way until each child has been introduced. If desired, guide youngsters to stand next to new individuals and play another round of this fun game!

Carole Watkins
Crown Point, IN

Off to School

Store in a backpack several cards labeled with directions such as "Count to ten" and "Sing 'The Alphabet Song.'" Invite a student to wear the backpack and walk around the circle as you lead the rest of the group in singing the song shown. At the end of the song, have the student hand the backpack to the nearest classmate. That child removes a card from the backpack and gives it to you to read aloud. Then he leads the group in completing the directions. He then wears the backpack for the next round of the activity.

Count to ten.

(sung to the tune of "The Muffin Man")

[Child's name] is off to school,
Is off to school, is off to school.
[Child's name] is off to school.
[Her] backpack's on [her] back.

Circle Time

Color Sticks

Give each child a jumbo craft stick with a different-colored sticky dot on each end. To begin, sing the first verse of the song shown. After singing the last line, prompt students who have the named color to wave that end of the stick in the air as you lead them in singing the last verse. Repeat the activity two or three times; then have students exchange sticks. 🖥

(sung to the tune of "The Muffin Man")

If you have the color [red],
The color [red], the color [red],
If you have the color [red],
Please wave it in the air.

Yes, I have the color [red],
The color [red], the color [red].
Yes, I have the color [red].
It's waving in the air.

Beth Lemke
Highland Family Center Head Start
Columbia Heights, MN

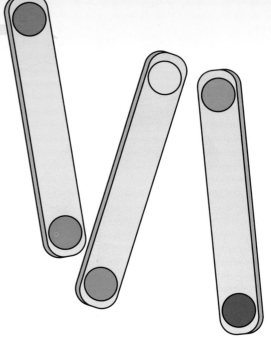

Jumbo Jack-in-the-Box

To prepare, tie a knot in one end of a tube sock (crank); then pull the loose end through a hole in the side of a child-size box. To play, have a child leave the group and close his eyes. Quietly signal a classmate to squat inside the box; then close the flaps above her. Have the first child return to the group and guess who is in the box. When the classmate is guessed or an appropriate number of guesses are made, have the group count aloud as the child turns the crank. On the count of three, the classmate pops out of the box!

Hollie O'Connor, 1st Presbyterian Preschool, Columbus, IN

Making a Scarecrow

Gather two garden gloves, two boots, a straw hat, and an oversize shirt. Ask a volunteer to stand and pretend to be a scarecrow. Then lead students in singing the first verse of the song shown. Have a child pick the shirt from the other accessories. Then help the scarecrow put on the shirt. Continue singing the song until the scarecrow is dressed in the remaining clothes. Then lead youngsters in singing the final verse. At the end of the song, prompt the scarecrow to make his scariest face! 💻

(sung to the tune of "Shoo Fly")

Scarecrow, what should you wear?
Scarecrow, what should you wear?
Scarecrow, what should you wear?
Wear [a shirt], I do declare!

Continue with the following: *a hat, some boots, some gloves*

Scarecrow, what should you do?
Scarecrow, what should you do?
Scarecrow, what should you do?
Scare those crows away from you!

Pumpkin Picking

Set out two containers labeled as shown. Scatter several large and small pumpkin cutouts nearby so the area resembles a pumpkin patch. (See page 268 for pumpkin patterns and enlarge them as needed.) Have youngsters walk in a circle around the pumpkin patch as you sing the song shown. At the end of the song, instruct the designated child to pick a pumpkin and hold it in the air. Ask students to identify the pumpkin as big or small. Then have the child put the pumpkin in the appropriate container. Repeat the activity until each pumpkin has been picked. 💻

(sung to the tune of "Pop! Goes the Weasel")

All around the pumpkin patch
Are pumpkins big and small.
[Lucus], pick the one you like best.
Show it to all!

Thumbs-Up, Thumbs-Down

Teach and reinforce appropriate social skills with this simple idea! Program paper strips with statements such as "Use your words when you get angry" and "Leave trash on the table when you finish eating," and store them in a container. To begin, remove a strip from the container and read it aloud. Prompt each youngster to give a thumbs-up if he agrees with the statement or a thumbs-down if he disagrees; then encourage students to explain their responses. After discussing the appropriate response, continue with other strips. 🖥

Joy Smith, Mother Goose Daycare and Preschool, Muncie, IN

Which House?

Cut out colorful copies of the house pattern on page 54. Also cut out a copy of the gingerbread man pattern on page 54. Mount the houses to a board or wall so they can be lifted like a flap. Have little ones close their eyes while you hide the gingerbread man beneath a house using Sticky-Tac adhesive or tape. Instruct students to open their eyes, and then lead them in reciting the chant shown. Invite youngsters to take turns choosing a house, identifying the color, and lifting it to look for the gingerbread man. When the gingerbread man is found, have children say, "You can't hide from us, Gingerbread Man!" 🖥

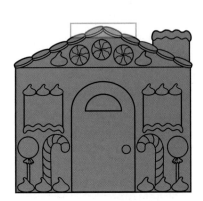

Gingerbread Man,
Quiet as a mouse,
Where are you hiding—
In which little house?

Kim Segerson
YMCA Discovery Center
West Bend, WI

What Should You Wear?

Gather several articles of winter wear, such as a pair of mittens, a hat, a scarf, a jacket, and boots. Also gather items you would wear in the summer, such as a bathing suit, shorts, and sandals. Choose an item and hold it in the air as you sing the first verse of the song shown. Then have students respond by singing the second verse and inserting the appropriate words. Repeat the activity with different items. 🖥

(sung to the tune of "For He's a Jolly Good Fellow")

Do you think you should wear [sandals],
Do you think you should wear [sandals],
Do you think you should wear [sandals]
When it is cold outside?

Oh, [yes/no], we [should/shouldn't] wear [sandals]!
Oh, [yes/no], we [should/shouldn't] wear [sandals]!
Oh, [yes/no], we [should/shouldn't] wear [sandals]
When it is cold outside!

Freeze and Melt

Youngsters learn to follow visual cues with this fun activity! Obtain a die-cut snowflake and sun. Have little ones pretend to be ice-skating snowmen. After a few moments, hold the snowflake in the air, prompting the snowmen to freeze in place. Then lower the snowflake, signaling them to skate again. After a few moments, hold the sun in the air, prompting the snowmen to melt to the ground. Repeat the activity several times. 🖥

Diane L. Flohr
Orchard Trails Elementary
Kent City, MI

Circle Time

Blowing Kisses

Youngsters practice number identification with this fun activity! Place numbered heart cutouts in a gift bag. To begin, take a heart from the bag and show it to the group. Have students identify the number. Then lead them in singing the song shown. (If a one is drawn, alter the last line of the song appropriately.) At the end of the song, encourage little ones to blow that many kisses. Continue with each remaining heart. 💻

(sung to the tune of "The Farmer in the Dell")

I know that number's name.
I bet you know it too!
It is the number [five].
I'll blow kisses to you!

adapted from an idea by Jeri Gardner
Reid Memorial Preschool
Augusta, GA

Who Took the Gold?

Invite a child (leprechaun) to sit in a chair facing away from the group. Provide a holiday-related hat for the leprechaun to wear, if desired. Place a yellow tagboard circle (gold coin) under the chair. To play, secretly choose a child to be the gold snatcher. Signal him to quietly take the coin and hide it from view as you lead the rest of the group in saying the chant shown. At the end of the chant, have the leprechaun face the group. Then help her guess who took her gold. After the classmate is revealed, he becomes the leprechaun and a new gold snatcher is chosen.

Leprechaun, leprechaun,
Someone took your gold!
Who do you think
Would be so bold?

Tanya Tschombor
Childtime Learning Center
Brea, CA

Special Shamrocks

Make two sets of shamrock cutouts (pattern on page 48) labeled with matching letters. Arrange one set of shamrocks faceup on the floor and stack the other set near you. Recite the rhyme shown. At the appropriate time during the rhyme, take a shamrock from the stack and hold it in the air, prompting students to say the letter's name. At the end of the rhyme, invite a volunteer to find a shamrock with the matching letter. When a match is found, set the pair of shamrocks aside. Continue until all the shamrocks are matched. 🖥

I have a special shamrock.
It shows the letter [*B*].
Search the shamrocks on the floor
And find one more for me!

adapted from an idea by Marie E. Cecchini
West Dundee, IL

Follow the Map!

Before youngsters arrive, hide a teddy bear somewhere in the classroom. Also make sure there is a clear path around the perimeter of your classroom. To begin, tell little ones there is a bear hidden in the room and that they are going to use a map to find it! Then give each child a copy of page 55 and keep one for yourself. Review the map with students and have youngsters stand. Have a student name the first site they will "walk through" on the map. Then lead youngsters a few feet from the circle-time area and prompt them to pantomime climbing mountains. Continue with each remaining imaginary landscape, guiding youngsters around the room until they reach the bear!

Shelley Hoster
Jack & Jill Early Learning Center
Norcross, GA

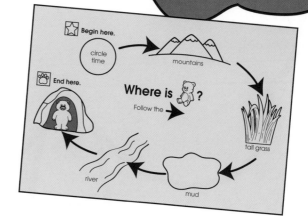

Circle Time

Hop?

With this idea, little ones develop listening and critical-thinking skills while getting a gross-motor workout! Invite youngsters to hop around as you name several things that hop, such as a bunny, a kangaroo, a grasshopper, and a frog. Then name something that does not hop, such as a rock or a cookie, prompting students to stop hopping and sit on the floor. Continue the activity with other gross-motor movements, such as crawling, swimming, and flying.

Keely Saunders
Bonney Lake Early Childhood Education and Assistance Program
Bonney Lake, WA

Shamrock Pattern
Use with "Spicy Shamrock" on page 13, "Special Shamrocks" on page 47, and "Lots o' Lucky Preschoolers!" on page 64.

TEC41053

Circle Time

/a/ for [apple].
/a/, /a/, /a/.

Rhythmic Sounds

Here's a no-prep activity that reinforces beginning sounds! To begin, invite youngsters to name a word that begins with /a/. After confirming the word begins with /a/, lead students in rhythmically reciting the chant shown. At the end of the second line, prompt youngsters to name a word that begins with /b/. Recite the chant again, inserting the /b/ sound and the word that youngsters have chosen. Continue in the same manner with several letters.

/a/ for [apple]. /a/, /a/, /a/.
/a/ for [apple]. /a/, /a/, /a/.

Karla Broad, Our Savior Preschool
Naples, FL

Where's the Bee?

Challenge youngsters' observation skills with this fun idea! Obtain two hexagonal pattern blocks. Attach a bee sticker to one block; then place it facedown on a beehive cutout with the remaining block, making sure students see where the programmed block is placed. Have youngsters watch carefully as you move the blocks around. Then ask a volunteer to pick the block that has the bee. If he is correct, youngsters buzz around the room like bees. If he is not, repeat the activity with a different volunteer. To increase the challenge, add another block! 🖥

Jennie Jensen
North Cedar Elementary
Lowden, IA

Circle Time

Swat!

Youngsters will be eager to play this letter-identification game! Cut out copies of the bug cards on page 56 and program each one with a letter. Attach the bugs to a wall in your circle-time area. Give a child a rolled-up newspaper (bug swatter). Then lead the group in reciting the rhyme shown. At the end of the rhyme, display a letter card that matches a letter on one of the bugs and say the letter's name. Then the child with the swatter swats the corresponding bug!

See the "alpha-bugs"
Sitting on the wall.
Swat the bug
With the letter I call!

Julie Vickery, International Children's Language School
Goam-dong, Yangju-si, Gyeonggi-do, South Korea

Feeding Time

Place an oversized brown circle (bird nest) on the floor. Have half the group (baby birds) sit in the center of the nest and the remaining students (adult birds) sit around the edge. Scatter lengths of yarn (worms) some distance from the nest. Turn down the lights and have all the birds pretend to be asleep. After a few moments, turn up the lights, signaling the baby birds to wake up and chirp to let the adults know they are hungry. Then prompt each of the adult birds to "fly" away and bring back a worm for one of the babies. After each baby bird is fed, have youngsters switch roles. What a fun way to investigate living things!

Mary Chidester
Hadnot Point Child Development Center
Jacksonville, NC

Rain Dance

Program each of several raindrop cutouts with a gross-motor movement. Place the raindrops in a bag with a paper cloud attached. Also obtain an instrument—such as a rain stick, a maraca, or a tambourine—to simulate rain sounds. Invite a student to take a raindrop from the bag for you to read aloud. Then play the instrument, encouraging youngsters to perform the directions at a pace that corresponds to the tempo of the rain. After a few moments, stop the rain and have students stand still. Continue with each remaining raindrop. 💻

Shelli Hurlocker
Busy Bees Christian Preschool
Kokomo, IN

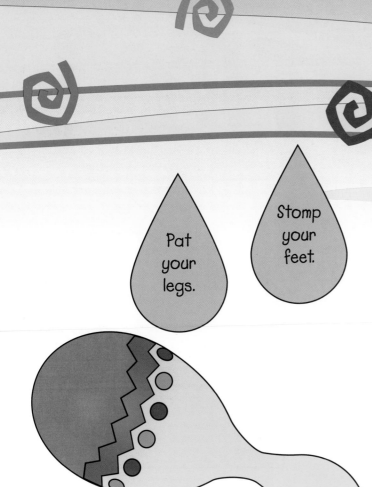

Pat your legs.

Stomp your feet.

From Caterpillar to Butterfly

After youngsters are familiar with the life cycle of a butterfly, lead them in singing the song shown. Next, invite a volunteer to act out the song. Provide her with a green paper leaf and a small blanket (chrysalis) to wrap herself in. Then lead youngsters in singing the song again. As the group sings, prompt the child to act out crawling like a caterpillar, munching on the leaf, forming a chrysalis, and then flying away as a beautiful butterfly. Invite other students to act out the song; then put the props in a center for independent use. 💻

(sung to the tune of "Clementine")

Caterpillar, caterpillar,
Eating leaves and crawling round;
You are big and so you make a
Chrysalis far off the ground.

Caterpillar, caterpillar,
You are such a big surprise.
You have wings and you're so lovely!
Oh, I can't believe my eyes.

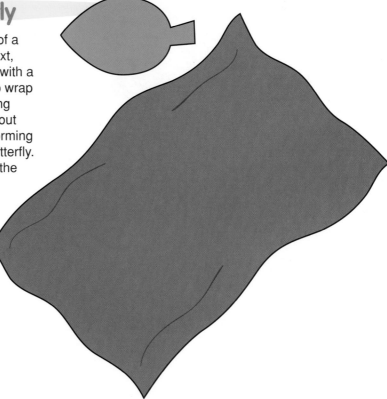

Circle Time

Make a Wish

Place a box (wishing well) in the center of the circle and provide each child with a craft foam coin. Briefly discuss what a wish is and then ask volunteers to tell something they've wished for and if their wishes came true. Next, have little ones walk around the wishing well as you lead them in singing the song shown. At the end of the song, signal youngsters to stand still. Then have the designated child make a wish and toss her coin into the well. Continue until each child has had a turn to make a wish.

(sung to the tune of "The Mulberry Bush")

Here we go round the wishing well,
The wishing well, the wishing well.
Here we go round the wishing well.
[Child's name], make a wish!

Mary Ann Craven, Fallbrook United Methodist School, Fallbrook, CA

Milk Shake Shimmy

Youngsters practice counting and get a gross-motor workout with this fun idea. Obtain a large lidded tumbler (milk shake cup) and a pair of medium-size dice. Place the dice in the cup and snap on the lid. Invite a child to dance around and shake the cup as you lead the rest of the group in the chant shown. At the end of the chant, have the youngster remove the lid and spill the dice. Then have her count the number of dots on top of the dice aloud. Replace the dice and repeat the activity.

Shake it up; shake it up! Yes sirree!
Make a tasty milk shake for you and me!

Rebecca Stalvey, Benson, NC

Ants in Your Pants!

To prepare, program a supply of cards with desired symbols, such as letters, numbers, or shapes. Draw a large ant on a few additional cards. Mix the cards and stack them facedown. To play, take a card from the stack and show it to the group. If the card shows a symbol, have youngsters identify it. If the card shows an ant, prompt little ones to say, "Ants in your pants!" and then wiggle around pretending they have ants in their pants. Set the card aside and repeat the activity.

Jenny Walser
Memories and Milestones
New Prague, MN

Share It or Not?

Place in a basket a collection of items that students can share—such as a doll, a building block, a toy car, and a marker—along with items they should not share, such as a toothbrush, an adhesive bandage, a plastic water bottle, and a lollipop. Elicit a short discussion about how germs get passed from one person to another, and then lead youngsters in singing the song shown. At the end of the song, invite a volunteer to take an item from the basket and identify it. Ask him to tell if the item should or should not be shared and explain why. Repeat the activity with each remaining item.

(sung to the tune of "Clementine")

There are some things
That we can share.
There are some things
That we can't.

There are some things
That we can share.
There are some things
That we can't.

Lindsey Bachman, YWCA Early Learning Center, Duluth, MN

Gingerbread Man and House Patterns
Use with "Which House?" on page 44 and "Where's the Gingerbread Man?" on page 78.

TEC41052

TEC41052

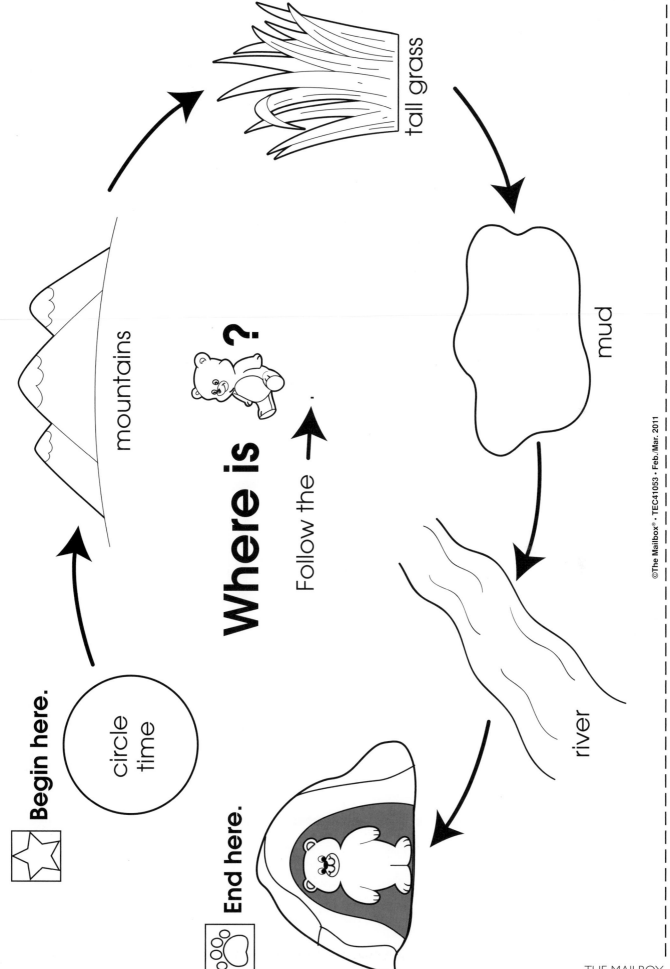

tall grass

mountains

mud

Where is ?

Follow the .

river

Begin here.

circle time

End here.

Note to the teacher: Use with "Follow the Map!" on page 47.

Bug Cards
Use with "Swat!" on page 50. 🖥️

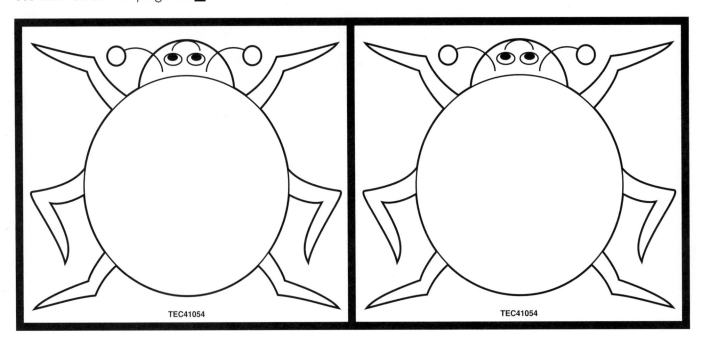

TEC41054

TEC41054

Truck Pattern
Use with "After You Read" on page 157.

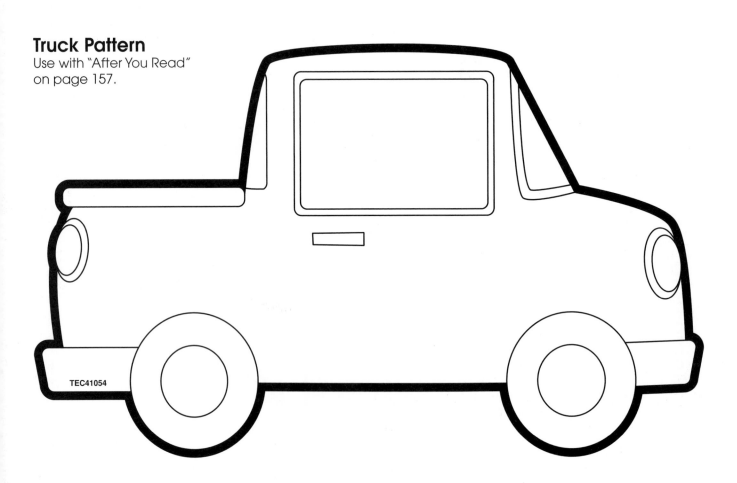

TEC41054

Classroom Displays

CLASSROOM DISPLAYS

Wrap a large box with plain paper (gift). Invite youngsters to decorate the gift using stickers or craft materials appropriate for the month. Label each of 12 balloon cutouts with a different month; then record the appropriate names and birthdates on each balloon. Attach the gift and balloons to a wall or board with the title shown. Then, each month, have students redecorate the box using materials that correspond to that month. 🖥

June Bass, Gatewood, Eatonton, GA

Inspire young weather watchers with this interactive display! Invite youngsters to decorate bulletin board paper trimmed so it resembles curtains. Attach the curtains to a board or wall with the title shown. Nearby, place weather-related cutouts for students to post on the display after checking the day's weather. 🖥

Jennifer Smith
Western Elementary Preschool
Georgetown, KY

Let's Make Letters!

For this unique display, help students arrange themselves on the floor to make several letters. Take a photo of the students. Then mount each photo near a corresponding letter cutout. Use this handy display to help youngsters practice letter skills.

Linda Culley
St. Mark's Nurturing Center
St. Charles, IL

Invite each child to decorate a T-shirt cutout (pattern on page 70) by dipping pom-poms in tinted water and then making prints on the shirt. When the projects are dry, help each child write his name on his shirt. Then display the shirts as shown.

Joy Mosley, Waynesboro Primary School, Waynesboro, GA

CLASSROOM DISPLAYS

Trick or Treat, Smell Our Feet!

Help each child make a white footprint on a sheet of black paper. Encourage her to sprinkle cinnamon over the white paint. When the paint is dry, trim around the footprint. Then have the child draw two eyes on the print. To complete the project, mount these aromatic crafts on a board with the title shown.

Loretta Swisher, Little Rainbows Daycare Ministry, Frankton, IN

Help each child cut out a photo of himself and attach it to a corn cutout (pattern on page 71). Encourage him to add torn paper husks and yarn (corn silk) to the cutout. Then attach the ears of corn to a display with cornstalk cutouts similar to those shown.

Sarah Booth
Messiah Nursery School
South Williamsport, PA

Families Are Handcrafted With LOVE

For this sweet display, have each child glue a family photo to a sheet of colorful paper (quilt patch); then invite her to decorate her patch with stickers, craft foam shapes, and markers or crayons. Attach the projects to a sheet of bulletin board paper (quilt); then add wide lace around the edges. Display this family-centered project with the title shown.

Donna Foss, Little People of Southbury, Southbury, CT

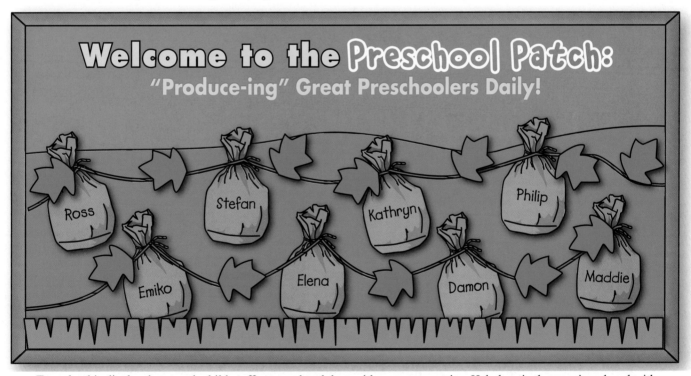

To make this display, have each child stuff a paper lunch bag with newspaper strips. Help her tie the opening closed with a piece of yarn and then have her paint the bag so it resembles a pumpkin. When the paint dries, write her name on the bag. Mount the projects on a board decorated as shown.

Brenda Ethridge, Bleckley County Primary School, Cochran, GA
Shannon Geer, Hawaii Kai Church Early Learning Center, Honolulu, HI

CLASSROOM DISPLAYS

Pick Up the Holiday Spirit in Our Preschool Classroom!

Jump-start the holiday spirit with this unique display! Help each child trace and cut out a construction paper evergreen tree. Help him glue lengths of twine to the tree and then glue the tree to a pickup truck cutout (pattern on page 72, enlarged). Display the projects as shown. 🖥

Sara Denardo, Cradles to Crayons LLC, Dayton, OH

Prepare for Santa's arrival with this scrumptious display! Have each child paint a tagboard cookie (patterns on page 72) with a mixture of flour and paint. Then have him press mini pom-poms (sprinkles) into the mixture. Glue the cookies to an oversize plate cutout and display the plate with the details shown. 🖥

Deborah Garmon, Groton, CT, and Amy D'Agostino, Syracuse, NY

Our Class Is Really Taking Shape!

This simple display is colorful and eye-catching! Have each youngster glue small shape cutouts to a large circle cutout to make a self-portrait. Have her name each shape she used. Then help her add her name to her project. Display the projects on a board with the title shown.

Cassidy Fountain, Mt. Washington, KY

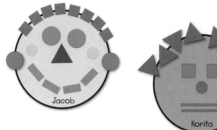

Editor's Tip:
Instead of using die-cut shapes for the features, use self-adhesive craft foam shapes. You can buy them by the bucket in many craft stores, and youngsters get an extra fine-motor workout removing the adhesive backing!

Our Little Snow Angels

To make this adorable display, have youngsters dress in winter outerwear; then take a photo of each child pretending to make a snow angel. Cut around each photo and attach it to a board covered with white paper. Draw angel details around each child. Then enlist youngsters' help in attaching cotton batting (snow) to the board.

Tammy Oveson, Learn 'n' Play Preschool, Waite Park, MN

CLASSROOM DISPLAYS

Put an international twist on this fun display! Share with youngsters how to say "I love you" in several different languages. Have each child make a self-portrait heart. Then write on a speech bubble her favorite way to say "I love you" from the languages shared with the group. Mount the projects and speech bubbles on a board titled as shown. 🖥

Cassandra Poritz, Elm Grove Lutheran Child Care, Elm Grove, WI

Invite youngsters to sponge-paint rainbow and sun cutouts. Then have each child color a shamrock cutout (patterns on page 48, reduced in size). Help him cut out a photo of himself; then encourage him to attach the shamrock to the photo so it looks as though he's holding it in his hand. Display the projects with the details and title shown. 🖥

Keely Saunders, Bonney Lake ECEAP, Bonney Lake, WA

Brushing Up on Dental Health!

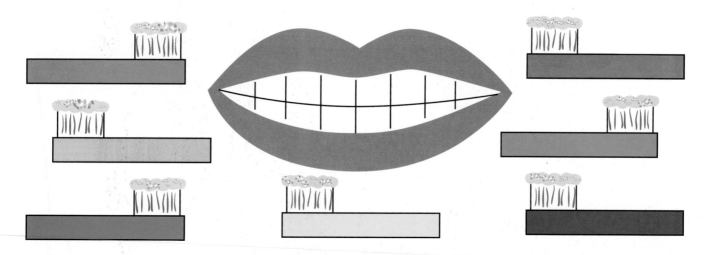

To make a toothbrush, help each child attach a blank index card to one end of a tagboard strip. Encourage him to draw lines on the card to represent bristles. Next, help him apply a thick layer of shaving cream mixed with glue (toothpaste) to the edge of the card. Then have him sprinkle the mixture with glitter. Mount the dried projects on a board decorated as shown.

Claudine Fredy, Iola-Scandinavia School District, Iola, WI

For this sweet display, have each child wrap a tagboard candy kiss cutout with aluminum foil. Have her tell something about winter that she will miss. Then record her thoughts on a paper strip and attach it to the kiss. Display the projects above a bowl-shaped cutout with the title shown.

Gina Petrassi
Bergen County Special Services
Hackensack, NJ

CLASSROOM DISPLAYS

Hopping Down the Preschool Trail!

For this personalized display, help each child glue a head shot photo of himself to the center of a paper plate. Invite each child to glue torn white facial tissue around the edge of the plate. Attach a pair of bunny ear cutouts to the project. Then display the crafts with the details and title shown. 🖥

Azucena Delgado
Jacksonville, FL

Keep Our Earth Clean and Green!

Celebrate Earth Day with this earth-friendly display! Retrieve paper, such as used reproducibles or newspapers, from your recycling bin. For each child, cut out a circle and fold it in half. Help each youngster unfold her circle and drizzle blue paint on one half and green paint on the other. Then have her refold the circle, gently rub her hand across it, and unfold it again. Display the projects as shown. 🖥

Janice Minton
Little Husky Childcare & Preschool
Oelwein, IA

Is It a Drizzle or a Downpour?

For this interactive display, have students use bingo daubers to decorate a large umbrella cutout. Mount the umbrella on a board or wall decorated as shown. Copy and cut out a supply of raindrop patterns from page 73. Each day, post a different number of raindrops on the board and have students count them to determine the total number. Then attach the appropriate number card to the umbrella.

C. Welwood, Woodbine, Calgary, Alberta, Canada

Nice, Gray Mice
(sung to the tune of "Three Blind Mice")

Nice, gray mice; nice, gray mice.
Small and sweet, small and sweet.
They all ran after the farmer's wife
To give her a hug and a kiss goodnight.
Have you ever seen such a loving sight as
Nice, gray mice?

This display presents a kinder, gentler version of a traditional song! To make these adorable mice, help each child glue two gray teardrop-shaped cutouts (ears) to a larger gray teardrop cutout (body) as shown. Have him use a marker to draw eyes. Then glue a yarn tail and whiskers in place. Display the mice with the version of the song shown.

Christine Cavin, YMCA of Frederick Preschool Center, Frederick, MD

CLASSROOM DISPLAYS

The Dog Days of Summer Are HERE!

To make this cute display, have youngsters make fingerprints in varying shades of brown on a length of kraft paper so it resembles a beach. Then invite each child to color a dog cutout (enlarge the patterns on page 74). Attach the beach and projects to a board or wall with other desired details and the title shown. 🖥

Kim Dessel, Pixie Preschool and Kindergarten, Spotswood, NJ

Someday I Hope to Fill Your Shoes!

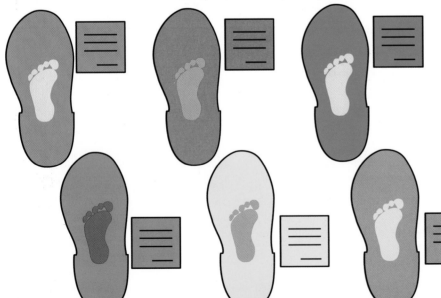

For this heartfelt display, paint the bottom of each child's foot and have her press it on an adult-size male shoeprint cutout. Then have her discuss why her father (or other special man) is a fantastic person. Write her words on a colorful paper square. Display the projects on a wall or board in your classroom.

Adriana Lopez
St. Gregory School
Tres Rios, Costa Rica

Preschool Is a Picnic!

Invite each child to cut out a picture of his favorite food from a magazine and glue it to a paper plate. Have him use a black ink pad to make thumbprint ants on his plate and a black marker to draw legs and antennae on each ant. Cut the bottom portion from a paper grocery bag. Attach a strip to the bag so it resembles a picnic basket with a handle. Then display the items as shown.

Sarah Booth, Hughesville, PA

We Are GROWING Like WEEDS!

In advance, find out each child's birth height. Have each youngster make a small and large flower craft as shown. Write her birth height and current height on the appropriate flowers. (If desired, have each child embellish her flowers with headshot photos of herself then and now.) Then mount the flowers on a board with this catchy title and any desired details.

Elizabeth Cook, St. Louis, MO

T-Shirt Pattern

Use with "Preschool Fits Us to a T!" on page 59.

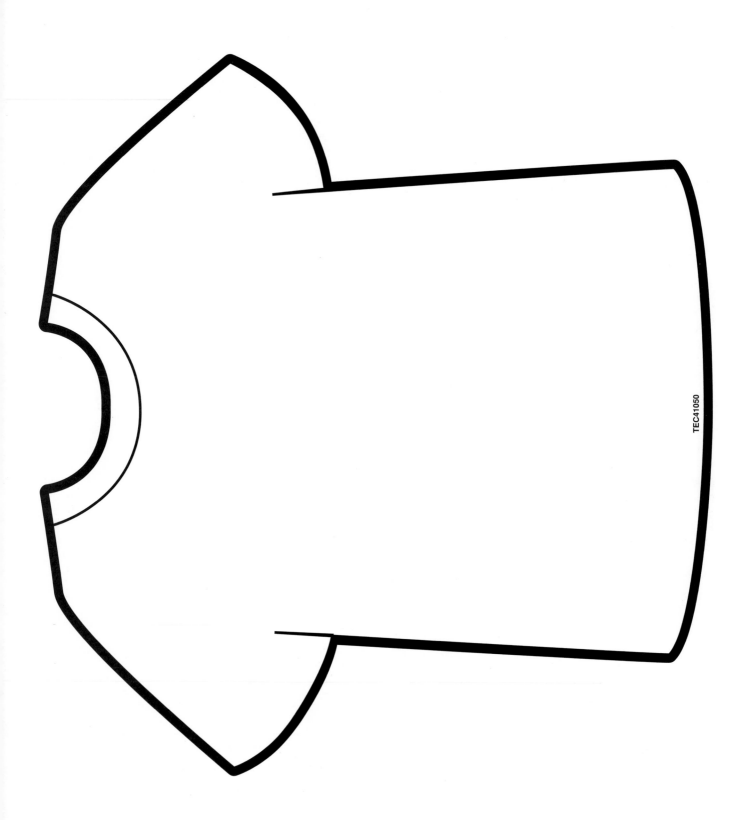

TEC41050

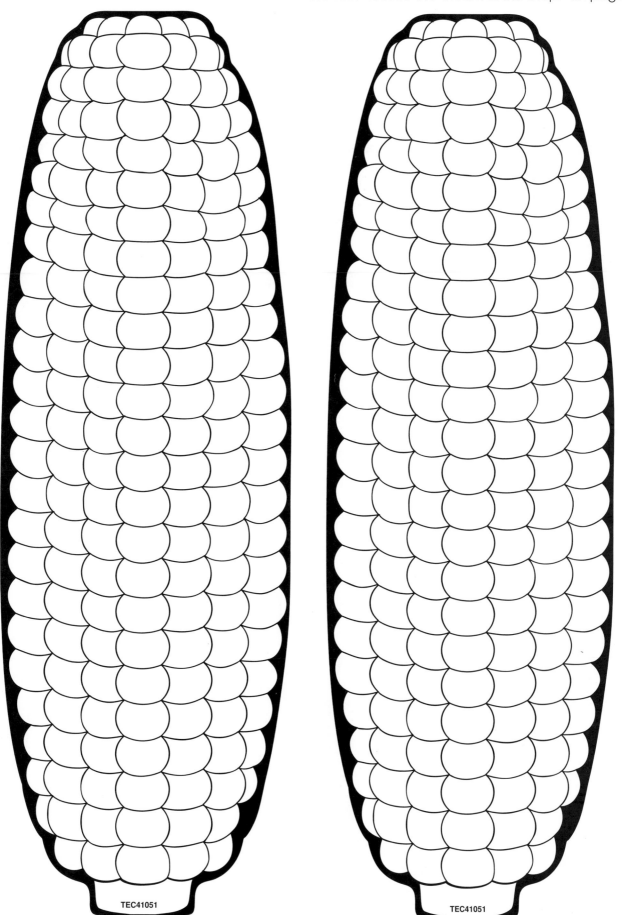

TEC41051

TEC41051

Pickup Truck Pattern
Use with the first display on page 62.

TEC41052

Cookie Patterns
Use with the second display on page 62.

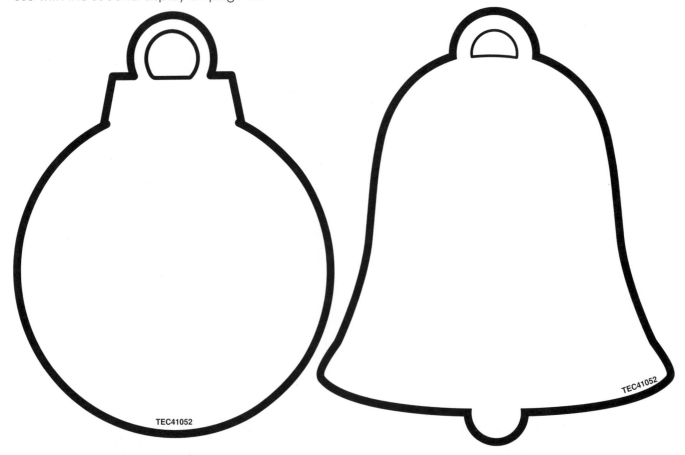

TEC41052

TEC41052

TEC41052

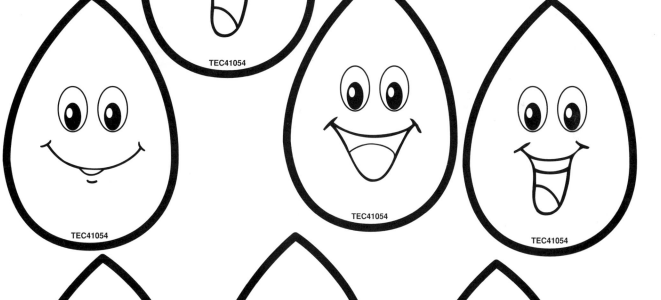

TEC41054
TEC41054
TEC41054
TEC41054
TEC41054
TEC41054
TEC41054
TEC41054
TEC41054
TEC41054

Instant Seasonal Activities

Instant Seasonal Activities

The Preschool Bus

Arrange youngsters in a circle. Then give a youngster (bus driver) a paper plate (steering wheel) and lead her around the circle, reciting the rhyme shown. At the end of the rhyme, have her stop and point to the youngster nearest her. Prompt the child to say his name and then "board" the bus by walking behind the driver. Continue until the entire class is on the bus.

> It's big! It's yellow! It's shiny and new!
> The preschool bus is here for you!

I'm a Seed!

Prompt each youngster to curl into a little ball and pretend to be an apple seed. Pretend to plant and water the seeds. (If desired, use a spray bottle for a realistic watering effect!) Then encourage youngsters to grow into very tall apple trees. Finally, walk around the classroom and pretend to pick the lovely ripe apples.

Find the As

Write several letters on a sheet of chart paper, including a class supply of As. Explain that the word *apple* begins with letter A. Have a child use a red bingo dauber to make an apple on a letter A. If desired, draw a stem and leaf on the apple. Continue until each child has made on apple on an A.

A	T	M	A
L	🍎	D	C
A	B	A	C
N	A	V	A
O	P	A	A

Crayon Color Match

Have a child pull a crayon out of a box and name its color. Prompt each youngster to find and touch something in the room that is that color. Check for accuracy. Then play another round.

COLORFUL CRAYONS

8 LARGE CRAYONS

Flashlight Fun!

Youngsters get to know the classroom and classmates with this simple activity! Dim the lights and give a child a flashlight. Ask her a question, such as "Where is the block center?" Prompt her to shine the light on the block center and then pass the flashlight to a classmate. Continue asking questions, such as "Where is [child's name]?" and "Where is your cubby?" until each child has a turn. *Karen Eiben, The Learning House Preschool, La Salle, IL*

Instant Seasonal Activities

What's Missing?

Gather several different fall-themed objects, such as a leaf, a small pumpkin, an apple, and an ear of Indian corn. Display the objects and have youngsters explain how each one relates to fall. Then direct youngsters to cover their eyes. Remove and hide one of the objects. Then invite little ones to open their eyes and prompt them to name the missing object. After the correct object is named, return it and play another round. *Roxanne LaBell Dearman, Western NC Early Intervention Program for Children Who Are Deaf or Hard of Hearing, Charlotte, NC*

Gathering Nuts

For each child, hide three brown pom-poms (nuts) around the classroom. Invite youngsters to pretend to be squirrels. Direct each squirrel to gather three nuts and then return to her place in the group area. After all the little squirrels have returned, have them pretend to sleep next to their winter supply of nuts. *Roxanne LaBell Dearman*

Falling Leaves

Gather youngsters in a circle and throw a handful of fall leaves in the middle of the group. Have students estimate how many leaves are on the floor. Then have little ones help you count the leaves aloud. Prompt students to revisit their estimates. Then play another round!

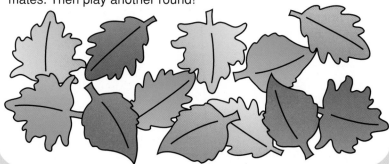

Build a Jack-o'-Lantern

Ask a child a question, prompting him to name a number, letter, or color in the room. After he answers the question correctly (with help as needed), draw a pumpkin on the board. Continue in the same way, adding a stem, eyes, a nose, and a mouth. When the mouth is finished, say, "Eek! It's a jack-o'-lantern!" Prompt students to cover their eyes as if scared by this frightening fruit. Erase the pumpkin and say, "Phew, it's gone!" Then play another round of the activity!

Time to Rake

Name a word, such as *rhino*. Prompt students to identify whether the word begins with /r/. If it does, say, "Yes, *rhino* begins with /r/, /r/, /r/, just like *rake!*" When little ones hear the word *rake,* encourage them to jump up and pretend to use a rake. Continue with other words. *Roxanne LaBell Dearman*

Instant Seasonal Activities

What's That Scent?

Poke a few holes in a lunch bag containing a few unwrapped candy canes. Have each child smell the bag and secretly guess its contents. After everyone has smelled the bag, encourage youngsters to voice their guesses. Then reveal the contents of the bag and give each child a wrapped candy cane treat! *Adapted from an idea by Lucia Kemp Henry, Fallon, NV*

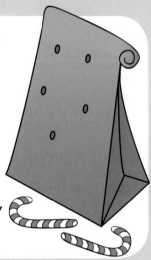

Cookie-Making 101

Tell little ones you need their help to make holiday cookies. Ask youngsters to name ingredients and kitchenware you will need to make the cookie dough and list the items on chart paper. Then encourage students to describe how to make the cookies, leading them to use words such as *measure, pour, stir, mix, roll, cut,* and *bake. Lucia Kemp Henry*

Great Guess!

Challenge youngsters' critical-thinking skills with this winter-related idea! Choose a word from the suggestions shown. Then provide students with clues to help them guess the word.

Suggested words: *snow, snowball, shovel, mittens, gloves, boots, scarf, earmuffs, ice skates, sled*

Super Snowman!

Youngsters practice color and shape identification with this simple activity! Draw a large snowman outline on chart paper or a whiteboard. Then draw colorful snowman details that include shapes. As you draw, prompt youngsters to identify the colors and shapes.

Where's the Gingerbread Man?

Arrange youngsters in a circle. Have a child walk around the circle with a gingerbread man cutout (pattern on page 54) as you lead the group in the chant shown. At the end of the chant, encourage the student to place the gingerbread man on, in front of, behind, above, or beside the child nearest her. Then prompt the group to name the gingerbread man's position in relation to the child. Have the two youngsters switch places and continue the activity. *Lucia Kemp Henry*

Walk, walk as nice as you can—
Where will you put the gingerbread man?

Instant Seasonal Activities

On the Move or Not

Display items that will or will not move when someone blows on them, such as those shown. Ask students to predict whether each item will or will not move when blown on. Finally, invite youngsters to test their predictions and compare the results. To challenge students' critical thinking, wet the lightest items and repeat the activity with just those items.
Karen Guess, St. Richard's School, Indianapolis, IN

Colorful Lambs

Invite each child to create an adapted version of "Mary Had a Little Lamb." Simply have her name a color and a color-coordinated item. Then lead the group in singing the song shown. *Karen Guess* 💻

[Courtney] had a little lamb,
Little lamb, little lamb.
[Courtney] had a little lamb.
Its fleece was [blue] as [sky].

The Letter L

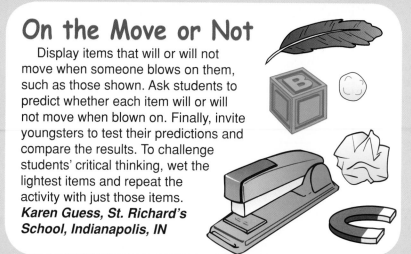

Write the words *lion* and *lamb* on a large sheet of paper. Say the words. Then circle the letter *l* and have youngsters say its sound. Help little ones brainstorm other words that begin with *l* and list them on the paper. Finally, point to a word and invite a student to circle the *l*. Encourage him to scan the word for any additional *l*'s to circle. Continue with the remaining words.
Karen Guess

Wind Chimes

Give each child an instrument that rings or chimes, such as a handbell, jingle bells, or a triangle. Fan youngsters with a large piece of poster board, encouraging students to play their instruments when they feel the breeze. Abruptly stop fanning, prompting students to stop playing the instruments. Continue for several rounds. What lovely wind chimes! *Karen Guess*

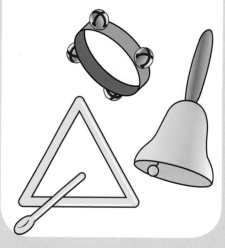

Valentine Rhymes

Prompt students to turn up the volume on their listening ears. Then say two words. If the words rhyme, youngsters blow a valentine kiss. If not, they sit still. See below for rhyming word pair suggestions! *Ada Goren, Winston-Salem, NC*

Suggestions: *love, dove; heart, tart; sweet, treat; kiss, bliss; honey, funny; candy, dandy; friend, bend; kind, mind*

Instant Seasonal Activities

One Spring Day

Write a spring-related story starter on chart paper. Read the words aloud and invite a student to complete the sentence. Record his words on the paper. Then encourage the remaining youngsters to add to the story. After each child has an opportunity to contribute to the story, read it aloud to the group. *Tricia Kylene Brown, Bowling Green, KY*

One spring day, I went for a walk and...saw baby ducks swimming in a pond. There were five baby ducks. They said, "Quack!" The mommy was swimming too.

Still as a Stone

Ask students to pretend they are sitting around a pond. Tell them to sit as still as stones. Then invite a child (frog) to hop to a classmate and make a funny frog face. If the child remains as still as a stone, she becomes the frog. If not, the frog hops to another classmate. *Tricia Kylene Brown*

Time for a Bus Ride

Tell students that spring is here and it's time to take a pretend bus ride. Have youngsters pretend to board a bus and then lead them around the room. Stop the bus and say, "I see a bear eating a...," pausing to allow students to name a real or nonsense word that rhymes with *bear*. After confirming that the two words rhyme, continue the activity, sighting other entertaining creatures and items. *Tricia Kylene Brown*

I see a bear eating a chair!

Rabbit Race

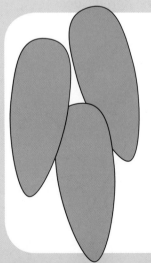

Divide the group in half and have each team stand in a separate line. Place a class supply of paper carrots a distance from the students (rabbits). On your signal, the first rabbit on each team hops to the carrot patch, "picks" a carrot, and then hops to the end of his line. The race continues until each rabbit has a carrot. *Adapted from an idea by Tricia Kylene Brown*

Buzz, Bees, Buzz!

Have youngsters huddle together pretending to be bees in a beehive. Announce a word and have students identify whether the word begins like *bee*. If it does, prompt your little bees to buzz around the room and then return to the hive. If it does not, the bees stay in the hive.

KIDS IN THE KITCHEN

Invite little ones to make and enjoy this pleasing pig treat. If desired, incorporate this snack into the pig literature unit. (See pages 162–166.) 💻

To prepare for the snack:

- Collect the necessary ingredients and utensils using the lists on the recipe card below.
- Photocopy the step-by-step recipe cards on page 83.
- Color the cards; then cut them out and display them in the snack area.
- Follow the teacher preparation guidelines for the snack.

Pretty Pink Piggie

Ingredients for one:
half a bagel
strawberry cream cheese
two mini chocolate chips
banana slice
two strawberry slices
red string licorice

Utensils and supplies:
plastic knife
paper plate for each child

Teacher preparation:
Arrange the ingredients and supplies near the step-by-step recipe cards.

Cindy Hubbard
Bunche Early Childhood Development Center
Tulsa, OK

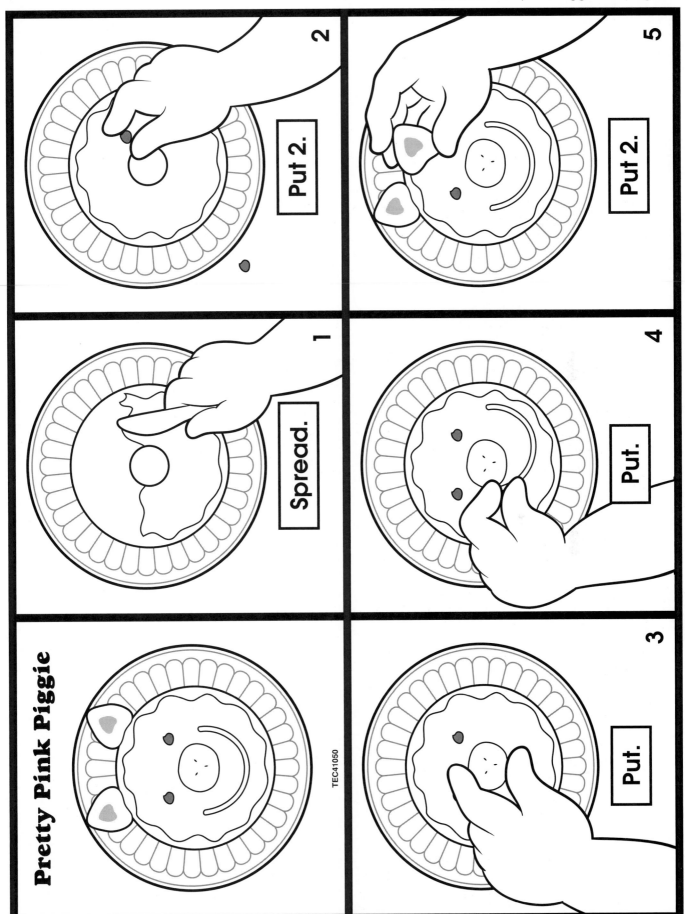

2 Put 2.

5 Put 2.

1 Spread.

4 Put.

Pretty Pink Piggie

3 Put.

TEC41050

KIDS IN THE KITCHEN

Conclude Fire Prevention Week by mixing up this tasty treat. 🖥️

To prepare for the snack:

- Collect the necessary ingredients and utensils using the lists on the recipe card below.
- Photocopy the step-by-step recipe cards on page 85.
- Color the cards; then cut them out and display them in the snack area.
- Follow the teacher preparation guidelines for the snack.

Dalmatian Pudding

Ingredients for one:
½ c. milk
2 tbsp. instant vanilla pudding mix
miniature chocolate chips

Utensils and supplies:
permanent markers
ear cutouts
tape
clear plastic cup for each child
plastic spoon for each child
tablespoon
measuring cup

Teacher preparation:
Arrange the ingredients and supplies near the step-by-step recipe cards.

Jennie Jensen
North Cedar Elementary
Lowden, IA

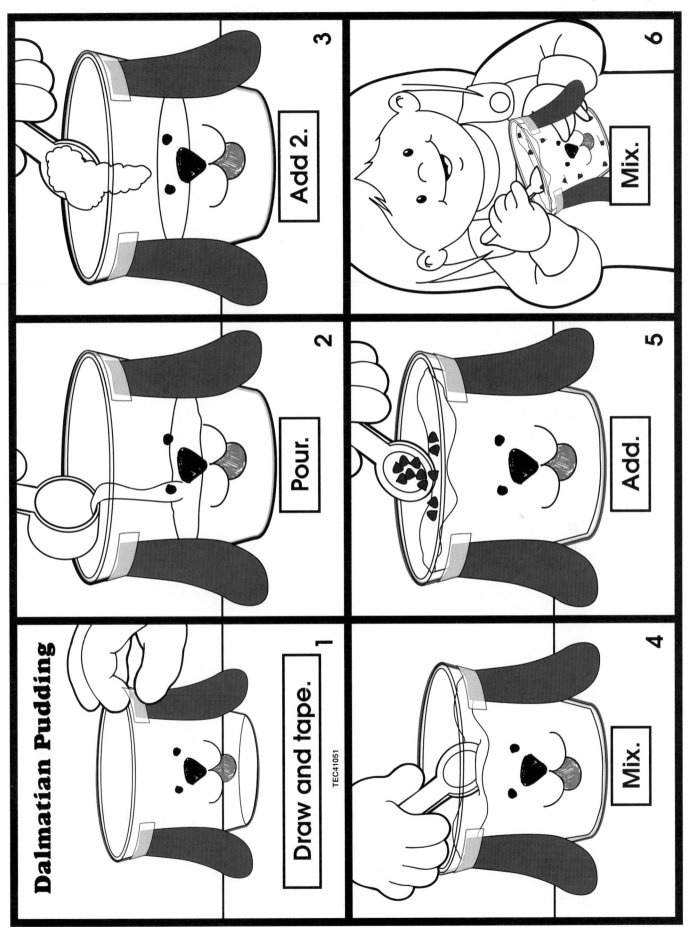

Dalmatian Pudding

1 — Draw and tape.

TEC41051

2 — Pour.

3 — Add 2.

4 — Mix.

5 — Add.

6 — Mix.

KIDS IN THE KITCHEN

Little ones stay warm and dry while building this tasty snowpal. If desired, serve hot chocolate with these yummy snacks. 🖳

To prepare for the snack:

- Collect the necessary ingredients and utensils using the lists on the recipe card below.
- Photocopy the step-by-step recipe cards on page 87.
- Color the cards; then cut them out and display them in the snack area.
- Follow the teacher preparation guidelines for the snack.

Snowpal Snack

Ingredients for one:
slice of bread
marshmallow fluff (or cream cheese)
miniature chocolate chips

Utensils and supplies:
snowpal-shaped cookie cutter
paper plate for each child
plastic knife for each child

Teacher preparation:
Arrange the ingredients and supplies near the step-by-step recipe cards.

Bonnie McBennett
ABC Childcare Center
Stratford, CT

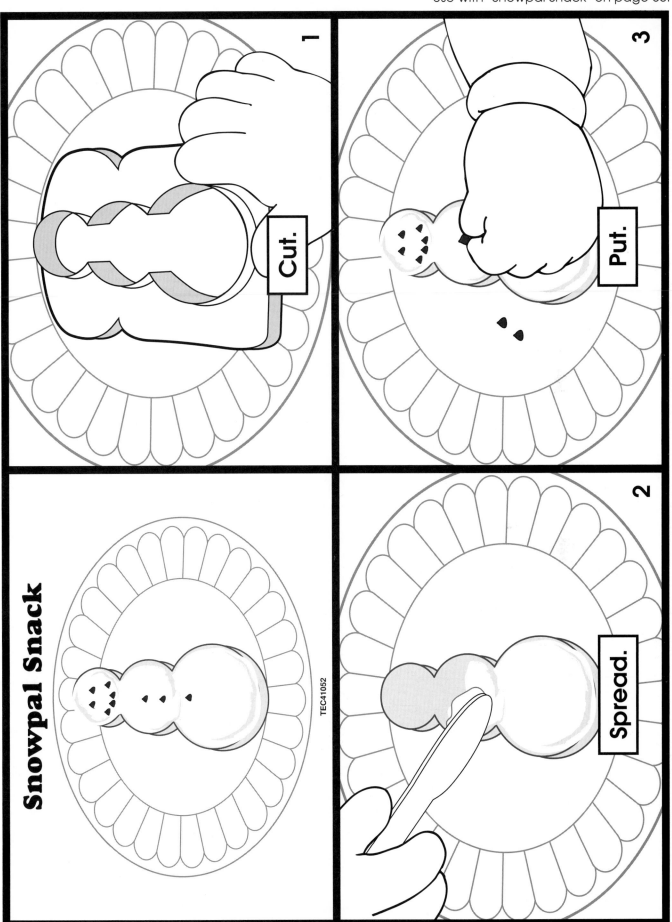

Snowpal Snack

1 — Cut.

2 — Spread.

3 — Put.

TEC41052

KIDS IN THE KITCHEN

This snack, along with a cup of green juice, is the perfect treat for a St. Patrick's Day celebration! 💻

To prepare for the snack:

- Collect the necessary ingredients and utensils using the lists on the recipe card below.
- Photocopy the step-by-step recipe cards on page 89.
- Color the cards; then cut them out and display them in the snack area.
- Follow the teacher preparation guidelines for the snack.

A Leprechaun's Lunch

Ingredients for one:
3 kiwi slices
thin celery stick
Ritz Bits cracker sandwiches (gold coins)

Utensils and supplies:
paper plate for each child

Teacher preparation:
Arrange the ingredients and supplies near the step-by-step recipe cards.

Nancy Morgan
Care-a-Lot In-home Daycare and Preschool
Bremerton, WA

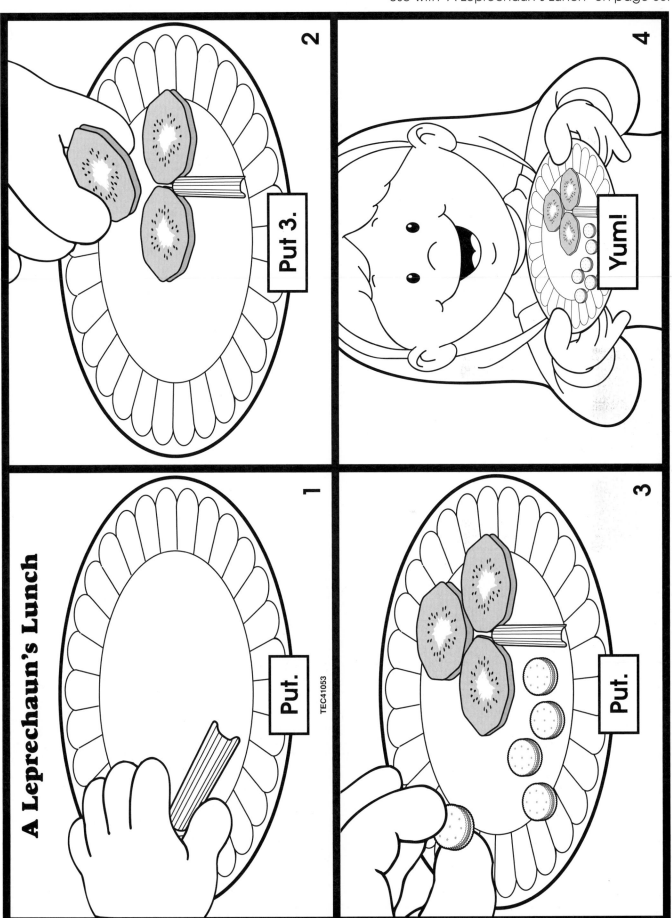

Plant the seeds of learning with this fun gardening snack. 🖥

To prepare for the snack:

- Collect the necessary ingredients and utensils using the lists on the recipe card below.
- Photocopy the step-by-step recipe cards on page 91.
- Color the cards; then cut them out and display them in the snack area.
- Follow the teacher preparation guidelines for the snack.

Planting Seeds

Ingredients for one:

chocolate pudding (soil)
M&M's Minis candy (seeds)

Utensils and supplies:

small scoop for the pudding
small paper plate for each child
plastic spoon for each child

Teacher preparation:

Arrange the ingredients and supplies near the step-by-step recipe cards.

Janet Boyce
Cokato, MN

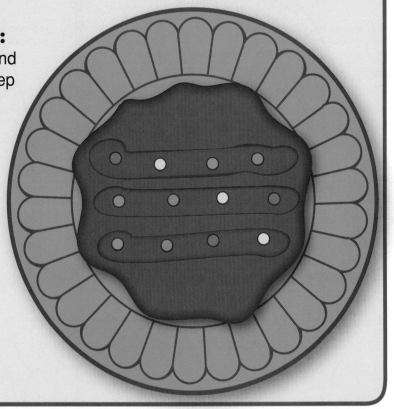

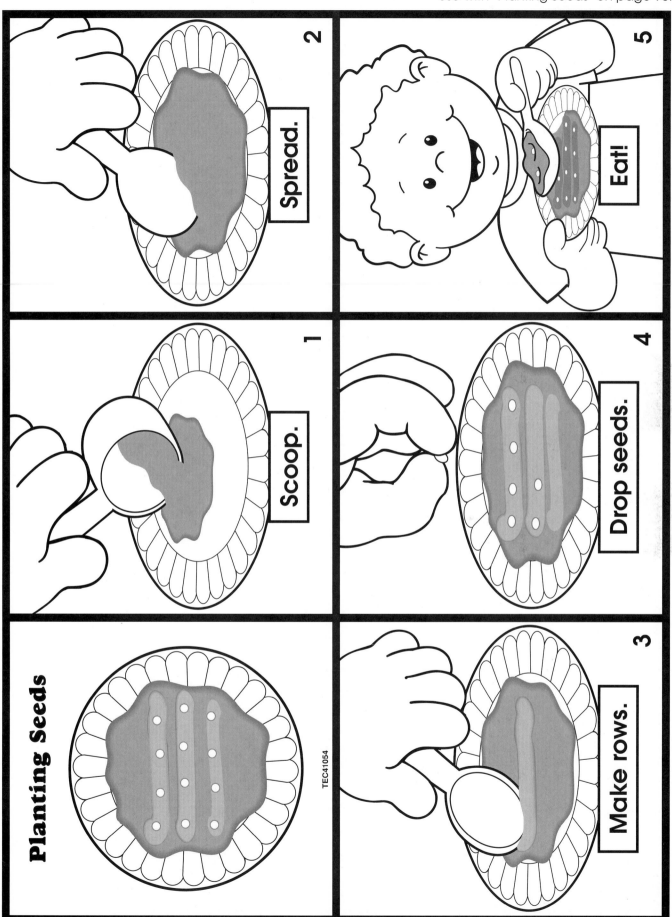

2 Spread.

5 Eat!

1 Scoop.

4 Drop seeds.

Planting Seeds

3 Make rows.

TEC41054

Dear Parent/Guardian,
We are making a snack titled "Planting Seeds." We would be grateful if you could help by providing the following ingredient(s):

_____

_____

_____

We need the ingredient(s) listed above by _____ .
                                                    date
Please let me know whether you are able to send the ingredient(s).

                            Thank you,

                    _____
                                teacher

☐ Yes, I am able to send the ingredient(s).
☐ No, I am unable to send the ingredient(s) this time.

                    _____
                            parent/guardian signature

Dear Parent/Guardian,
We are making a snack titled "Planting Seeds." We would be grateful if you could help by providing the following ingredient(s):

_____

_____

_____

We need the ingredient(s) listed above by _____ .
                                                    date
Please let me know whether you are able to send the ingredient(s).

                            Thank you,

                    _____
                                teacher

☐ Yes, I am able to send the ingredient(s).
☐ No, I am unable to send the ingredient(s) this time.

                    _____
                            parent/guardian signature

This festive fireworks treat is just perfect for a Fourth of July celebration! 🖥

To prepare for the snack:

- Collect the necessary ingredients and utensils using the lists on the recipe card below.
- Photocopy the step-by-step recipe cards on page 94.
- Color the cards; then cut them out and display them in the snack area.
- Follow the teacher preparation guidelines for the snack.

Splendid Sparkler

Ingredients for one:
pretzel rod half
white icing (or cream cheese)
red, white, and blue sprinkles

Utensils and supplies:
paper plate for each child

Teacher preparation:
Arrange the ingredients and supplies near the step-by-step recipe cards.

Jennifer Lange
Little People's School
Naples, FL

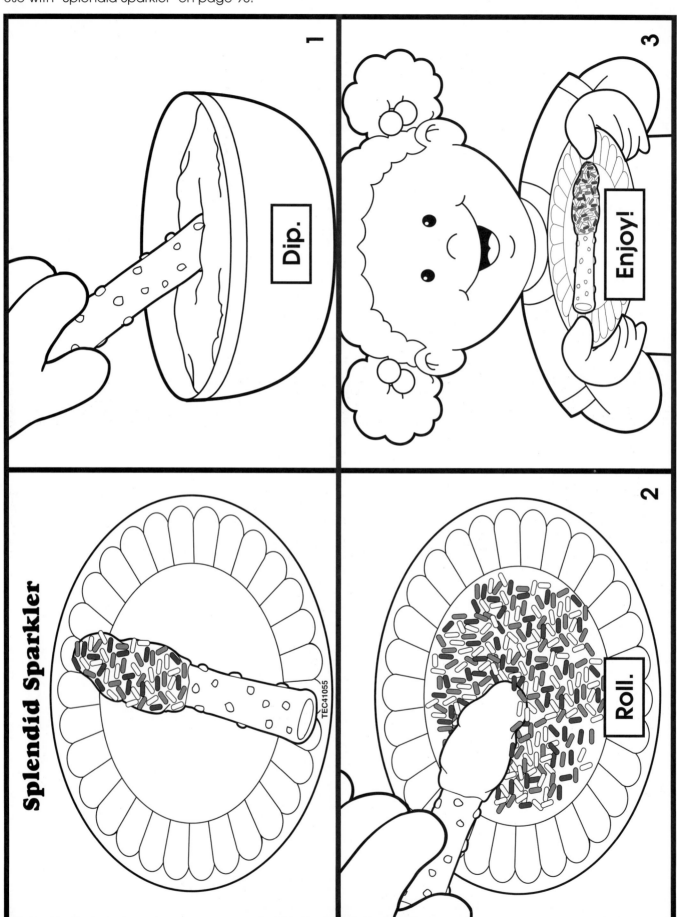

Splendid Sparkler

1 Dip.

2 Roll.

3 Enjoy!

TEC41055

LEARNING CENTERS

Learning Centers

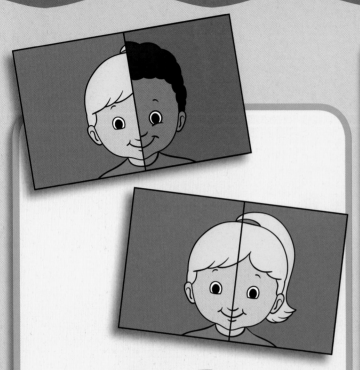

Hungry Worm
Art Center

Set out white paper, containers of red and green paint, two paintbrushes, and brown and green paper scraps. A child paints the palm of her hand red (apple) and her thumb green (worm); then she presses her hand on a sheet of paper. She cuts or tears a stem and leaf from the paper scraps and glues them to the apple. Then she draws details on the worm.

Tina MacKay
Rose Hill United Methodist Youth Center
Rose Hill, KS

Photo Fun
Social Studies Center

Cut a head-shot photo of each child in half and then store the halves in a container. A student assembles halves from different photos to create funny faces. Then he finds the matching halves of each classmate's photo, puts them together, and identifies the classmate.

Tricia Brown
Bowling Green, KY

Squeeze, Pop, and Poke
Fine-Motor Area

Provide handheld squishy balls, Bubble Wrap cushioning material, a foam block, and golf tees. A youngster gets a fine-motor workout by squeezing the balls, popping the bubbles, and poking the golf tees into the foam. What fun!

Diane Kovac
Capital Area Intermediate Unit #15
Summerdale, PA

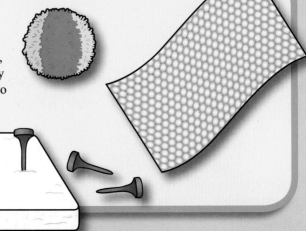

Shape Mats
Math Center

Cut out an oversize circle and square from colorful construction paper. Place the resulting mats at a center along with a bag of matching cutouts in smaller sizes. A student takes a shape from the bag and places it on the appropriate mat. She continues until all the shapes have been sorted. **For a greater challenge,** add another shape to the center.

Beth Deki
Carebear Preschool
Chandler, AZ

Seasonal Name Fun
Literacy Center

To prepare, write each letter of a child's name on identical seasonal cutouts, such as apples. Then write his name on an envelope and store the cutouts inside. A youngster removes the cutouts from their envelope. Then he spells his name by arranging the cutouts in the correct order. Repeat this activity each month, changing the cutouts to correspond to the season! 🖥

Cathy Mansfield
The Springhouse Learning Station
Eighty Four, PA

Nifty Neighborhood
Block Center

Take photos of buildings in your community. Print enlarged copies of the photos and attach them to empty food boxes covered with paper. Place the resulting buildings in your block center. A youngster uses the buildings, along with classroom blocks and accessories, to create a neighborhood.

Vanessa Mininger
Family Educational Network of Weld County
Greeley, CO

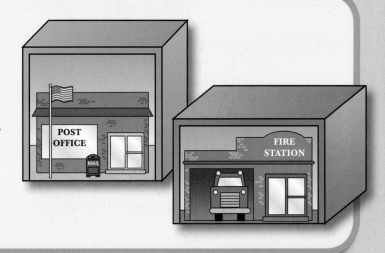

Learning Centers

Find and Match
Sensory Center

Fill a sensory table or plastic tub with tinted rice. Gather pairs of random items in your classroom. Place one object from each pair on a tray. Hide the remaining objects in the rice. A child searches for the items. Each time he finds an item, he places it on the tray next to the matching item.

Erin Hedstrom
Bright Beginnings Childcare
Princeton, MN

Trick or Treat?
Play Dough Center

Set out play dough along with tissue paper squares (candy wrappers) and a pumpkin candy bucket. A youngster molds the play dough into pretend candy and wraps each piece in a candy wrapper. Then he fills the bucket with the faux candy.

Picturesque Thanksgiving
Literacy Center

Cut out a copy of the picture cards on page 107. Set out the cards along with paper and markers or crayons. A student chooses a card (or cards) and identifies the picture. She dictates a Thanksgiving-related sentence using the featured picture. Then she draws a picture on the paper to illustrate her words. 🖥

Lynne Wilson
St. Augustine Manor Child Enrichment Center
Cleveland, OH

I like to eat turkey and corn on Thanksgiving Day!

Marly

Fine Feathers
Fine-Motor Area

Decorate a brown tagboard circle with eyes, a beak, and a red paper wattle. Punch holes in the circle as shown. Provide a large craft feather for each hole. A student inserts a feather into each hole.

Melie Fleming
Rhymes and Reasons Daycare Center
Lackawanna, NY

Top the Pies
Math Center

Decorate five orange paper circles so they resemble pumpkin pies. Program each pie with a different number from 1 to 5 and add a matching dot set to the back, if desired. Provide a supply of cotton balls (dollops of whipped cream). If desired, place the cotton balls in a clean whipped-cream container. A youngster chooses a pie and identifies the number. Then she places that number of whipped-cream dollops on the pie. 🖥

Henry Fergus, Phoenix, AZ

Preschool Painters
Dramatic-Play Area

Place clean paint cans in your dramatic-play area along with paint-related items, such as stir sticks, sample paint-color cards, clean paintbrushes, a clean paint roller and tray, clean rags, and overalls (with some washable paint smeared on them). A child visits the center and uses the props to pretend to paint. 🖥

Crystal Finley
Neosho Heights Elementary
Oswego, KS

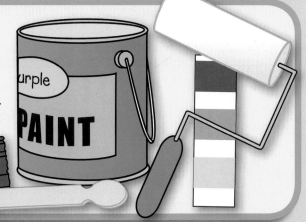

Learning Centers

Snow Writing
Literacy Center

Pour salt (snow) into a box lid, piling it up at one end to make a snowbank. Place several letter cards nearby. A youngster chooses a card and stands it in the snowbank. Then he uses his fingertip to practice writing the chosen letter in the shallow snow, smoothing out the snow each time he is finished writing the letter. 🖥

Janet Boyce
Cokato, MN

Tasty Headwear
Snack Center

Provide hat cutouts (pattern on page 108) along with spoons, napkins, and a bowl of cereal that includes colorful marshmallow shapes. A child takes a hat, spoons cereal onto a napkin, and then uses the cereal to decorate her hat. When she is finished, she munches on her cereal design. 🖥

Mary Robles
Little Acorns Preschool
Milwaukie, OR

Editor's Tip:
When the youngster is done with her snack, consider having her use the hat to make the cute project on page 11!

Student Snowpeople
Dramatic-Play Area

Youngsters make themselves into snowpeople at this center! Attach spring-style clothespins to the backs of tagboard circles to make buttons. (Add details to the buttons as desired.) Place the buttons in a tub along with hats, boots, mittens, scarves, and other accessories. Also provide a full-length mirror. A youngster dresses up in the items and clips the buttons to his outfit. Then he views his chilly snowpal self!

Rexann Roussel
Narrow Acres Preschool
Paulina, LA

Glistening Snowball
Art Center

For this group art project, cut white yarn into twelve-inch lengths. Youngsters dip the yarn pieces into a medium-consistency flour-and-water paste and then wrap them around an inflated balloon. They continue until the balloon is covered with layers of yarn. Then they shake iridescent glitter onto the wet mixture! (After the project is dry, pop the balloon and remove it.)

Katie Kawerski
Flin Flon Sweetgrass Aboriginal Head Start
Flin Flon, Manitoba, Canada

String of Lights
Math Center

Label each of ten lightbulb cutouts (pattern on page 108) with a number from 1 to 10. Attach a length of yarn to a wall and place the bulbs nearby along with spring-style clothespins. A student attaches the bulbs to the yarn in numerical order. **For a more challenging version,** provide lightbulbs with numbers from 1 to 20. 🖥

Tricia Kylene Brown
Bowling Green, KY

Authentic Snow Cones
Sensory Center

Fill your sensory table with freshly fallen snow. Provide disposable cups, an ice cream scoop, and pump bottles filled with tinted water (snow cone syrup). To make scented syrup, add a liquid baking extract to each bottle. A child scoops snow into a cup and then squirts syrup on the snow, pretending to make a snow cone.

Karen Tubbs
Malad Head Start
Malad, ID

Learning Centers

On Stage
Dramatic-Play Area

To create a performing arts theater, post black bulletin board paper on a wall (stage background). Then mount real or paper curtains to the background. Provide toy microphones (or attach foam balls to cardboard tubes), assorted stage props, costumes, and audience chairs. Youngsters use the costumes and props to engage in pretend theater play. Lights, cameras, action! 🖥

Natasha Pritchett, University Children's Center, Chicago, IL

Valentine Pairs
Game Center

Obtain a matching pair of valentines for each child, each pair different from the others. Label the backs of the card pair with the youngster's name. Place one card from each pair in a bag and put the remaining cards name-side down on a table. A youngster chooses a card from the bag and finds the match on the table. Then she flips both cards over to see the matching names. She identifies the name of the classmate, with help as needed. She continues until all the cards are matched.

Sharon King
Amarillo, TX

Go for the Gold!
Math Center

Attach several leprechaun cutouts (patterns on page 109) to a tabletop. Put a pot of gold at the opposite end of the table. Also provide enough leprechaun cutouts to extend the pattern to the pot. A child studies the pattern. Then she extends the pattern until the leprechauns reach the pot of gold. 🖥

Mary Robles, Little Acorns Preschool, Milwaukie, OR

Sweet Heart
Art Center

Place at a table an oversize poster board heart along with collage materials, such as red and pink pom-poms, tissue paper, and craft foam hearts. Also provide a class supply of valentines, each labeled with a different child's name. Each student visits the table, finds his valentine, and glues it to the heart. Then he decorates the heart with desired craft materials.

Norinne Weeks
Carrillo Elementary
Houston, TX

Shiny Gold
Literacy Center

Set out a large tagboard pot of gold labeled "Leprechaun Gold." Also provide tagboard coin cutouts labeled to match the letters on the pot. A youngster places a coin atop a matching letter. She continues until she spells each word with coins. For an easier version of this activity, only use one of the words.

Merilee Withrow
Dallas Christian School
Sunnyvale, TX

How Many Scoops?
Sand Table Center

Add to your sand table assorted transparent containers, each marked with a measuring line of equal height. Also provide a small scooper, such as a powdered drink mix scooper. Using the scooper, a child fills a container to the line with sand, counting the number of scoops it takes to fill it. He repeats the process with a different container and then compares the number of scoops it takes to fill each one.

Laetitia Bertrand, Hyde Park Child Development Center, Austin, TX

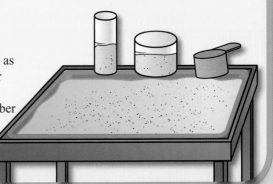

Learning Centers

Blend, Squeeze, and Paint
Art Center

Partially fill resealable plastic bags with shaving cream; then add powdered tempera paint to each bag. Seal the bag (making sure to squeeze out the air), and then reinforce the seal with masking tape. Put the bags at a table along with construction paper. A child manipulates a bag to blend its contents. When she is finished, snip a corner off the bag. Then have her gently squeeze the shaving cream onto a sheet of paper and fingerpaint a design.

Jackie Page
Jackie's Family Day Care
Columbus, WI

Recycled Blocks
Block Center

Collect a supply of clean, plastic containers, such as margarine tubs, whipped topping containers, jars, and juice bottles. Place the collection in your block center. A youngster uses the recycled items, along with classroom blocks, to create a unique structure.

Lydia Hayes-Rumbaugh
Beginnings Family Childcare
Pine, CO

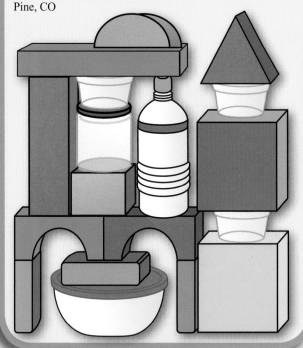

Frog Fun
Math Center

Cut apart the cards on page 110 and attach a small magnetic strip to the back of each one. Also flip a twelve-cup muffin tin upside down and label the cups in sequential order from 1 to 12. A student attaches each frog to the appropriate cup. When he is finished, he touches each frog as he counts them in sequential order. 💻

Paula Grimes
Westbay Children's Center
Saint Warwick, RI

Learning Centers

Terrific Tomato
Sensory Center

Set out a shallow container of condensed tomato soup along with a supply of large tomato-shaped cutouts. A youngster finger-paints a cutout with the soup, sniffing the aroma as he paints. When he is finished painting, he glues green paper leaves to the top of the tomato.

Maria Kipper
Willard Model Elementary
Norfolk, VA

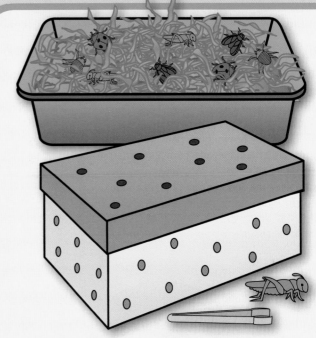

Bug Collection
Fine-Motor Area

Fill your sensory table or a plastic tub with Easter grass. Hide a collection of plastic bugs in the grass. Poke holes in a cardboard box and put some leaves and twigs in the box. Then place the items at a center along with a pair of tweezers. A child searches through the grass for bugs. When he finds one, he picks it up with the tweezers and puts it in the box. Then he continues searching for bugs to add to his collection.

Kristy Pulcher
First United Methodist Church—The Weekday Program
Plano, TX

Reading Nest
Literacy Center

Drape a brown blanket over a kiddie pool so it resembles a bird's nest. Place the nest in your reading area and put a soft, comfy blanket inside. Also provide a few stuffed toy birds or bird puppets. A student nestles down inside the cozy nest to read a book or uses the props to tell a story. 💻

Patricia Absec, Absec Daycare, Post Falls, ID

Alphabet Tree
Literacy Center

After reading aloud Bill Martin Jr. and John Archambault's *Chicka Chicka Boom Boom*, try this fun idea! Fill your sensory table or a plastic tub with green paper shreds. Hide among the shreds brown pom-poms (coconuts) and alphabet letters. Provide a simple palm tree cutout and a pair of tongs. A student uses the tongs to place the coconuts and letters on the tree, identifying each letter as he works. 🖥

Jennifer Stephen, Carmel Baptist Wee School
Matthews, NC

Modern Art
Fine-Motor Center

Place regular and decorative scissors at a table along with construction paper and a variety of paper scraps. A child cuts the paper scraps using the scissors and then glues his clippings to a sheet of paper. When he is finished, he showcases his modern art by mounting it to a larger sheet of contrasting paper.

Jean Gentile
Prairieview School
Hainesville, IL

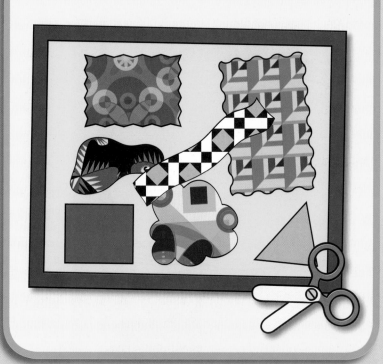

Perfect Pool
Reading Area

Put a blue blanket (water) in a small wading pool and place the pool in your reading area. Provide a few pool-related items, such as a child's swim tube; a beach ball; a beach towel and bag; sunglasses; and a clean, empty sunblock container. Also stock the area with summer-related books. A youngster pretends to relax in the pool while he reads a favorite book. How fun! 🖥

Rebecca L. Mason, Word of Life Christian Preschool, Baldwinsville, NY

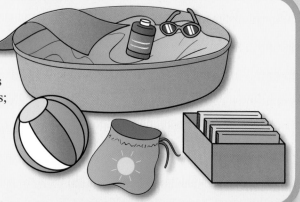

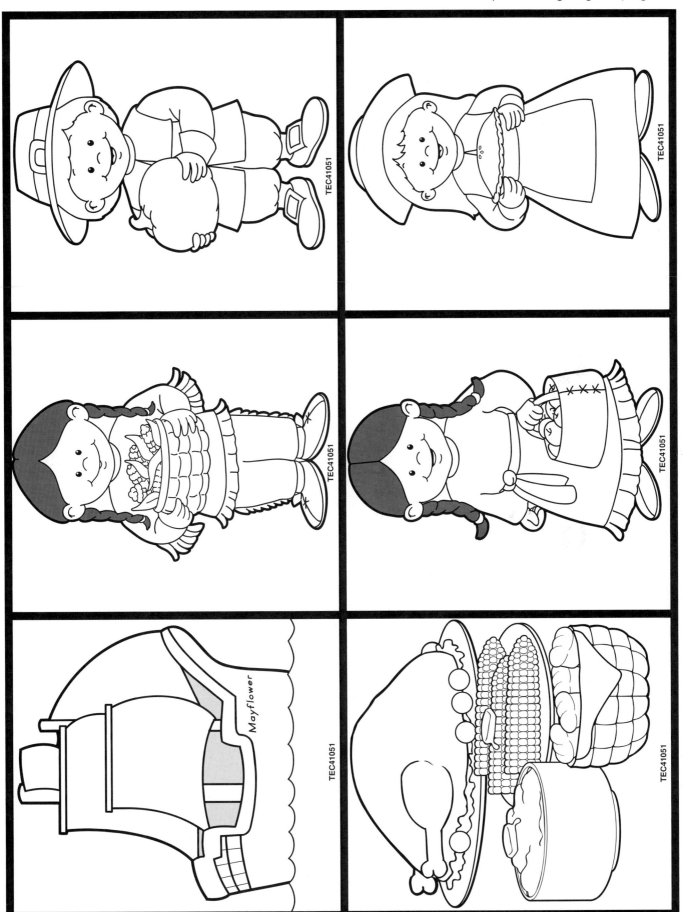

Mayflower

Winter Hat Pattern
Use with "Cozy Winter Hat" on page 11 and "Tasty Headwear" on page 100.

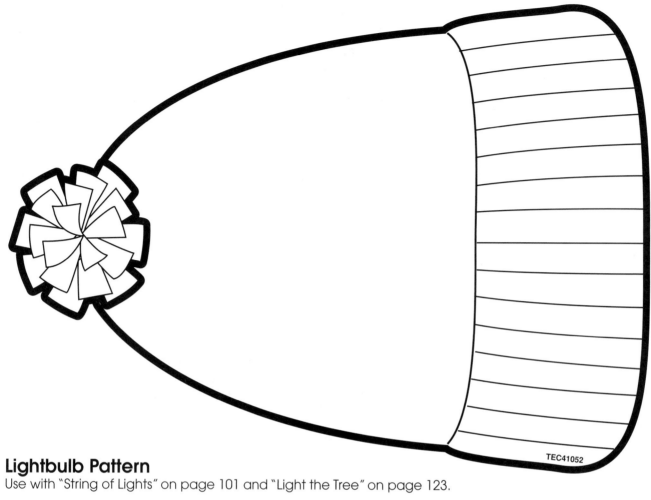

TEC41052

Lightbulb Pattern
Use with "String of Lights" on page 101 and "Light the Tree" on page 123.

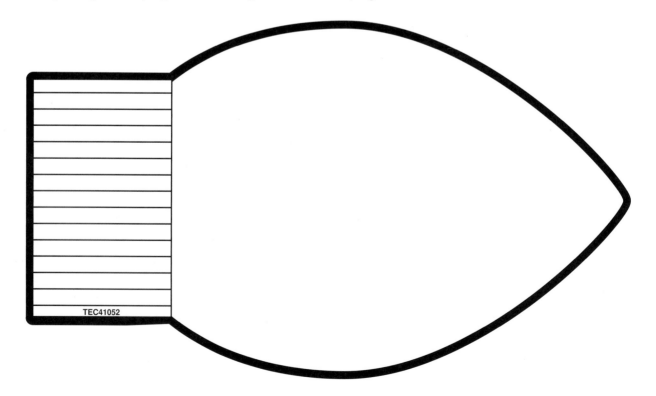

TEC41052

Leprechaun Patterns

Use with "Find the Leprechauns" on page 29, "Go for the Gold!" on page 102, and "Look! A Leprechaun!" on page 141.

TEC41053

TEC41053

Frog Number Cards
Use with "Frog Fun" on page 104.

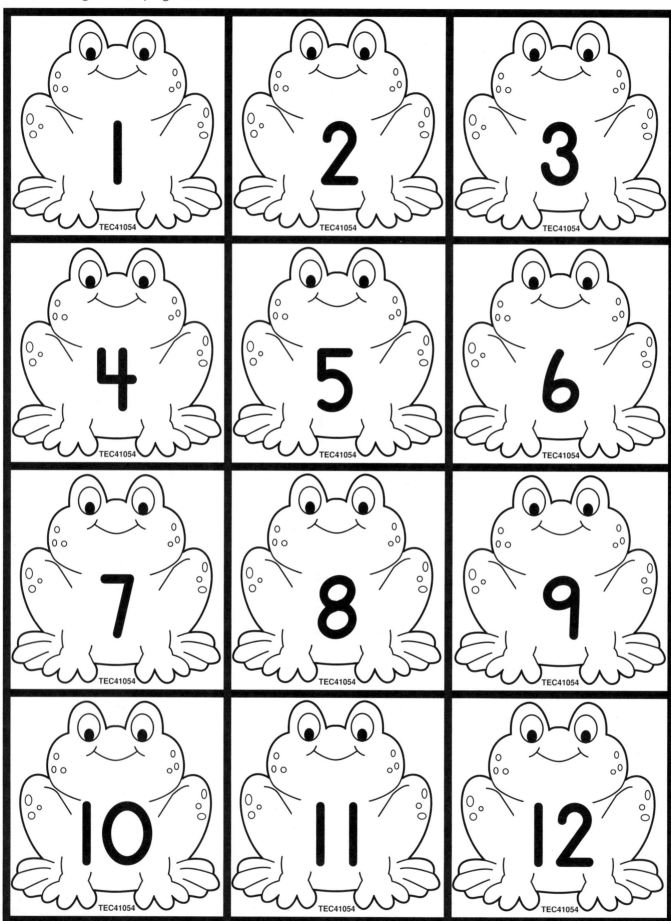

MANAGEMENT TIPS & TIMESAVERS

Management Tips & Timesavers

Hang It Up

Organize big books in a snap with this tip. Gather a supply of pant hangers and attach a book to each. Then hang the books in a desired location, such as along the sides of an easel. *Junetta Hudson, New Castle County Head Start, Newark, DE*

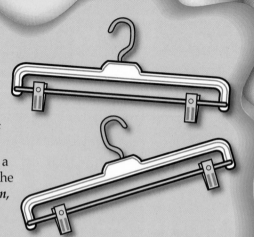

Ready to Nap

Help little ones drift off to sleep in minutes with this routine. Ask a youngster to choose a book from a provided selection. Invite youngsters to sit in their naptime spots and snuggle with their blankets as the story is read aloud. Then, before each child lies down, use an empty spray bottle to "mist" each youngster's pillow with pretend dream spray. *Cynthia Obrien, Miss Cindy's Daycare, Greentown, PA*

A Complimentary Tune

Sing the song shown to compliment students on a fine cleaning job. (If desired, sing the song to celebrate other accomplishments, changing the third line.) *Molly Wiard, Honeyville Buzzy Bees Preschool, Topeka, IN*

(sung to the tune of "The Farmer in the Dell")

Oh, I'm so proud of you.
Just look what you can do.
You worked to clean our room!
Oh, I'm so proud of you!

Juice Box Handles

Avoid juice box messes with this novel idea. Simply pull up the flaps near the top of the juice box to make handles. Then encourage each child to hold the handles when he drinks. No more messes from enthusiastically squeezed juice boxes! *Jennifer Lamy, Chestnut Children's Center, Needham, MA*

Name Flap

Here's a tip to prevent youngsters from covering their names on their artwork. Fold the top inch of the paper back to make a flap. Write the child's name on the flap. Keeping the flap behind the paper, place the paper on an easel or table for your little artist to use. *Cheryl Young, Miss Cheryl's House, Fruita, CO*

Management Tips & Timesavers

Seating Arrangements

To avoid circle-time arguments, use this tip for easy seating! Take a photo of each seat available on your rug. Laminate the photos for durability. When it is time to sit on the rug, give each child a card and direct her to find the seat on the rug that matches her card. *Tammy Stapley, The Preschool Club, Eugene, OR*

Finger Jackets

Keep cleanup to a minimum after fingerprinting and finger-painting activities with finger jackets. To make finger jackets, cut the fingers from several latex-free rubber gloves. Have the youngster slip on a finger jacket, make the necessary fingerprints, and then simply dispose of the finger jacket. Simple! *Kate Burley, Lakewood Preschool, White Lake, MI*

Clean Sleeves

Adult-size hair scrunchies are perfect for keeping long sleeves out of messy things such as paint, shaving cream, or food. Slide a scrunchie onto a child's wrist over his sleeve. Then push up his sleeve. The scrunchie keeps the sleeve from sliding back down his arm. *Evonrose Todd, Mid Cities Head Start, Euless, TX*

Flashlight Letters

This relaxing game is perfect for transitioning youngsters to naptime. Dim the lights and use a flashlight to draw a letter on the ceiling. Have students name the letter. Then invite little ones whose names begin with that letter to quietly move to their naptime spots. Continue until everyone is at her naptime spot. *Heather Musholt, Blessing Child Care Center, Quincy, IL*

Quiet Play

Little ones enjoy using beans and corn kernels at a sensory table, but they can be noisy. To muffle the noise, cover the bottom of your sensory table bin with felt squares. Then line the bin with a sheet, tucking the excess sheet under the bin. No more noise! *Deena Brants, Lyle PreK, Kewanee, IL*

Management Tips &Timesavers

Hand-Wear Dryer

Here's a quick way to dry little ones' mittens and gloves after recess. When a youngster comes in from recess with wet hand wear, have him slip each mitten or glove on a shoe rack as shown. Students' mittens and gloves should be dry in no time! *Jeannie Pavlik, Pittsville Elementary, Pittsville, WI*

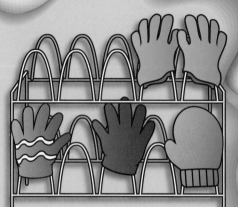

Supercleaners

Designate two of your youngsters to be supercleaners: dynamic superheroes searching for messes! Allow each super-cleaner to wear a cape and a button labeled with a large *S*. After students have finished cleaning, have the super-cleaners swoop in to evaluate the cleaning, reporting on nicely cleaned areas as well as those that need more work. *Michele Sears, Northeast R-IV Cairo/Jacksonville, Cairo, MO*

Marble Painting Made Easy

For a less-messy option for marble painting, try this! Obtain a disposable aluminum pan with a clear plastic lid. Place the paper and paint-covered marbles in the pan and secure the lid. Then have the youngster shake the pan until the desired effect is reached. *Linda Owen, Protestant Preschool and Kindergarten, Goldsboro, NC*

Positive Identity

While little ones are completing an art project, take photos of small groups working. If any artwork is missing a name, simply refer to the photos to identify the artist! *Suzanne Foote, East Ithaca Preschool, Ithaca NY*

Sticky Materials

Here's a way to make the most of patterns and cards found in your copy of *The Mailbox* magazine! Cut out and laminate the reproducibles. Then spray the backs of the patterns and cards with repositional adhesive. Youngsters can now stick the items on your board to tell stories, make patterns, and do sorting activities! *Halli Sutton, El Monte PreK, Concord, CA*

Management Tips & Timesavers

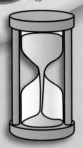

In Record Time

To encourage a quick cleanup, try this! Gather sand timers for four different times (one minute, three minutes, five minutes, and ten minutes) and assign a point value to each one. To begin cleanup, turn over the four timers. Youngsters try to finish cleaning before the timers run out. Award the group points for each timer they beat. After the group earns a designated number of points, reward them with a special storytime, a fun snack, or a new classroom toy. *Jackie Engvaldsen, Hawley 1 Head Start, Hawley, PA*

Wiggle Worms

Use wiggle worms to get the wiggles out before storytime or other whole-group activities. Give each child a length of hazard tape (worm). Then play a recording of a favorite song and direct little ones to energetically wiggle their worms through the air! *Teri Lavelle, Zion Lutheran Preschool, Indiana, PA*

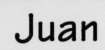

To the Moon

To prepare for this behavior incentive, display a row of star cutouts leading to a moon cutout. Place rockets personalized with student names before the first star in the row. At the end of each day, invite students who have demonstrated good behavior to move their rockets to the next star. When a student places his rocket on the moon, reward him with a small treat or special privilege. *Evelyn Bosques, Angel De La Guarda, San Sebastian, Puerto Rico*

Clip and Snip

Help youngsters fringe-cut paper with this quick tip. Attach a large chip clip to the side of the paper opposite the side that needs to be cut. A child cuts the paper, stopping when she reaches the clip! *Barbara Roach, Aldersgate Dayschool, Alexandria, VA*

Seasonal Snapshots

To help with planning for the next school year, take photos of displays, art projects, and other decorations used throughout the year. Store the photos on your computer in files labeled for the seasons. So simple! *Tommie Haga, St. John's Christian Preschool, Rockville, MD*

Management Tips & Timesavers

Ready to Go

Use this tip to keep your favorite activities from *The Mailbox®* magazine organized and at your fingertips. Attach a copy of the activity to the front of a pocket folder. Place inside the folder items needed for the activity, such as patterns, reproducibles, and game cards. Store the folder with your materials on the same theme. *Rhonda Burke, Ms. Rhonda's Day Camp, LaCombe, LA*

Movin' On

This idea is perfect for transition time and developing letter knowledge. Give each child a different alphabet card. Keep a duplicate set for yourself. Display a card and have students identify the letter. Then have the child with the matching letter move to the next activity! To dismiss students in small groups, simply hand out sets of identical cards! *Jill Story, The Growing Tree Preschool, Chambersburg, PA*

Tearing Tip

When little fingers have difficulty tearing paper for an art project, simply give them paper that's been cut with pinking sheers. The sheers create a zigzag edge that makes the paper easier to tear. Now that's frustration-free! *Bridget Williamson, Bridget's Childcare, Sewell, NJ*

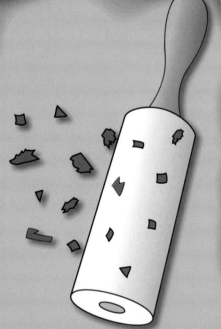

Roll It Up!

Do you have little bits of paper left on the floor after cutting activities? No problem! Give a youngster a lint roller and encourage her to roll it over the scraps. What a simple cleanup! *Lori LaLonde, Discovery Time Childcare, Hastings, MN*

Sticker Stationary

Keep reward stickers from getting lost or attached in unwanted places! Write each child's name on a separate paper and put the papers in a class binder. When a youngster receives a sticker, have her attach it to her page. When the page is full, write an encouraging note on it and send it home with the child to share with her family. Then insert a new page in the book. *Carole Schultz, Cedar Springs Weekday School, Knoxville, TN*

Our Readers Write

Our Readers Write

First-Week Memories

On the first day of school, I take a photo of each child at play. I glue the photo to a sheet of construction paper and caption it as shown. Then I invite the child to add a few stickers of her choice around the photo. It is a simple keepsake that parents will treasure for years to come.

Amy Pylant
Rosemont Elementary
Orlando, FL

Anna had a great first day of school!

Today's News

Encourage little ones to tell about newsworthy classroom happenings! Each day prior to dismissal, I gather youngsters and invite volunteers to tell about different events that happened that day; then I write their responses on a sheet of paper. I find it helpful to keep the papers and refer to them when writing our class newsletter.

Maria Prayner
Riverside Preschool
Painesville, OH

Morning Mail

Outside my classroom door, I place seasonal stationary, pens, and a small box decorated like a mailbox. Above the materials, I post an invitation to parents and staff members to write a note to a specific child or the entire group. During morning group time, I ask a child to bring in the mail. Then I read aloud each note.

Evon Rose Todd
Mid Cities Head Start
Euless, TX

Dear Alaina,
I hope you have a great day at school. I know you will have lots of fun.

Love, Mom

Painting With Watercolors

To assist little ones in learning to paint with watercolors, I teach them the three Ws—water, wipe, and wiggle. I instruct youngsters to dip the brush in the water, wipe off the extra water, and then wiggle the brush in the paint. This technique results in excited painters with beautiful, bold paintings.

Melissa Nething
Ewing School
Marietta, OH

This is Ms. Miller. She works in the office.

Get to Know the Staff

I invite a different staff member to visit our class each day. The visitor shares a book with the class and tells about the job she does in our school. I take a photo of her to place in a class book titled "Inside Our School." Then I enlist students' help in creating a caption for the photo.

Jean Gentile
Prairieview School
Hainesville, IL

In the Huddle

To encourage teamwork, I invite youngsters to make a huddle after morning circle time. I ask each child to place one hand in the huddle. Then I say a sentence such as "Be good friends and work together." The children repeat the sentence, lift their hands, and break up the huddle.

Karen Eiben
The Learning House
La Salle, IL

Apples All Around

When it isn't possible to take my youngsters to a farm to pick apples, I bring the apple picking to them. On the day of the apple picking, I give each child a small bag to decorate. While they are busy decorating, an adult scatters donated apples around the playground. Then each little one takes his bag to the playground, and the apple-picking fun begins!

Gena Moronio
Happy Campers Children's Center
Hopewell Junction, NY

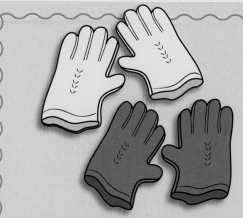

Colorful Hands

For a unique way to reinforce color recognition, try this! I purchase several pairs of gloves in different solid colors. Prior to circle time, I slip on a pair of gloves. I wear the gloves throughout circle time and incorporate the glove color with our activities as much as possible.

Kim Burd
J. L. Hensey School
Washington, IL

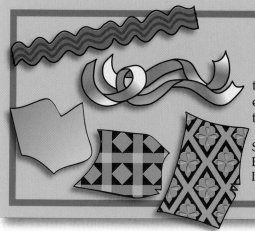

Oodles of Collage Materials

At the beginning of the year, I send a note home asking parents to donate scraps of fabric, ribbon, trim, or decorative paper. This ensures that youngsters always have just the right items to glue on their papers when they make one-of-a-kind collages.

Suzanne Foote
East Ithaca Preschool
Ithaca, NY

Our Readers Write

Pumpkin Spy

To prepare for this giggle-inducing math activity, I tape small pumpkin cutouts to the lenses of a few flashlights. Then I gather youngsters in the circle-time area and pass out some of the flashlights. To signal the little ones to shine their flashlights on a wall, I say, "Pumpkins, pumpkins in the sky. How many pumpkins do we spy?" I lead youngsters in counting the pumpkins. Then I collect the flashlights and redistribute a different number of them to students.

Danielle Lockwood
Colchester, CT

Colorful Glue

Here's a use for felt-tip markers that will no longer write. I use a pair of pliers to remove the tip from the marker. Then I drop the tip into a bottle of white glue. I let the glue sit for a few days so it can absorb the color from the tip. Now I have colorful glue to use during craft projects! If I am planning to store the glue for a while, I remove the tip from the bottle.

Cindy Burt
La Petite Academy
Madison, WI

Halloween Wear

This is a fun dress-up option for schools that prefer to avoid Halloween costumes. I help a child use puffy fabric paint to draw a spider in a spiderweb on a T-shirt. I hot-glue a pin to the back of a plastic bug and attach it to the shirt so it looks as if the bug has been caught in the web. My youngsters just love wearing these shirts for our fall celebrations!

Gisele Accardo, Pac Preschool, Mandeville, LA

Mr. Pumpkin Head

My little ones love this entertaining Halloween center activity. In advance, I make holes in a pumpkin where the ears, eyes, nose, and mouth will go. Then I place the pumpkin at a center along with Mr. Potato Head toy facial features. A child places the features in the pumpkin to make a variety of silly faces.

Carissa Dwyer
Discovery Kids Preschool
Maple Plain, MN

Edible Indian Corn

To make this treat, I follow the traditional Rice Krispies Treats snack recipe, substituting Fruity Pebbles cereal. I place a scoop of the mixture on a piece of waxed paper for each child. When the mixture reaches a touchable temperature, I spray each child's hands with a small amount of cooking spray and invite him to shape his mixture so it resembles an ear of corn. Allow the mixture to harden for a few minutes before eating.

Karen Eiben
The Learning House Preschool
La Salle, IL

Not Just for Cookies

Here's an inexpensive way to have magnetic boards in several centers! I use lines of Velcro fasteners to attach cookie sheets to walls or other hard surfaces. Then I place letter, number, or picture magnets near each board.

Kathy Gobble
Louisburg United Methodist Preschool
Louisburg, NC

Spell It Out

To create a special thank-you card, I gather large letter cards to spell "thank you" and give each card to a child. I ask any remaining students to hold a related prop. Then I arrange the youngsters appropriately, take a photo, and glue the photo to a card. I invite each child to write his name on the inside of the card. 💻

Sarah Booth, Messiah Nursery School
South Williamsport, PA

Leafy Bouquets

To make these fall decorations, I have each child place a blob of play dough in a clean laundry detergent cap. I encourage her to push the stems of fall leaves into the dough. Then I tie a piece of ribbon around each cap and display the bouquets throughout the room. How lovely!

Mary Di Domenico, Creative Playcare
Briarcliff Manor, NY

Happy "Thumbs-giving"

Happy "Thumbs-giving"

This card is sure to get a thumbs-up! I have each child make thumbprints on a card programmed as shown. Then I help her add a head, feathers, and legs to each print to make a turkey. I encourage students to dictate a message to a loved one for me to write inside the card. 💻

Jennifer McMurrain Stafford
Wesley Preschool Playcare and Kindergarten
Evans, GA

No More Trays

Here's a great alternative to trays of watercolors. In each of several baby food containers, I mix a different color of tempera paint and water. These mixtures make beautiful, vibrant watercolors for little ones to use. This idea also makes cleanup and storage a snap. 💻

Molly Kremnitzer, Kids in Christ Preschool, Las Cruces, NM

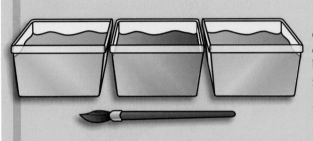

The Traffic Song

To teach my little ones about right and left, I invite them to look at the traffic outside our classroom window! When a vehicle passes, I lead youngsters in singing the song, substituting the type of vehicle and direction as needed. 💻

(sung to the tune of "The Farmer in the Dell")

The [car] went to the [right].
The [car] went to the [right].
We saw it with our eyes.
The [car] went to the [right].

Seasonal Fishing

This activity is the perfect way to introduce events or characteristics of each month. At the beginning of each month, I attach paper clips to seasonal patterns. Then I place the patterns facedown on a pond cutout. I invite a volunteer to use a magnetic fishing pole to "catch" a pattern. Then I display the pattern, and we discuss what it is and how it is related to the month. We continue until all the patterns have been caught. 💻

Michelle Joyce
Michelle's Family Daycare
Lancaster, MA

On Their Bellies!

My youngsters find it fascinating that penguins slide on the ice on their bellies! To simulate this, I place fish cutouts in our gross-motor area. Then I allow a few youngsters at a time to lie on their bellies on scooters and scoot themselves along to pick up the fish. They have such fun learning about penguins! 💻

Megan Blevins, Murray-Lasaine Elementary, Charleston, SC

Holiday Traditions

I send home with each child a blank folded card and a note explaining this card-making activity. I ask each child's family to help her create a holiday card that shows how her family celebrates the holidays. On a designated day, I invite youngsters to share their cards with the group before displaying them. 🖥

Colleen Brumley, Carlsbad, NM

The Gift of Reading

Instead of doing a gift exchange near the holidays, I invite my class to do a book exchange. I ask each family to wrap an inexpensive or gently used book and send it to school by a certain date. (I keep a few extras on hand in case someone is unable to bring a book.) This exchange is always appreciated by parents!

Katie Greenhaw
Growing Minds Learning Center
Fayetteville, GA

Special Skin

For this diversity activity, I gather paint sample cards (from home improvement stores) in a variety of skin tones. Then I attach the cards to a wall. My youngsters love to look at the cards, admire the colors, and find the ones that most closely match their own skin.

Hollie O'Connor
First Presbyterian Preschool
Columbus, IN

Santa's Nice List
Orlando
Kaley
Laura
Andrew
Lucero
Marcy
Olivia
Jacob

Santa's Nice List

To make this adorable holiday decoration, I paint two cardboard tubes gold. I write "Santa's Nice List" on a length of paper, and then I have each child write his name below the title. I attach the tubes to the paper so it resembles a scroll. Then I display the list on our door. I always get a lot of compliments on this cute decoration!

Susan Price
Little Precious Ones
Farmington, WV

Light the Tree

Promote kindness in your classroom with this holiday display! I post a large evergreen tree cutout on the wall. Each time a student witnesses a kind act, she gives a lightbulb cutout (pattern on page 108) to the child who was kind. That child writes his name on the bulb and attaches it to the tree. 🖥

Christine Vohs, College Church Preschool, Olathe, KS

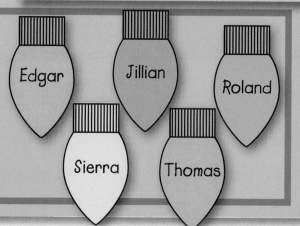

Our Readers Write

Friendship Fruit Salad

Celebrate Valentine's Day with this fun and healthy snack. Prior to celebration day, I send home a note asking each child to bring to the class party a small amount of fresh, ripe fruit, such as a banana, an apple, an orange, or a few grapes or strawberries. I help each child wash and cut his fruit. We mix the fruits in a large bowl to make a fruit salad. Then we add whipped topping and have it for our snack!

Jeanette Anderson
Jeanette's Tots
Otsego, MN

Literature in the Spotlight

Many times, after reading a good book with my class, I have students do a follow-up activity or art project. When I display the finished projects, I post a copy of the book cover nearby. This helps parents notice the connection between the book and the project. It also encourages parents to find other books by that author or illustrator to read at home with their child.

Aletha Scheck, Crown of Life Lutheran School, Colleyville, TX

Colorful Blocks

Here's a quick way to add a festive flair to your block area. For each season or holiday, I set out blocks in related colors. For example, I provide red, pink, and white blocks for Valentine's Day, green blocks for St. Patrick's Day, and pastel blocks for Easter! My students love the variety.

Nancy Jandreau
Ballston Spa, NY

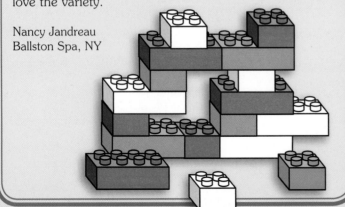

Shapely Stories

When a puzzle is missing pieces, most of us just throw it away. I found a great way to use the leftover pieces from wooden puzzles to spark students' imaginations. I place the remaining puzzle pieces near my sand table. My youngsters stand the pieces in the sand and use them to tell creative stories.

Janice Sutherland
Louisiana Schnell Elementary
Placerville, CA

Snapshot Sequencing

I take photos of my students doing something in sequence, such as completing their morning routine, getting ready for lunch, or making a play dough creation. After printing the photos, we practice sequencing the event. Then I glue each photo to a sheet of blank paper, and we write a caption about each page. I bind the pages between two covers and place the book in the reading center.

Kimberly Torson
University of Michigan-Dearborn Early Childhood Education Center
Dearborn, MI

A Fresh Scent

To keep my room smelling fresh, I simply place fabric softener sheets in various locations. I place them where I store students' extra clothes, in the bathroom, and under the plastic liners in the trashcans!

Danielle Lockwood, Colchester, CT

Fruit Salsa

Youngsters love to help prepare this salsa for a sweet Cinco de Mayo celebration! Have students chop some of the soft fruits with a butter knife. They can also help add ingredients and stir! 🖥️

2 tart apples, finely chopped	2 kiwifruits, peeled and finely chopped
1 tsp. lemon juice	2 tbsp. brown sugar
1 c. fresh strawberries, finely chopped	2 tbsp. strawberry jelly
1 c. blueberries, finely chopped	1 tsp. cinnamon

In a large bowl, toss the apples with the lemon juice. Add the other fruits and mix thoroughly. Stir in the remaining ingredients. Chill the salsa in the refrigerator for 30 minutes before serving it with cinnamon pita chips.

Kathleen Majewski, Penfield Village Nursery School and Kindergarten
Penfield, NY

A Flower for Mom

Mothers love this simple-to-make Mother's Day gift. In advance, I cut the tops from a class supply of water bottles to make vases. For each student, I tie a ribbon of his choice around his vase. Then he decorates it with foam flower and heart shapes. Finally, I help him plant a flower in the vase.

Sharon McDonough
Buttonwood Preschool
Lumberton, NJ

Headgear

I encourage youngsters to wear hats in the dramatic-play area without worry of lice. I purchase a class supply of inexpensive shower caps (headgear). On the inside of each cap, I write a different student's name. During dramatic play, I have each child wear his headgear under the hat of his choice!

Darlene Beam
Bowdon Elementary
Bowdon, GA

Our Readers Write

Zip It!

Instead of binding our class books with metal binder rings (which are usually too small or too big and fairly expensive), I use plastic zip ties. They can be found in hardware and dollar stores in a variety of colors. After binding a book with zip ties, I simply snip off any unused portion of each tie. I'm so happy to have found such an economical alternative to binder rings!

Molly Drake
Blackheath Pre-Kindergarten Center
Long Beach, NY

Parent Information Board

I rarely get the chance to share our daily activities with every parent at the end of the day. To solve this problem, I mounted a dry-erase board to my classroom door. On the board, I highlight the day's activities, such as a book we read, a craft we made, or a game we played. The parents love the daily information center and appreciate how it keeps them in the loop!

Julie Haskins
TLC's Small Blessings Child Care & Preschool
Tulelake, CA

Personal Clipboards

Here's a great way to teach students about recycling and provide them with individual clipboards. I ask each youngster to bring in an empty cereal box. To make a clipboard, I cut both panels from a box and glue them together. Then I hot-glue two mini clothespins to the panels to hold the paper in place. My little ones just love having their own portable writing space!

Suzanne Foote
East Ithaca Preschool
Ithaca, NY

Scoot Through the Ocean

In my classroom, we use scooter boards for pretend ocean play! I tape blue crepe paper streamers to the sides of the classroom tables. Positioning himself on his stomach, a child rides a scooter board under the tables, pretending to be a shark swimming through the ocean. If desired, enhance the experience by suspending ocean critter cutouts under the tables.

Diane Postman
Abingdon Elementary
Hayes, VA

SCIENCE EXPLORATIONS

Science Explorations

Fresh Apples

With this simple investigation, youngsters explore how to keep apples from turning brown.

Materials:
2 apples
knife (for teacher use only)
3 plastic containers
lemon juice
milk
water
paper towel

STEP 1

Present an apple to your youngsters and have them identify it. Explain that apples do something very interesting when they are cut open. Cut the apple in half and have students describe its interior. Engage youngsters in a quick group game or activity. Then revisit the apple and guide students to notice that the white flesh of the apple is now brown.

STEP 2

Say, "Let's find out whether there is a way to keep the apple from turning brown." Have youngsters help you pour a little lemon juice, milk, and water into separate containers. Ask youngsters to predict which liquid will help keep the apples from browning.

STEP 3

Slice the second apple and have volunteers place a slice in each container. When the slices are coated with the liquids, remove them from the containers and place them on a paper towel. Encourage students to observe the slices and identify the liquid that was most effective in keeping the apple from browning. Then have students revisit their predictions.

What Now?

Are there other fruits that behave this way? Gather a banana, an orange, and grapes. Slice each fruit and then have students observe the slices to determine whether any turn brown as apples do.

Science Explorations

Shake, Shake, Shake!

What happens when stones and water are shaken in a container? Your little ones find out with this preschool investigation of erosion!

Materials:
smooth stone
angular stones
plastic lidded container
water

STEP 1

Show youngsters the smooth stone and an angular stone. Have students touch the stones. Then ask, "Why are some stones smooth while others are rough and pointed?" Have students share their thoughts.

STEP 2

Encourage youngsters to help you place water and the angular stones in the container. Secure the lid, using tape if needed. Then prompt each youngster to shake the container. Leave the container out for the week, encouraging students to shake the container vigorously whenever possible.

STEP 3

Remove the lid from the container and have students study the water, prompting them to notice that there are bits of stone present. Ask, "How did the little pieces of stone get in the water?" Lead them to conclude that shaking the container caused the stones to bang together. The banging caused little pieces to break off.

STEP 4

Show youngsters the smooth stone again. Explain that it is possible that the stone banged against other stones in a river or a lake. It banged against stones for a long, long time, and that's why it's smooth.

What Now?

Have students shake a container of water and smooth stones. Are there as many little pieces of stone in the water? Why not?

Science Explorations

Repelling Pepper
Your little ones will be amazed with this splendid surface tension exploration!

Materials:
bowls of water
pepper
cinnamon
dish soap

STEP 1
Gather youngsters around the container of water. Have each child shake pepper onto the surface of the water. Encourage youngsters to observe the pepper, leading them to conclude that the pepper floats on the water.

STEP 2
Have youngsters observe closely as you squeeze a drop of dish detergent into the middle of the bowl. The pepper immediately scoots to the sides of the bowl! Ask, "Do you think the same thing will happen if we use cinnamon instead of pepper?" Repeat the experiment using cinnamon and a new bowl of water. Youngsters will be amazed when this spice behaves in the same way!

STEP 3
Have students suggest other substances they could test. (You may consider trying confetti, crayon shavings, and bottle caps.) Encourage students to predict whether these things will act the same way. Gather the substances and then test them in clean bowls of water. Do they react in the same way as the pepper and cinnamon?

This Is Why
Water has a "skin" on top of it that we call surface tension. When you add soap to the water, it reduces the surface tension near the area where the soap was added. The pepper scoots away, staying near areas of high surface tension.

Science Explorations

Freefall Fun!
Youngsters explore gravity when they drop a variety of objects!

Materials:
2 sheets of paper
large feather
small ball

STEP 1

Ask students if they've noticed that things fall when they are dropped. Drop a few common classroom objects to give students examples. Say, "I wonder if some things fall faster than others."

STEP 2

Next, show students the paper. Then crumple one sheet in a ball. Ask, "If we drop the sheet of paper and the crumpled paper, do you think they will hit the floor at the same time?" Have students share their predictions. Give a child the sheet of paper and another child the crumpled paper. Have them stand next to each other and drop the papers on your command. Then have students share their observations, noting that the crumpled paper hit the floor first.

STEP 3

Repeat the activity with the feather and ball, having youngsters make predictions as they did before. When students notice that the ball hits the floor first, help them discuss why they believe this happened.

STEP 4

If desired, place a variety of droppable objects in a tub at a center or take the tub out to the playground for youngsters to independently continue this exploration of gravity.

This Is Why
Objects push air out of the way as they fall. The sheet of paper is larger than the crumpled paper and must push more air out of the way before it reaches the floor. The ball of paper has less air resistance and falls faster. A large feather also falls slowly, much like the sheet of paper.

From Carrot to Plant

Youngsters investigate growing plants from carrot tops with this easy experiment!

Materials:
packet of seeds (any type)
carrots
pebbles
shallow pan
water
knife (for teacher use)

STEP 1

Show students the packet of seeds. Open the packet and have students touch and observe the seeds. Review with students that, when planted, the seeds will sprout roots and then a stem and leaves. Then explain that they're going to explore a different way to make a plant.

STEP 2

Show students a carrot and help them identify the vegetable. Then tell them that they're going to see whether they can make a plant from a carrot. (Mention that this will make a lovely plant, but it will not grow new carrots.) Cut off the top inch from several carrots and also cut off any greens. Have youngsters place pebbles in the shallow pan. Then encourage them to place the carrot tops on the pebbles, cut side down. Pour water in the pan to cover the bottoms of the carrots and place the pan in a sunny location.

STEP 3

Have students observe the carrots each day and make sure that water always covers the bottoms of the carrots. (If they dry out, they will not sprout.) Soon roots will sprout from the bottoms of the carrots and bushy green leaves will sprout from the tops!

What Now?

Do similar sprouting activities with beets and turnips. Simply follow the procedure given. What a fun way to investigate plant growth and make attractive plants for the classroom!

Songs & Such

SONGS & SUCH

What's the Weather?

Add this snappy song to the weather segment of your morning calendar time! 🖥

(sung to the tune of "If You're Happy and You Know It")

Oh, what type of weather do we have today?
Is it sunny? Is it rainy, dark, and gray?
Is it cold, or is it hot?
Should I wear a hat or not?
Oh, what type of weather do we have today?

adapted from an idea by Jenny Drewnowski
Peekaboo Playhouse
Cranberry, PA

Nine Little Apples

This adorable fingerplay is sure to be a favorite with your little ones. Guide students to hold up both hands with their fingers folded down. Then lead them in singing the fingerplay, prompting them to put up one finger per apple. During the final line, have students form a fist (an apple) and pretend to take a bite. Crunch! 🖥

(sung to the tune of "Ten Little Indians")

One little, two little, three little apples;
Four little, five little, six little apples;
Seven little, eight little, nine little apples—
Delicious as can be. Crunch!

Jeanette Gray
Epworth Preschool and Kindergarten
Gaithersburg, MD

Have You Seen My Friend?

Youngsters learn their classmates' names with this toe-tapping song! Place student name cards in a bag. Draw a card and help youngsters identify the name. Then lead them in singing the song, inserting the name and then pointing to that youngster during the final line. 🖥

(sung to the tune of "The Muffin Man")

Have you seen my friend [child's name],
My friend [child's name], my friend [child's name]?
Have you seen my friend [child's name]?
[She's/He's] sitting over there!

LeeAnn Collins, Sunshine House Preschool, Lansing, MI

Are You Ready?

Is it time for little ones to listen? Get their attention with this little song! 🖥

(sung to the tune of "Are You Sleeping?")

Are you ready? Are you ready?
Let me see; let me see.
Show me if you're ready; show me if you're ready.
One, two, three,
Eyes on me!

Wendy Turner
Rockford Child Care Preschool
Rockford, MI

SONGS & SUCH

Autumn in the Air

This short and satisfying action rhyme reviews body parts! Give each youngster a leaf cutout. Then lead students in performing the poem shown. 🖥

Autumn leaf in the air,	*Move leaf through air.*
Autumn leaf in my hair,	*Touch leaf to hair.*
Autumn leaf on my knee,	*Touch leaf to knee.*
Autumn leaf floating free,	*Move leaf through air.*
Autumn leaf on my nose.	*Touch leaf to nose.*
Whoops! There it goes!	*Throw leaf in air.*

Tiffany Dart
St. Paul Lutheran School
Luxemburg, WI

Four Alley Cats

What do alley cats do on a fall night? Your youngsters will find out with this action rhyme! 🖥

Four alley cats on a late-night prowl—	*Hold up four fingers.*
They pounce and hiss	*Pretend to pounce.*
And scratch and growl.	*Make scratching motions.*
The first alley cat says, "The stars are bright!"	*Hold up one finger.*
The second alley cat says, "It's cold tonight!"	*Hold up two fingers.*
The third alley cat says, "Autumn's in the air."	*Hold up three fingers.*
The fourth alley cat says, "Mice, beware!"	*Hold up four fingers.*
Four alley cats on a late-night prowl—	*Hold up four fingers.*
They pounce and hiss	*Pretend to pounce.*
And scratch and growl!	*Make scratching motions.*

Elizabeth MacKinnon, Duluth, MN

The Doughnut Song

This fun little song is sure to be a favorite among your youngsters! If desired, have each child make a sweet little shaker instrument by placing colorful candy sprinkles in a small, plastic, baby food container. Secure the lid with tape. Then lead students in singing the song and shaking their instruments! 🖥

(sung to the tune of "Twinkle, Twinkle, Little Star")

Yum, yum, doughnuts,
Sweet and nice—
Chocolate, glazed,
Or filled and iced.
Sprinkles on the top, so sweet;
What a tasty treat to eat!
Yum, yum, doughnuts,
Sweet and nice—
Chocolate, glazed,
Or filled and iced.

Ellen Roberts, Altoona, PA

Boo-Boos!

This silly song is just perfect to incorporate into a health-related unit! If desired, let each child put a self-adhesive bandage on her index finger. Then, during the fifth and sixth lines, have her wave her finger in the air. Repeat the song with the suggestions given. 🖥

(sung to the tune of "Old MacDonald Had a Farm")

[Little Sophie waved hello.]
E-I-E-I-O!
[She stumbled, and she scraped her toe.]
E-I-E-I-O!
With a boo-boo here and a boo-boo there—
Here a boo, there a boo, everywhere a boo-boo!
[Little Sophie waved hello.]
E-I-E-I-O!

Continue with the following:
Little Michael climbed a tree…He fell down and skinned his knee.
Little Maggie shut the door…She pinched her finger, and it's sore.
Little Sam jumped on the bed…He fell off and bonked his head.

Jeanine Dupler
Gainesville, FL

SONGS & SUCH

Polar Bears!

This action rhyme is sure to be "bear-y" fun for your little ones! 🖥

A polar bear is big and white.   *Stretch arms upward.*
To all the seals he is a fright!   *Make scary face.*
He likes to swim in chilly seas   *Make paddling motions.*
Without a sniffle, cough, or sneeze!   *Tap nose.*
His furry paws won't slip on ice.   *Walk like a bear.*
To be that bear would sure be nice!   *Shake finger.*

Sarah Booth
Hughesville, PA

Holiday Colors

Lead youngsters in singing this catchy holiday song. Then help students name colors associated with Christmas *(green and red)*. Repeat the song two more times, replacing *Christmas* with each suggestion given. 🖥

(sung to the tune of "Clementine")

[Christmas] colors, [Christmas] colors,
They are lovely—what a sight!
Can you name some [Christmas] colors
Looking festive, looking bright?

Continue with the following: *Kwanzaa* (green, red, and black); *Hanukkah* (blue and white)

adapted from an idea by Jacqueline Schiff
Moline, IL

It's January!

Have youngsters ring in the New Year with this celebratory song! For added fun, have students play noisemakers or instruments instead of clapping! 🖥️

(sung to the tune of "If You're Happy and You Know It")

January is the first month of the year.   *(clap, clap)*
At the stroke of midnight everyone will cheer.   *(clap, clap)*
Oh, the weather's very cold.
Hello, new year; goodbye, old!
January is the first month of the year.   *(clap, clap)*

Sherri Rhyne
Mount Pisgah Weekday School
Greensboro, NC

Itsy-Bitsy Snowman

What's more pleasant than an itsy-bitsy spider? Why, an itsy-bitsy snowman, of course! 🖥️

(sung to the tune of "The Itsy-Bitsy Spider")

The itsy-bitsy snowman   *Hold arms in circle (snowman tummy).*
    was standing in the snow.
Down came some flakes—   *Wiggle fingers downward.*
    it made the snowman grow.
Out came the sun   *Hold arms to make sun.*
    to shine its golden rays
Which warmed the little snowman *Hug self and slump to the floor.*
    and melted him away.

Victoria Silberstein
Johnson Early Childhood Center
Weymouth, MA

SONGS & SUCH

Red, Yellow, Green

Youngsters learn the meanings of stoplight colors with this catchy tune. 🖥️

(sung to the tune of "Three Blind Mice")

Red, yellow, green.
Red, yellow, green.
What do they mean?
What do they mean?
Red means stop and yellow means slow;
Green means go and now we know
What this colorful stoplight means.
It's red, yellow, green.

Courtney Pate, Burlington, NC

Hello, Mr. Moon!

This splendid tune is sure to be a favorite. If desired, display a construction paper moon while you lead youngsters in singing the song. 🖥️

(sung to the tune of "If You're Happy and You Know It")

Oh, hello, Mr. Moon, how are you?
Oh, hello, Mr. Moon, how are you?
We're so glad you're out tonight.
You are such a silvery sight.
We just love to see your light, yes, we do!

Oh, goodnight, Mr. Moon, yes, goodnight.
Oh, goodnight, Mr. Moon, yes, goodnight.
Oh, our eyes are closing tight.
It is time to say goodnight.
Oh, goodnight, Mr. Moon, yes, goodnight.

Jackie Harad, Wilmington, DE

Look! A Leprechaun!

Those tricky leprechauns disappear as soon as they are spotted! Lead youngsters in singing this song about those mysterious little creatures. If desired, have students decorate a leprechaun cutout to use as a prop as they sing the song. (See page 109 for leprechaun patterns.) 🖥

(sung to the tune of "The Muffin Man")

Look! I see a leprechaun, a leprechaun, a leprechaun!
Look! I see a leprechaun! He's standing very near.
Poof! There goes the leprechaun, the leprechaun, the leprechaun!
Leprechauns won't stay around; they always disappear!

Winter Is Done!

These snowmen know that spring is on its way! Give each child five cotton balls (melting snowmen). Have him place his cotton balls in a row. Then lead youngsters in reciting the rhyme, picking up each snowman from left to right when indicated. 🖥

Five melting snowmen, made of snow and ice.
The first one says, "This day is very nice!"
The second one says, "I think it's time for spring."
The third one says, "I can hear the birds sing."
The fourth one says, "I can feel the warm sun."
The fifth one says, "I think winter is done!"
Then drip, drip, drop, they melt away
As snowmen do on a nice warm day.

Marie E. Cecchini
West Dundee, IL

SONGS & SUCH

It's the Easter Bunny!

Here's a sweet little Easter song! Encourage a volunteer to be the Easter Bunny and prompt him to hop about the room as you lead students in singing the song. Repeat the song several times, inviting a different youngster to be the bunny each time. 🖥

(sung to the tune of "Are You Sleeping?")

Easter Bunny, Easter Bunny,
Bringing treats, bringing treats.
Jelly beans are dandy!
So are eggs with candy!
Oh, what fun! Yum, yum, yum.

Jacqueline Schiff, Moline, IL

Five Little Hats

This adorable chant is sure to be a favorite with your little ones. In advance, make five simple hat cutouts in the colors shown. Lead students in reciting the chant shown, inserting a child's name in each line and encouraging that child to remove the appropriate hat. 🖥

Five little hats, sitting in the store.
[Child's name] bought the yellow hat, and now there are four.
Four little hats, as pretty as can be.
[Child's name] bought the green hat, and now there are three.
Three little hats—red, pink, and blue.
[Child's name] bought the red hat, and now there are two.
Two little hats—one and two.
[Child's name] bought the pink hat, and now there's just blue.

Marie E. Cecchini, West Dundee, IL

Spring Planting

Sing this song with youngsters before a planting activity or seed exploration. 💻

(sung to the tune of "London Bridge")

It is spring—let's plant some seeds,
Plant some seeds, plant some seeds.
It is spring—let's plant some seeds.
What do they need?

Seeds need water, sun, and air,
Sun and air, sun and air.
And they need some gentle care.
That's what they need.

adapted from an idea by Janet Boyce, Cokato, MN

Be a Helper!

Remind youngsters to be helpful with this catchy song! After leading students in singing the song, encourage them to name jobs they can help with both at home and at school. 💻

(sung to the tune of "Clementine")

Be a helper, be a helper.
There are lots of things to do!
Think of jobs that you can help with.
Raise your hand and
Name a few!

Jacqueline Schiff, Moline, IL

SONGS & SUCH

Mystery Melon

Here's a sweet little song about a favorite summer-time treat! Lead youngsters in singing the song several times. Then have them guess the name of the treat. Why, it's watermelon, of course! 🖥️

(sung to the tune of "Are You Sleeping?")

Red and juicy, red and juicy.
Nice and sweet, nice and sweet.
Dripping on your fingers, dripping on your fingers.
Good to eat, good to eat.

adapted from an idea by Heather Leverett, Nashville, TN

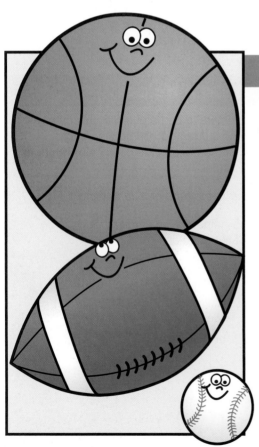

Lots of Sports!

Your little sports lovers are sure to enjoy this action rhyme. If desired, have youngsters share sports-related experiences before they perform the rhyme. 🖥️

If you're a [basketball] player, how do you play?   *Throw arms out to sides.*
You [dribble] the ball—it's the [basketball] way!   *Pretend to [dribble].*
[Basketball, basketball] is so much fun!   *Pretend to [dribble].*
It's a great game for everyone!   *Clap hands to the beat.*

Continue with the following:
soccer, kick
football, run with
baseball, swing at

adapted from an idea by Cindy Norman
YWCA Early Learning Center
Topeka, KS

Five Little Hot Dogs

For this adorable action rhyme, number five cylindrical building blocks (hot dogs) and place them in a frying pan. Obtain a pair of tongs. Recite the rhyme, holding up each appropriate hot dog. 🖥

Five little hot dogs frying in a pan.
The first one said, "I'm working on a tan."
The second one said, "I'm almost done!"
The third one said, "Well, it's been fun."
The fourth one said, "There's mustard, I see."
The fifth one said, "It's ketchup for me!"
"Lunch is ready!" they heard someone shout
Then the tongs went in, and the dogs came out.

Amanda Brinkman
Tea Sprouts Preschool
Tea, SD

Swinging Is Super!

Have youngsters sway enthusiastically as they sing this song. Then encourage them to sing it again when they swing during outdoor play! 🖥

(sung to the tune of "Clementine")

I am swinging, I am swinging.
I am way up in the air.
I am swinging, I am swinging.
Feel the breeze blow through my hair!

I am swinging, I am swinging.
I am way up in the sky.
I am swinging, I am swinging.
Watch the ground go speeding by!

Vicki Padgett
Mouzon United Methodist Church Preschool
Charlotte, NC

Fourth of July March

Spotlight the Fourth of July with this patriotic marching song! If desired, give each child a small American flag to wave. Or have students pretend to wave a flag. 🖥

(sung to the tune of "Yankee Doodle")

Let's all wave the Stars and Stripes
As we all sing this song.
Pick your knees up, wave your flag,
And let's all march along.
Four steps to the front we go;
Four steps back again.
Four steps to the front we go
And four steps back again!

Wave flag.

March in place and wave flag.

March four steps forward and four back.

March four steps forward and four back.

Donna Olp
St. Gregory the Great Preschool
South Euclid, OH

Ant Antics

Your little ones are sure to be on the lookout for ants after they sing this splendid song! Lead students in singing the song. Then continue with the suggested verses. 🖥

(sung to the tune of "Did You Ever See a Lassie?")

Did you ever see an ant, an ant, an ant?
Did you ever see an ant at your picnic lunch?
He'll take all your [cookies].
He'll take all your [cookies].
Did you ever see an ant at your picnic lunch?

Continue with the following: hamburgers, potato chips, cake, apples, watermelon, hot dogs, ice cream

Virginia Lopez, Grace Mission State Pre-K, Chicago, IL

STORYTIME

Storytime

A Splendid Friend, Indeed
Written and illustrated by Suzanne Bloom

A talkative goose likes doing all the things Bear is doing—so much so that it takes over all of Bear's activities, leading Bear to feel quite annoyed! Then Goose does something touching, sparking an unlikely friendship between the pair.

ideas contributed by Elizabeth Cook
Glendale Lutheran Early Learning Center
St. Louis, MO

Yes, because they are reading together!

Before You Read

Display the cover of the book and have students describe what they see. Direct their attention to how the animals are sitting and the way they are looking at each other. Then say, "Bear and Goose are very different. Do you think they can be friends?" After youngsters share their thoughts, have them settle in for this entertaining read with a very special ending.

I have a friend named Carly.
We are different because...

she likes to swing and I like to go down the slide.

kristy

After You Read

Elicit a discussion about friendship, leading youngsters to understand that people can be friends whether they are alike or different. Next, give each child a paper programmed as shown. Encourage her to dictate to complete the prompt. Then have her illustrate her words. If desired, bind the pages between two covers with the title "We Are Friends: Alike or Different!"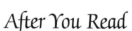

Buzz

Written by Janet S. Wong and illustrated by
Margaret Chodos-Irvine

*A young boy starts his day with the sound of a
bee buzzing around outside his bedroom window.
His day continues with a morning routine filled
with buzzing!*

My daddy's razor buzzes!

Before You Read

Before revealing the cover of the book, invite little ones to
name things at home, at school, or outdoors that make buzzing
sounds. Write youngsters' responses on chart paper. Tell students
the book you are about to read is filled with pictures of things that
buzz. Then read the story aloud, checking each item on the chart
paper that appears in the book.

After You Read

Obtain one item that makes a buzzing sound, such as an
alarm clock or a timer, along with a few items that make
different sounds. Have little ones curl up on the floor and
pretend to be asleep. Instruct youngsters to listen carefully as you use each item to make a sound. Tell them
when they hear the buzzing sound, they are to pretend
to wake up and fly around, buzzing like bees. After a
few moments, signal your little bees to curl up on the
floor; then repeat the activity.

Storytime

Nuts to You!

Written and illustrated by Lois Ehlert

Youngsters will be nuts about this tale of a mischievous squirrel that will stop at nothing to get food—including sneaking into an apartment through a tear in a window screen!

ideas contributed by Ada Goren, Winston-Salem, NC

Squirrels like to eat nuts!

Before You Read

Before revealing the cover of the book, invite each child to name her favorite food. After youngsters have had a chance to share, tell them that today's story is about an animal that likes to eat nuts. Then ask students to predict what the animal is. After students share their thoughts, reveal the cover of the book so they can see if their predictions are true. Finally, have little ones settle in for this delightfully nutty tale!

After You Read

The narrator gives the squirrel peanuts and says, "Nuts to you!" Invite your little ones to say the same phrase with this simple counting game! Gather a container of brown pom-poms (nuts). Choose a child to be the narrator and tell the remaining students that they are going to pretend to be squirrels. Have the narrator take a handful of nuts and walk around the interior of the circle. Invite him to drop the nuts in front of a squirrel and say, "Nuts to you!" Invite the squirrel to count the nuts aloud and then pretend to gobble them up. Continue with a different narrator.

Snip Snap! What's That?

Written by Mara Bergman
Illustrated by Nick Maland

Three young children watch as an alligator slowly creeps through their apartment. Are they scared? You bet they are! But then they courageously turn the tables and order the alligator to get out!

Alligator!

Before You Read

Explain that the story you are about to read features a wild animal. Then read the clues shown to help youngsters guess what it is. After all the clues have been read, display the book's cover as the final clue.

If you see me in a river, you will surely quiver!
I am shades of green, and my face looks mean.
My tail is long, and my jaws are strong.
You might say, "See ya later!" because I'm an…

Is Ethan afraid of a spider?

After You Read

This adorable project mimics the repetitive words in the story. Give each child a sheet of paper. On the right half of the page, have him draw a picture of something that frightens him. On the left half of the page, help him glue a photo of himself making a frightened face. To complete the project, help him place a half sheet of paper, programmed on the front and back as shown, atop the photo. Then staple the sheets along the left side.

You bet he is!

Storytime

Snowmen at Christmas
Written by Caralyn Buehner
Illustrated by Mark Buehner

On Christmas Eve, after the townspeople are snug in their beds and fast asleep, all the snow families gather for a Christmas celebration that includes a visit from a very special guest!

> Build a snow tree and decorate it!

Before You Read
Inspire youngsters' imaginations with this prereading activity! Display the cover of the book and read the title aloud. Then ask, "If snowmen could come to life, what things might they do to celebrate the holidays?" After little ones share their thoughts, have them settle in for this very festive tale!

After You Read
Youngsters decorate this tree with snowballs—just as the snowmen in the story do! Attach a tree cutout to a wall and then gather little ones around the tree. Ask each child to name something she likes to do on Christmas Eve (or the night before a different holiday for youngsters who do not celebrate Christmas). Write each child's response on a separate snowball cutout and help her attach it to the tree.

Sammy Spider's First Hanukkah

Written by Sylvia A. Rouss
Illustrated by Katherine Janus Kahn

Sammy the spider watches from above as the Shapiro family celebrates Hanukkah. Each night, Josh Shapiro gets a colorful new dreidel from his parents. Sammy wants a dreidel too, but spiders spin webs, not dreidels. At the end of the Hanukkah celebration, Sammy gets a big surprise from his mother!

There are lots of candles!

Before You Read

Ask youngsters what they know about Hanukkah. Write their thoughts on a sheet of chart paper. Then show students the cover of the book. Explain that Sammy the spider doesn't know anything about Hanukkah. In fact, this is his first Hanukkah. Then have students settle in to hear about Sammy's first Hanukkah experience.

After You Read

Youngsters get color-matching practice with these colorful dreidels! Make dreidel cutouts in the colors shown in the story. Place the cutouts at a table along with paper scraps and magazines. Encourage youngsters to search for and cut out scraps and magazine pictures that match the dreidel colors. Then have them glue the pieces to the dreidels. Soon your youngsters will see colorful dreidels just as Sammy does!

Storytime

Russell the Sheep
Written and illustrated by Rob Scotton

After a long, busy day, all the sheep fall fast asleep—all except Russell, that is! He tries everything from sleeping in a tree to counting the stars. Finally, he finds the perfect solution to end his sleepless night.

ideas contributed by Ada Goren, Winston-Salem, NC

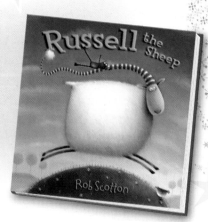

Before You Read

Conceal in a pillowcase several bedtime-related items, such as a toothbrush, a nightlight, a teddy bear, and a small pillow and blanket. Remove each item, in turn, and have students identify it. After all the items have been identified, ask youngsters what the items have in common, leading students to understand that they are all used at bedtime. Finally, have little ones settle in for this humorous tale about a sheep that has trouble falling asleep!

After You Read

Little ones will be eager to imitate Russell with this fun counting idea! Arrange youngsters in a circle. Have students count from one to ten around the circle. Direct the child who says ten to lie down on the floor and pretend to be Russell falling asleep. (Encourage him to use his best fake snore!) Then, on your signal, have the group call out, "Wake up, Russell!" prompting him to sit up and begin a new round of counting.

Guess How Much I Love You

Written by Sam McBratney
Illustrated by Anita Jeram

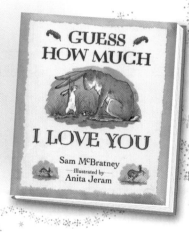

Little Nutbrown Hare attempts to show Big Nutbrown Hare how far-reaching his love is for him. Then, as they share just how much they love one another, this adorable little bunny realizes that love can be quite difficult to measure!

I tell my nana I love her every time I see her!

Before You Read

Display the cover of the book and read its title aloud. Tell youngsters that today's story is about a little rabbit that tries different ways to show a big rabbit how much he loves him. Next, hand a child a heart cutout. Ask her to name someone she loves and tell how she shows him or her. Then have her pass the heart to a classmate. After each child has had the opportunity to share her thoughts, read aloud this loving tale. 🖥

Do You Know How Much I Love You?

After You Read

Invite each child to show how much he loves someone special with this adorable valentine! Take a photo of each child holding a heart cutout. Help him glue the photo to the front of a construction paper card programmed as shown. Then have him attach a copy of the poem shown to the inside of the card. Finally, encourage him to dictate words to complete the poem and then illustrate his thoughts. 🖥

I love you up to the stars,
And that is quite a lot!
So have a happy
Valentine's Day
From your loving tot!

Quinn

Flower Garden
Written by Eve Bunting
Illustrated by Kathryn Hewitt

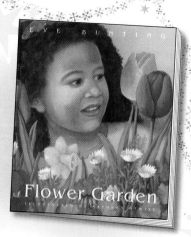

With her father's help, a little girl creates a breathtaking window box as a birthday gift for her mother. When her mom arrives home at the end of the day, she is welcomed with a heartwarming surprise!

ideas contributed by Ada Goren, Winston-Salem, NC

> She could plant flowers at her grandma's house and pick some when they visit!

Before You Read

Display the cover of the book and read the title aloud. Tell youngsters that today's story is about a little girl who wants to plant a flower garden for her mother's birthday, but she lives in a city apartment where she does not have a yard for planting. Then challenge students' critical thinking by inviting them to brainstorm how the little girl could plant a garden. After students share their thoughts, have them settle in for this heartwarming story.

This beautiful flower box,
As pretty as can be,
Was handmade just for you
Because you're special to me!

Shantae

After You Read

Invite each child to make a window box for someone special to her! For each child, program a window box cutout with the poem shown and then have her glue the box to a sheet of construction paper. Encourage each child to use cupcake liners, pom-poms, craft sticks, and leaf cutouts to make flowers above the box. Then encourage her to sign her name near the poem. What a lovely gift! 🖥

Editor's Tip:
Are you looking for the perfect Mother's Day present? Look no further! Little ones' mothers will be thrilled with this vibrant project!

Sakes Alive! A Cattle Drive

Written by Karma Wilson
Illustrated by Karla Firehammer

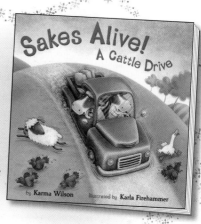

Mabel and Molly, two adventurous cows, sneak Farmer's truck keys out of his back pocket. Then off they tear on a wild joyride! Soon after, a parade of police cars follows closely behind, desperately trying to corral this crazy pair of bovines!

The cows will go on a picnic!

Before You Read

Before revealing the cover of the book, ask youngsters to tell what they know about a cow. For example, they might share what it sounds like, what it eats, where it lives, and what it might do. Next, tell little ones the story you are going to read is about two cows that do something very unusual! Then ask little ones to predict what they think the cows will do. After everyone has the opportunity to make a prediction, display the book's cover and then read aloud this hilarious adventure.

After You Read

Give each child an enlarged truck cutout (pattern on page 56) and have him color the truck. Cut out the window. Then help him attach a photo of himself to the back of the truck so his face peeks through the window. Encourage him to glue the truck to construction paper programmed as shown. To complete the truck, have him glue brown crinkle shreds (hay) above the truck bed. Then encourage him to draw details. If desired, bind the pages together to make a class book titled "Sakes Alive! Preschoolers Drive!" 🖥

Sakes alive!

See Caleb drive!

Storytime

Sheila Rae, the Brave

Written and illustrated by Kevin Henkes

Sheila Rae always acts brave in front of her scaredy-cat little sister. But when Sheila Rae gets lost, it's her little sister who comes to the rescue!

ideas contributed by Roxanne LaBell Dearman
Western NC Early Intervention Program for Children Who Are Deaf or Hard of Hearing
Charlotte, NC

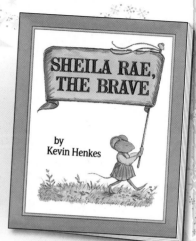

> I climbed up a really, really tall slide and then went down it!

Before You Read

Display the cover of the book and read its title aloud. Tell little ones that today's story is about a mouse who likes to show how brave she is. Then ask students to tell about a time they acted brave, inviting each child to hold a Badge of Courage (pattern on page 160) as she shares her story. After each child has had the opportunity to share, have youngsters settle in for this delightful tale with a sweet ending. 🖥️

> I am not afraid of big dogs or tall trees or monsters!

After You Read

What would Sheila Rae say? Youngsters are sure to tell you with this cute project! Have each child cut a gray heart cutout in half and attach the halves (ears) to either side of a gray teardrop cutout (head) so it resembles Sheila Rae. Have her color a nose and the insides of the ears. Then direct her to add eyes to the project. Next, have her dictate something Sheila Rae would say. Write her words on a speech bubble. Then display the projects and bubbles with the title "What Would Sheila Rae Say?"

My Lucky Day

Written and illustrated by Keiko Kasza

When Mr. Fox answers a knock at the door, he is thrilled to see a delicious-looking piglet standing there. However, this wise little piglet keeps Mr. Fox so busy and distracted that there's no chance he's getting his pork dinner.

The fox has the lucky day because it eats the pig!

Before You Read

Show youngsters the cover of the book and have them describe what they see. Ask students to study each animal's expression and tell what it might be thinking. Then read aloud the title and ask "Which animal do you think has the lucky day? Why?" After youngsters share their thoughts, have them settle in for this entertaining read-aloud with a surprising twist!

After You Read

Encourage little ones to reenact the story using story-related props. Provide items such as a stuffed toy pig, a roasting pan, a pail for bathing the pig, a bath brush, a towel, empty salt and pepper shakers, and other cooking and food-related items. To inspire story extensions, provide other stuffed animals, such as a bear and a wolf.

Badge of Courage

TEC41055

BOOK UNITS

Perfectly Pleasing Pig Characters!

These fabulous books have one thing in common—
a splendid selection of swine!

ideas contributed by Ada Goren, Winston-Salem, NC

Pigs Aplenty, Pigs Galore

Written and illustrated by David McPhail

The narrator of this story has a quiet evening interrupted by the antics of a pack of pigs that take over his kitchen, order pizzas, and bring in their pig pals by the busload!

What Would You Do?
Dictating information

Youngsters put themselves in the story with this simple project and display. Print an expressive photo of each youngster in your class and then trim around the photo. Have each child color a copy of page 165 and then attach her photo to the page. Next, encourage her to dictate what she would do if she found pigs aplenty in her kitchen. Write her words on the page. If desired, display youngsters' work with the title of the book.

If there were pigs in my kitchen, I would have them make cookies.

Rhymes Aplenty
Identifying rhyming words

Youngsters supply rhyming words during a second reading of the story. In advance, cut out several copies of the pigs on page 166. Then read the book aloud, pausing before each word that completes a rhyme and encouraging youngsters to supply the word. Each time they provide the rhyming word, have a child attach a pig cutout to your board. By the time the story is finished, you'll have pigs aplenty! 🖥

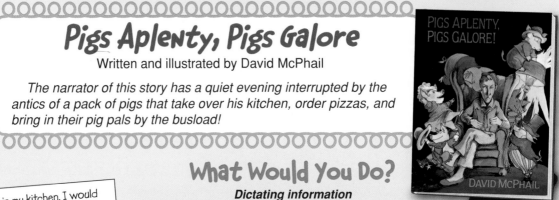

How Many Pigs?
Counting

With this giggle-inducing activity, youngsters get to be the pigs from the story! Choose a small group of youngsters and encourage them to act like the pigs. Say, "There are pigs here on our floor. Pigs aplenty, pigs galore!" Have the pigs freeze momentarily and prompt the remaining students to help you count the pigs. Then pretend to give the pigs pizza and encourage them to go back to their seats. Repeat the process with different numbers of pigs.

Piggies

Written by Audrey Wood
Illustrated by Don Wood

This delightfully illustrated story features smart, long, silly, fat, and wee pigs dancing on a child's fingers.

My Five Piggies

Trisha

Fingertip Piggies

Responding to a story through art

Invite each youngster to make a simple version of the pigs found in the story! Trace each youngster's hand and wrist as shown. Encourage her to color the tracing. Then prompt her to make two pink fingerprints above each finger. Use a fine-tip marker to add details to the fingerprints so they resemble pigs. Then title the page as shown.

We All Have Piggies!

Performing a fingerplay

A quick examination will show youngsters that they have the same types of fingers as the child in the story. Lead youngsters in this fingerplay to get those piggies wigglin'!

I have two fat piggies,	*Hold up thumbs.*
Two smart piggies,	*Also raise index fingers.*
And two long piggies too.	*Also raise middle fingers.*
I have two silly piggies	*Also raise ring fingers.*
And two wee piggies	*Also raise little fingers.*
Waving right at you!	*Wave both hands.*

Clean and Dirty

Exploring the sense of touch

The pigs in this story are cute when they're clean and when they're dirty as well! Youngsters experience both clean and dirty pigs at this sensory center! Place a tub of soapy water and a tub of mud at a table along with plastic or craft foam pigs. Also provide scrub brushes, if desired. A youngster helps a pig roll around in the mud. Then she washes it in the sudsy water. Ah, sparkling clean!

Oink?

Written by Margie Palatini
Illustrated by Henry Cole

Two pigs are living a happy life on the farm, but the other animals think the pigs are too messy, too lazy, and too stinky. Will the pigs end up improving themselves—or will the other animals do it for them?

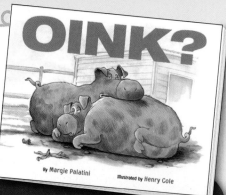

What Happened?

Dramatizing the story

After a read-aloud of the story, place a few simple props in your dramatic-play area to encourage story retellings! Provide an empty paint can and brushes, baskets and plastic vegetables, and a blue blanket or sheet (watering hole). Also provide a copy of the book. Youngsters are sure to enjoy using the props to dramatize and extend the story.

Baa?

Developing connections between spoken and written words

Write the sentences shown on sentence strips and cut the words apart. Place the sentences in your pocket chart. Also write each suggestion below on two separate sentence strip pieces. Begin reading the story, running your fingers below the sentence strips the first time the pigs respond in such a manner. The next time this occurs in the story, replace "Oink?" with "Baa?" Once again read the words from the story and run your fingers below the sentence strips. When youngsters protest that this is incorrect, say, "I am so silly! Those letters don't make the word *oink;* they make the word *baa!*" Continue in the same way with the remaining options.

Suggestions: *baa, moo, woof, meow, tweet, roar*

Pigs in a Puddle

Responding to the story through art

To make the pigs in their nice, clean puddle, give each child enlarged copies of two of the pig patterns on page 166. Have him fingerpaint one pig pink and the remaining pig brown. Then have him glue the pigs and an aluminum foil watering hole cutout to a sheet of paper. If desired, attach speech bubbles as shown.

Note to the teacher: Use with "What Would You Do?" on page 162.

Pig Patterns

Use with "Rhymes Aplenty" on page 162 and "Pigs in a Puddle" on page 164.

TEC41050

TEC41050

TEC41050

TEC41050

WHERE THE WILD THINGS ARE

STORY AND PICTURES BY MAURICE SENDAK

Where the Wild Things Are

Written and illustrated by Maurice Sendak

Soon after a mischievous boy named Max is sent to his room, the room transforms into a forest and he "travels" to the land where the Wild Things are. Much to Max's delight, he is named king and has a grand time cavorting with the creatures. But, in the end, Max is lonely and returns home—the place where he is loved best of all.

Elizabeth Cook, St. Louis, MO

Moody Max

Making text-to-self connections

Throughout the story Max feels many different emotions! Revisit the story page by page and have youngsters name Max's emotions. Write each emotion on a sticky note and place it on the corresponding page. Then reread the story, pausing each time you come to a sticky note and prompting youngsters to mirror Max's emotions.

angry

happy

afraid

From Bedroom to Forest

Investigating the story's setting

Youngsters re-create Max's bedroom transformation with this activity! To prepare, draw a simple bedroom scene on a sheet of bulletin board paper. Place the scene on a table and gather youngsters around it. Ask them what happens to Max's bedroom in the story. After the answer is shared, take the group outside and invite each child to gather natural items, such as branches, leaves, grass, and rocks. Return to the classroom and have each child glue his items to the paper to transform Max's bedroom into a forest!

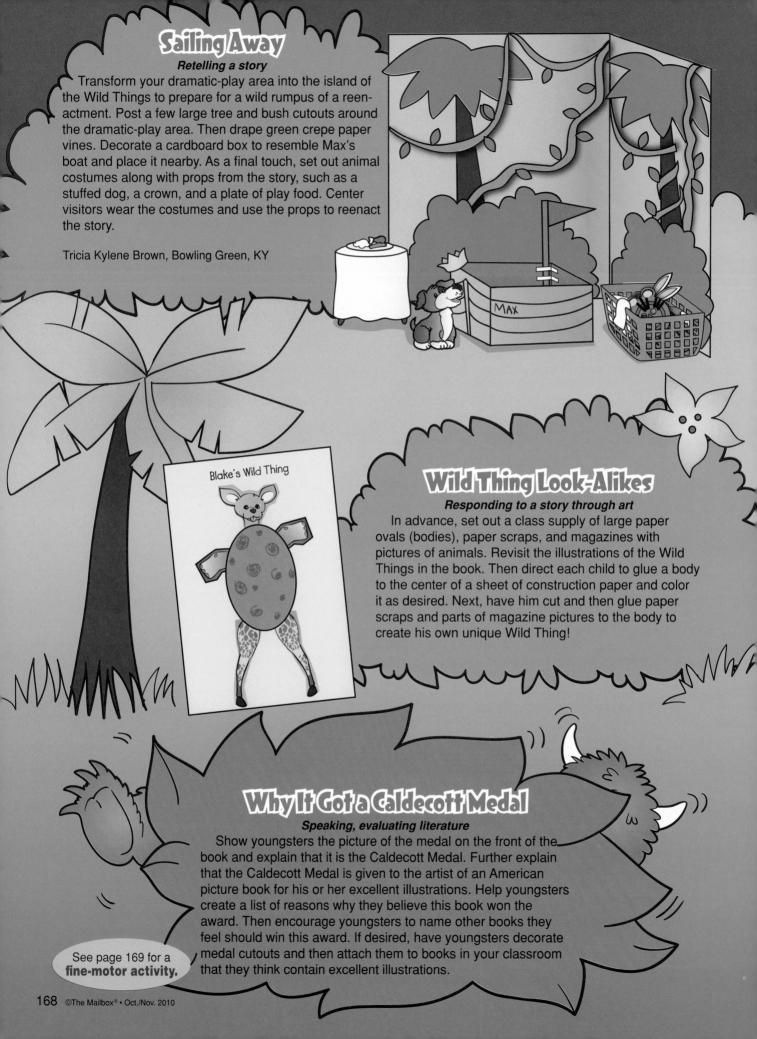

Sailing Away
Retelling a story

Transform your dramatic-play area into the island of the Wild Things to prepare for a wild rumpus of a reenactment. Post a few large tree and bush cutouts around the dramatic-play area. Then drape green crepe paper vines. Decorate a cardboard box to resemble Max's boat and place it nearby. As a final touch, set out animal costumes along with props from the story, such as a stuffed dog, a crown, and a plate of play food. Center visitors wear the costumes and use the props to reenact the story.

Tricia Kylene Brown, Bowling Green, KY

Blake's Wild Thing

Wild Thing Look-Alikes
Responding to a story through art

In advance, set out a class supply of large paper ovals (bodies), paper scraps, and magazines with pictures of animals. Revisit the illustrations of the Wild Things in the book. Then direct each child to glue a body to the center of a sheet of construction paper and color it as desired. Next, have him cut and then glue paper scraps and parts of magazine pictures to the body to create his own unique Wild Thing!

Why It Got a Caldecott Medal
Speaking, evaluating literature

Show youngsters the picture of the medal on the front of the book and explain that it is the Caldecott Medal. Further explain that the Caldecott Medal is given to the artist of an American picture book for his or her excellent illustrations. Help youngsters create a list of reasons why they believe this book won the award. Then encourage youngsters to name other books they feel should win this award. If desired, have youngsters decorate medal cutouts and then attach them to books in your classroom that they think contain excellent illustrations.

See page 169 for a **fine-motor activity.**

Terrible Teeth

Note to the teacher: Give each child a copy of this page and a strip of colorful construction paper. Have her color the page. Then teach her how to angle scissors so she can snip triangles from the strip. Have her glue the triangles (teeth) to the Wild Thing's mouth.

Books With Bear Characters

Youngsters will fall in love with the adorable bear characters in this super selection of books!

ideas contributed by Elizabeth Cook, St. Louis, MO

Bear Wants More

Written by Karma Wilson and illustrated by Jane Chapman

Bear sleeps through the winter. When springtime comes, Bear awakens with an enormous appetite! He eats a bounty of food but still wants more! So his friends plan a surprise feast to help satisfy Bear's insatiable hunger.

What Would You Eat?

Relating to a story character

After reading the story aloud, review with students the things Bear eats and list them on chart paper. Then have youngsters curl up on the floor and pretend to be asleep. Prompt little ones to wake up and pretend to be as hungry as Bear is after his long winter nap. Have students name foods they would want to eat and list them on the paper. Then compare the lists to see whether the children and Bear like to eat the same things.

What Bear Eats	Food We Would Want
grass	hot dogs
strawberries	macaroni and cheese
clover	pizza
fish	strawberries
honey cakes	pancakes

I'm So Hungry!

Role-playing, gross-motor skills

Youngsters pretend to be Bear waking up after a long winter nap! Have youngsters line up with their feet spread apart to form a cave. Direct the child at the back of the cave (Bear) to crawl through the cave, emerge from the front, and say, "I'm so hungry!" Then that child becomes the front of the cave and the child at the back becomes Bear. Continue until each child has played the part of Bear. Then invite your hungry little bears to snack on some teddy bear-shaped crackers.

Nibble, Nibble, Crunch!

Responding to a story through art

Give each child a yellow bear cutout (pattern on page 173). Have her paint the bear with a thick layer of brown paint and then drag the tines of a plastic fork through the paint to create the illusion of fur. To complete the project, have her glue a hole-punch dot (eye) and green crinkle shreds (clover) to the bear.

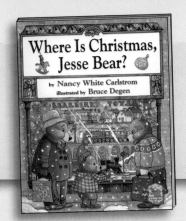

Where Is Christmas, Jesse Bear?
Written by Nancy White Carlstrom and illustrated by Bruce Degen

Jesse Bear explores wonderful holiday sights, smells, sounds, and activities and discovers that Christmas is all these things and much more!

Where Is Christmas?
Dictating information

Holiday traditions and special activities lead Jesse Bear to discover where Christmas truly is. Youngsters express their own ideas about where to find Christmas (or another special holiday) with this activity! Write the desired holiday name on a copy of page 174. Then help each child write his name. Read the prompt aloud. Encourage him to dictate something that has special meaning to him during the holiday and then have him illustrate his words.

Where is ___Christmas___,

___Joshua___ ?

___Christmas___ is...

at Grandma's house helping her decorate the tree!

Friendly Gifts
Making connections

Youngsters will feel the joy of giving just as the bears in the story do! Discuss the page spread that shows the bears wrapping Christmas cookies and read the tag on each plate. Then invite each child to make a similar gift for someone she knows. Have her decorate cookie cutouts and glue them to a holiday plate. Next, help her wrap the plate with clear cellophane and then tie the cellophane with a festive ribbon. Finally, help her label a tag for the intended recipient and attach it to the gift. 🖥

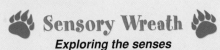

Sensory Wreath
Exploring the senses

Little ones experience some of the same textures, sights, smells, and sounds that Jesse Bear does at this sensory center! Provide an evergreen wreath (or evergreen branches) along with items such as plastic ornaments, jumbo bells, pinecones, and cinnamon sticks. A youngster uses his senses to investigate the items and then uses the items to decorate the wreath.

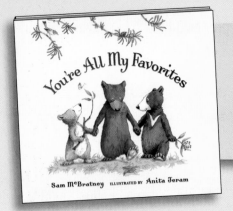

You're All My Favorites

Written by Sam McBratney and illustrated by Anita Jeram

Mommy and Daddy Bear tell their three cubs that they are the most wonderful baby bears in the whole world! Then each of the cubs begins to wonder how they could all be the best. But Mommy and Daddy Bear know just what to say!

🐾 Big or Little? 🐾

Sorting by size

The story has big bears and little bears! Have youngsters practice sorting big from little with the main characters and some of the special guests in the story! Cut out a copy of the cards on page 175 and place them faceup on a table. Have a child choose a card and decide whether it represents a big or little creature by using a big booming voice or a teeny tiny voice. For example, she might say in a loud voice, "Big butterfly!" Then have her place the card in your pocket chart. Continue with each card until all the pairs are on the chart. 💻

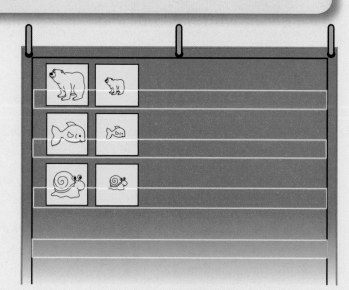

🐾 You Are So Wonderful! 🐾

Dictating information

Youngsters share why someone special to them is wonderful, just like the bears in the story! Ask a child to name someone he thinks is wonderful and why that is so. Write his words on a copy of the bear on page 173. Continue with each child. Then display the bears with the title "I Know Someone 'Bear-y' Wonderful!"

🐾 Let's Compare! 🐾

Evaluating literature, organizing data

After reading all three bear books in this unit, have little ones share which book is their favorite! Make three yarn circles on the floor and place each book in a circle. Help youngsters briefly summarize each story. Then give each child a copy of the bear on page 173, reduced in size. Encourage each child to write his name on his bear and then place it in the circle with his favorite bear book. Prompt youngsters to discuss the results using the words *fewer, more,* and *equal.* 💻

Bear Pattern
Use with "Nibble, Nibble, Crunch!" on page 170 and "You Are So Wonderful!" and
"Let's Compare!" on page 172.

TEC41052

Where is _____,

_____?

_____ is…

Note to the teacher: Use with "Where Is Christmas?" on page 171.

TEC41052

TEC41052

TEC41052

TEC41052

TEC41052

TEC41052

TEC41052

TEC41052

TEC41052

TEC41052

TEC41052

TEC41052

The Wind Blew

Written and illustrated by Pat Hutchins

Townspeople's belongings are whisked away by windy weather! The wind carries their belongings for a while. Then it throws the items down and blows out to sea.

ideas contributed by Roxanne LaBell Dearman
Western NC Early Intervention Program for Children Who Are Deaf or Hard of Hearing
Charlotte, NC

Wow, What Windy Weather!

Recognizing beginning sound /w/

After reading the story aloud, engage little ones in this fun wind-producing activity! Lead youngsters in saying the word *wind* and in practicing its beginning sound. Then give each child a small piece of tagboard. Say, "I see a [name of an object] blowing in the wind!" emphasizing the object's beginning sound. If the word begins like *wind*, youngsters make a breeze by fanning their piece of tagboard. If the word begins with a different sound, students stay still. Repeat the activity, choosing from the following for words with the beginning sound /w/: *wagon, wand, watermelon, watch, walnut, worm, wallet, whale, well,* and *wig.*

What Blew Next?

Sequencing story events

To prepare, color and cut out the picture cards on a copy of page 178. Mount a strip of blue paper (sky) on a wall and place the cards faceup nearby. Add details to the sky, if desired. Reread the story, keeping the pages of the book concealed. Pause on each page and prompt students to name the item that blew away. When the correct item is named, invite a child to attach the appropriate card to the sky. Continue until all the cards are displayed in the correct sequence. 💻

The Wind Took My...

Developing visual memory

Display items like the ones in the story, such as an umbrella, a hat, a shirt, a scarf, an envelope, and a newspaper. Review the items with the group. Next, have youngsters turn their backs to the items. Encourage students to pretend a big gust of wind blows through the classroom while you remove one of the items. Then say, "Oh no! One of my things blew away!" Prompt youngsters to turn around and name the missing item. Repeat the activity several times, removing a different item each time.

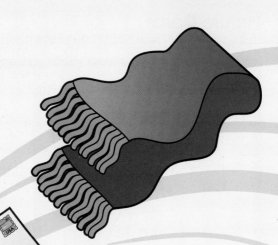

There It Goes!

Creating a story innovation

Help little ones act out a new version of the story! Have a child choose an item from the classroom, such as a stuffed toy, a dress-up item, or her own coat. Turn on an indoor fan. Then say, "The wind blew, and it took the [object] away from [child's name]!" Prompt the child to walk through the breeze created by the fan, holding her object in the air and leaving it on a table as if the wind has taken it away. Continue with each remaining child.

One windy day,...
I saw a lion
blow by!

One Windy Day

Contributing to a class book

Give each child a paper programmed with the prompt "One windy day,..." Also provide a variety of magazines. Invite each child to cut out a magazine picture of something she would like to see blowing in the wind. Then have her glue the picture to her page and add details as desired. Encourage her to dictate words to complete the prompt. Then bind the pages together along with a cover titled "One Windy Day." 💻

Picture Cards

Use with "What Blew Next?" on page 176.

TEC41053

TEC41053

TEC41053

TEC41053

TEC41053

TEC41053

TEC41053

TEC41053

TEC41053

TEC41053

TEC41053

The Tale of Peter Rabbit

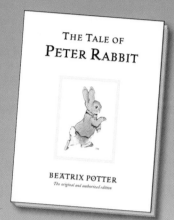

Written and illustrated by Beatrix Potter

This classic story tells the tale of Peter Rabbit, a naughty little bunny who sneaks into Mr. McGregor's garden despite his mother's warning to stay away. After helping himself to a bounty of veggies, Peter runs smack into Mr. McGregor! The lucky little rabbit escapes, but his gluttonous behavior results in a bellyache.

ideas contributed by Ada Goren, Winston-Salem, NC

The Green Thumb Award

Making text-to-self connections

Mr. McGregor's vegetables are irresistible to Peter, but how do your little ones feel about them? Prepare a few vegetables mentioned in the story—such as lettuce, green beans, and radishes—for youngsters to taste. Then write the name of each vegetable on a sheet of paper, as shown. Gather a small group of students and have each child taste the vegetables. Ask youngsters to share how they feel about the vegetables. Then have each child make a green thumbprint on the paper in the row of her favorite. Continue with other small groups of students. Then gather youngsters to count and compare the number of green thumbprints for each choice.

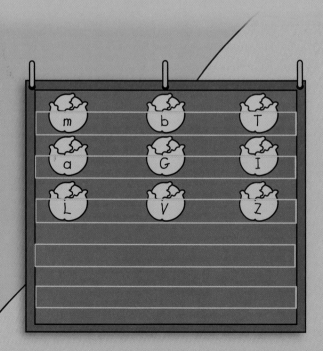

Shoe Search

Identifying letters

Help find one of Peter's shoes with this fun activity! Enlarge the cabbage pattern on page 181 and make several copies. Cut out the cabbages and label each one with a different letter. Also cut out a copy of the shoe on page 181. Place the cabbages in your pocket chart and hide the shoe behind a cabbage. Remind youngsters that Peter loses a shoe among the cabbages in Mr. McGregor's garden. Then have a child identify the letter on a cabbage and lift up the cutout. If he finds Peter's shoe, have him remove the shoe. If he doesn't, continue until the shoe is found. Then play another round of the game. 🖥

Mother Knows Best
Evaluating story events

Help little ones evaluate Peter's decision to go into Mr. McGregor's garden. On a board or chart paper, draw two columns. Label one column with a happy rabbit face and one with a sad rabbit face. Reread the story, stopping to list the good and bad things that happen to Peter as a result of his decision. At the end of the story, review the list with students to determine whether Peter makes a good decision. To conclude the activity, enlist youngsters' help in composing a class letter to Peter explaining why he should listen to his mother. 💻

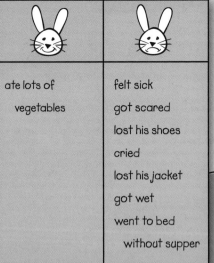

ate lots of vegetables	felt sick
	got scared
	lost his shoes
	cried
	lost his jacket
	got wet
	went to bed without supper

Flopsy, Mopsy
Rhyming

Recite the names of Peter's siblings. Then ask students what they notice about the names, leading them to conclude that the names *Flopsy* and *Mopsy* rhyme. Hand a stuffed toy rabbit to a youngster and encourage her to come up with another rhyming name for a future sibling of Peter's. Then prompt her to hand the rabbit to a classmate, who says an additional rhyming name. Continue in the same way until each child has a turn.

Peter's New Jacket
Responding to a story through art

Invite youngsters to make new jackets for Peter to replace the one he lost! Help each child cut out an enlarged copy of the jacket pattern on page 181. Encourage her to glue torn scrapbook paper or gift wrap scraps to the cutout. Trim any excess paper from the edges. Then have her glue craft foam circles (buttons) to the jacket. If desired, display the jackets with the title "New Jackets for Peter." 💻

TEC41054

TEC41054

Jacket Pattern
Use with "Peter's New Jacket" on page 180.

TEC41054

The Very Lonely Firefly

Eric Carle — The Very Lonely Firefly

Written and illustrated by Eric Carle

A little firefly searches for other fireflies because it is lonely. It sees many things that shine light, such as lightbulbs, candles flames, and fireworks. Only after much searching does it discover a group of fireflies. Now it isn't lonely anymore!

ideas contributed by Margaret Aumen
Emory United Methodist Nursery School
New Oxford, PA

Feeling Lonely?
Building prior knowledge

To enhance this prereading activity and read-aloud, drape a string of white holiday lights in your classroom. Then dim the classroom lights so the holiday lights resemble fireflies. Tell students the name of the book. Ask, "What does *lonely* mean?" and "How do you feel when you're lonely?" After you discuss the answers to these questions, encourage students to name things they could do so they don't feel lonely, such as talk to a friend, play, or read a book with their moms or dads. Then have students settle in for the read-aloud to find out what stops the firefly from feeling lonely.

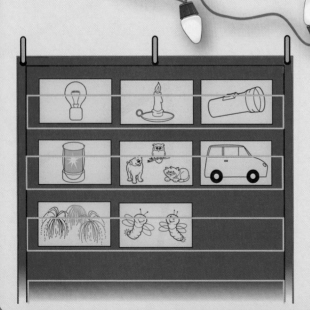

From Light to Light
Sequencing

Spotlight the events in the book with this brilliant activity! Cut out a copy of the cards on page 184. Place the cards faceup on a table. To begin, have students name which light the firefly flies to first, using the book as a reference if needed. Prompt a child to find the corresponding card and place it in your pocket chart. Say, "Is this what the firefly is looking for?" Encourage students to say, "No!" Then continue in the same way with each remaining card, prompting students to say, "Yes!" for the final card! 🖥️

Little Lights
Developing fine-motor skills
This easy process art looks similar to the group of fireflies at the end of the book! Have each child paint a sheet of paper with black paint so it resembles the night sky. Next, give her a ¼-inch-wide strip of paper and encourage her to snip it into little pieces over the painted paper. Now she has a sky filled with fireflies.

Fireflies or Lightning Bugs
Investigating living things
Might another name for this story be "The Very Lonely Lightning Bug"? Why, of course! Explain that fireflies also are called lightning bugs. Then ask youngsters which name they like better. If desired, graph the results! Then encourage students to sing this catchy little song! 💻

(sung to the tune of the chorus of "Jingle Bells")

Fireflies, lightning bugs. Which name will you use?
You can use the one you like. It's up to you to choose!
Fireflies, lightning bugs. They are both the same.
It's so strange that something small would end up with two names!

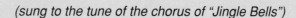

Act It Out!
Dramatizing a story
With this activity, youngsters "fly" from light to light, just like the very lonely firefly! In advance, cut out a copy of the cards on page 184. Remove the firefly card and then position the remaining cards in a loose path around the room in story order. Encourage half of your class (lonely fireflies) to stand at the beginning of the path and half (firefly friends) to stand at the end. Prompt the firefly friends to recite the chant shown. Then instruct each lonely firefly to "fly" from card to card until he joins the firefly friends. Continue with each lonely firefly. Then switch groups so the remaining youngsters get a chance to fly. Now that's some firefly fun! 💻

Don't be lonely anymore. Come find what you're looking for!

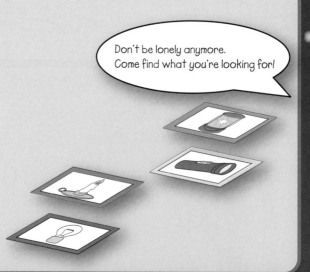

Story Cards

Use with "From Light to Light" on page 182 and "Act It Out!" on page 183.

TEC41055

TEC41055

TEC41055

TEC41055

TEC41055

TEC41055

TEC41055

TEC41055

CENTER UNITS

Center Time at the FAIR

Best "Baa"
Literacy Center

Label several pairs of sheep and prize-ribbon cutouts (patterns on pages 188 and 189) with matching letters. Sort the sheep and ribbons and spread them out faceup. A child chooses a sheep and traces the letter using her index finger. Next, she finds the prize ribbon with the matching letter and traces the letter in the same way. Then she puts the ribbon on the appropriate sheep.

Carole Watkins
Crown Point School Corporation & Northwest Indiana Special
 Education Cooperative
Crown Point, IN

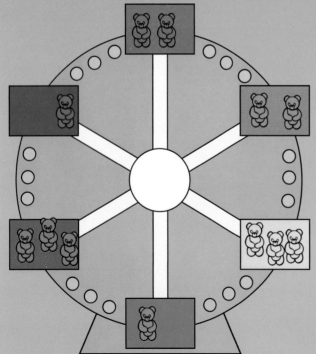

Colorful Ferris Wheel
Math Center

To make a Ferris wheel, attach strips of masking tape to a large tagboard circle as shown. Then tape several different-colored construction paper rectangles (seats) to the circle. Add details as desired. Place the Ferris wheel at a center along with a container of sorting bears. A student places the bears on the seats of the corresponding colors.

Candy Apples
Art Center

Place a supply of tagboard apple cutouts in your art center. Also provide a mixture of white corn syrup and red food coloring. A youngster paints an apple with the mixture so it appears glossy and red like a real candy apple! Then she glues a stick to the back of the cutout. She places her apple in a foil cupcake liner and flattens the liner around the apple. If desired, display these projects with other fair-related artwork and fair photos.

Squirt That Duck!
Water Table

Attach a length of masking tape across your water table to create a finish line. Provide a rubber duck and a squirt bottle filled with water. A child places a duck in the water. Then he uses the squirt bottle to squirt the duck, maneuvering it across the table and past the finish line.

Round and Round
Block Center

To make this faux fair ride, attach large condiment cups near the edge of a lazy Susan, as shown. Put the lazy Susan in the block area along with toy figures that will fit inside the cups. A youngster uses blocks and other accessories to build a pretend fairground. Then he puts a figure in each condiment cup and gives the lazy Susan a spin, pretending the figures are on a ride.

Mary Davis, Keokuk Christian Academy, Keokuk, IA

Face-Paint Designs

Writing Center

Have a student draw a self-portrait on a paper plate. Then have her use a marker or glitter pen to draw face-paint designs on her self-portrait. When she is finished, have her describe her face painting. Write her words on an index card. Then display the painting and the card.

Roxanne LaBell Dearman
Western NC Early Intervention Program for Children Who Are
  Deaf or Hard of Hearing
Charlotte, NC

If I went to a face-painting booth, I would get a butterfly painted on my cheek!

Alexis

Prize-Ribbon Patterns

Use with "Best 'Baa'" on page 186.

TEC41050

TEC41050

TEC41050

Candy Centers

No doubt your little ones will be delighted with this collection of sweet centers!

Caramel Apples
Play Dough Center

Set out red and brown play dough and a supply of craft sticks. A youngster molds red play dough into apple shapes and then adds brown play dough caramel to the apples. Then she inserts a craft stick into each apple. If desired, have students place their creations on waxed paper just like real caramel apples!

adapted from an idea by Marie E. Cecchini, West Dundee, IL

Peppermint Patty
Art Center

Mix a generous amount of peppermint extract into a container of brown paint. Trim a bite cutout from a tagboard circle for each child. A child paints the circle with the paint mixture. Then he wraps a large square of aluminum foil around his project so it resembles a peppermint patty.

Cool Candy Corn

Math Center

Students develop color-matching and sorting skills with this idea! Color a candy corn cutout as shown. Also fill a pumpkin pail with yellow, white, and orange pom-poms. A child sorts the pom-poms onto the appropriate sections of the candy corn.

My Favorite Treats

Fine-Motor Area

Set out store circulars or magazine pages featuring assorted candy and Halloween treats. Also provide scissors and a class supply of goody bags. A youngster looks through the advertisements, cuts or tears out items she would like to receive when she trick-or-treats, and puts them in a goody bag.

Tricia Brown
Bowling Green, KY

Letter Match

Literacy Center

To prepare for this activity, laminate several different candy wrappers for durability. Place the wrappers at the center along with letter cards or tiles that match the candy names. A student chooses a candy wrapper and finds the matching letters. Then he arranges the letters to form the candy name.

Wonderful Winter Centers

These splendid center activities are just perfect for the winter season!

Ice-Fishing Fun

Dramatic-Play Area

Place lengths of aluminum foil on your floor and then put a black circle atop the foil so it resembles an ice-fishing hole. Attach jumbo paper clips to fish cutouts and place the fish on the hole. Provide a magnetic fishing pole along with items such as a plastic pail, winter wear, camping chairs, a mock campfire, a frying pan, and cookware. A child uses the props to engage in pretend ice-fishing play. 🖥

Simonne Perry
Broad Street School
Nashua, NH

Textured Polar Bear

Sensory Center

To prepare, mix equal parts shaving cream and white glue; then add pieces of torn white facial tissue and cotton batting to the mixture. A youngster fingerpaints a paper plate with a thick layer of the mixture, noticing the texture as he paints. When he is finished, he glues two white semicircles (ears), a black circle (nose), and two jumbo wiggle eyes to the project.

Amanda Kasik
Wee Wisdom
Lincoln, NE

Fluffy Snowball

Fine-Motor Area

Provide sheets of paper—such as copy paper, writing paper, or newspaper—cotton balls, and glue. A child crumples a sheet of paper into a snowball shape. Then she stretches and tears cotton balls and glues the pieces to the paper ball. She continues until the entire surface is covered. The result is a soft, fluffy snowball!

adapted from an idea by Sarah Teacher
Broadway Learning Center
Longview, WA

Oh No, Too Slow!

I ran faster than the Gingerbread Man could!
I nibbled his _____leg_____, and it sure tasted good!

Jacob

Oh No, Too Slow!

Writing Center

After reading aloud a favorite version of *The Gingerbread Man,* give each child a copy of page 195 and a gingerbread man cookie. Also provide crayons. A youngster takes a bite of his gingerbread cookie and then dictates a word or words to complete the sentence. He draws a picture to illustrate the page and then enjoys the rest of his cookie.

Lisa Shroyer
Wee Wuns Weekday Ministries
Cypress, TX

Flurries or a Snowstorm?

Math Center

Set out a large construction paper cloud, number cards, and white linking cubes (or any type of white manipulative). A student takes a card and identifies the number. Then he counts aloud that many manipulatives (snowflakes) and places them below the cloud. When he is finished, he removes the snowflakes from beneath the cloud and sets the card aside. Then he repeats the activity with a different card.

Totally Tracks!

Play Dough Center

Set white play dough at a table along with a rolling pin and plastic woodland animals and trees. Also provide items such as rocks and small twigs. A child flattens a portion of dough so it resembles snow. Then she arranges the rocks and trees to complete the snowy scene. Finally, she engages in pretend forest play, pressing the animals' feet into the snow to make tracks.

Mary Ellen Moore
Miller Elementary
Canton, MI

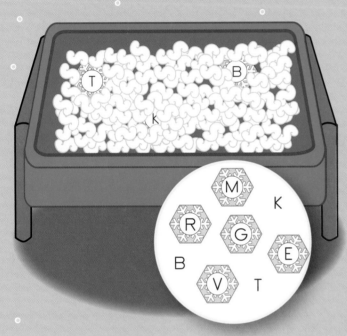

Letter Match

Literacy Center

Fill your sensory table with white packing peanuts or cotton balls to represent snow. Then hide die-cut snowflakes, each labeled with a different letter, in the table. Label a large snowball cutout with the matching letters and place it nearby. A youngster digs through the snow and places each snowflake he finds atop the matching letter on the snowball.

Rexann Roussel
Narrow Acres Preschool
Paulina, LA

It's Snowing!

Art Center

Set out construction paper, crayons, slightly diluted glue, and a container of instant potato flakes. A student uses a white crayon to draw an outdoor scene on a sheet of black paper. Then she spreads glue on a portion of the paper and sprinkles it with potato flakes (snowflakes). She repeats the process to create a snowy outdoor scene.

I ran faster than the Gingerbread Man could!

I nibbled his _____, and it sure

tasted good!

Fine-Motor Fun at Center Time

Every center in this fabulous collection gives youngsters an excellent fine-motor workout as well as targeting important preschool skills!

Clip and Drop
Math Center

Fill a large plastic jar with colorful, squishy balls (or crumpled balls of colorful paper). For each color, provide matching spring-style clothespins. A student spills the balls out of the jar. Then she chooses a clothespin, clips it to a matching ball, and releases the ball into the jar. She continues in the same way until all the balls are back in the jar.

Marnie Cooper
The Ark Preschool
Rockwall, TX

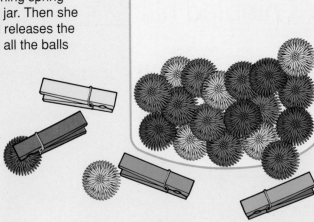

Freestyle Sculpture
Recycling Center

Obtain a large block of packing foam. Also provide a collection of milk caps, bottle tops, pipe cleaners, and unsharpened regular and fat pencils. A youngster visits the center and presses desired items into the foam. To make a curly stem, he wraps a pipe cleaner around a pencil and then slides it off. He presses one or both ends of the stem into the foam.

Jacqueline Higgins
Eastminster Presbyterian Preschool
Indialantic, FL

Zip, Snap, and Buckle!
Dramatic-Play Area
Stock the area with assorted carryalls—such as a purse, a backpack, a briefcase, a suitcase, and an athletic bag—along with items to fill each one. A child unfastens a carryall and puts several items inside. Then he refastens it and acts out a role appropriately suited for the carryall. When he is finished, he undoes the fastener and unpacks the carryall.

Marie E. Cecchini
West Dundee, IL

Plunger Person
Manipulative Center
Decorate the base of an unused plunger so it resembles a head, as shown. Provide a collection of items that will easily fit onto the plunger handle, such as elastic hair ties, plastic bracelets, napkin rings, and small cardboard tubes. Also provide lengths of colorful ribbon and a few silk scarves. A student decorates the plunger by sliding or tying items onto the handle.

Mary Davis, Ankeny Christian Academy, Ankeny, IA

Tactile Masterpiece
Art Center
In one end of a lidded box, cut a hole large enough for a child's hand to fit through. Put in the box a sheet of paper trimmed to fit. A child spoons paint onto the paper and then closes the lid of the box. She reaches through the hole and fingerpaints on the paper using only her sense of touch. Then she removes the painting from the box.

Ellen Maguire
Little Corner Schoolhouse
Brookline, MA

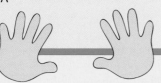

Designer Cakes

Play Dough Center

This simple idea takes the cake! Place several laminated copies of page 199 at a table. Also provide colorful play dough and birthday candles. A child uses the items to decorate the cake. 💻

adapted from an idea by Sandy Prosen
Early Childhood Family Education
Cottage Grove, MN

Chunky Noodles

Lacing Center

To prepare, cut foam pool noodles into three-inch chunks and put them in your sensory table. Attach a length of thick yarn (or ribbon) to a prepared piece of noodle. A student visits the table and strings the pieces onto the yarn. Now that's using her noodle!

Sandy Prosen

Perfect Punches

Writing Center

Set out an assortment of shape punches. A youngster punches desired shapes from scrap paper. Then he glues the shapes to a sheet of paper. After he draws desired details, he dictates a sentence or a story about his picture.

Katie Stephens
Macomb Christian Early Education Center
Warren, MI

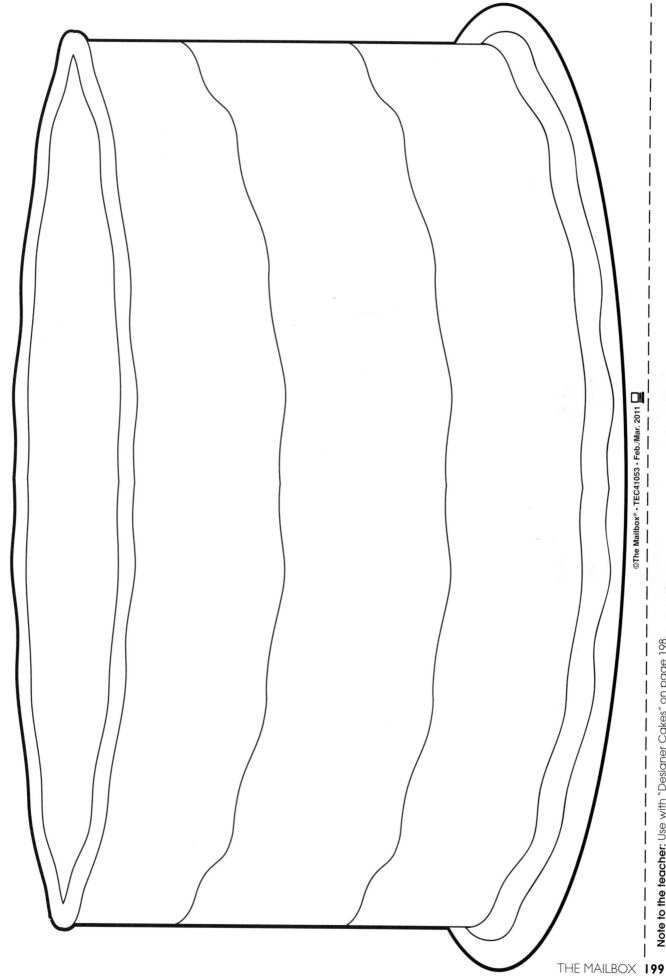

©The Mailbox® • TEC41053 • Feb./Mar. 2011

Note to the teacher: Use with "Designer Cakes" on page 198.

Fabulous Flower Centers!

Youngsters' knowledge will bloom with these vibrant ideas!

ideas contributed by Elizabeth Cook, Saint Louis, MO

Muffin Tin Prints
Art Center

A muffin tin is the key to this unique artwork! Have a child flip a six-cup muffin tin over and paint the bottom of each cup in one row. Encourage her to turn the tin over and press the painted cups against a sheet of paper to make a print. Prompt her to glue a pom-pom in the center of each print. Then have her paint a stem and leaves below each resulting flower.

Smelly Skunk
Games Center

Color a copy of the cards on page 203 so the flower pairs match. Then cut out the cards and laminate them for durability. Place the cards facedown at a center. To play, a youngster flips a card. If the card shows a flower, he flips a second card. If the flowers match, he sets the pair aside. If they do not, he turns the cards back over. If he flips a card that shows a skunk, he holds his nose and says, "Oh no, smelly skunk!" Then he flips the card back and his turn ends. Play continues, in turn, until all the flowers are matched.

Geometric Garden

Flannelboard Center

Place near a flannelboard an assortment of felt shapes—such as circles, squares, triangles, rectangles, and ovals—along with felt flower stems and leaves. Also provide felt soil, raindrops, clouds, and a sun. A child uses the shapes to create a geometric flower garden scene.

Beautiful Arrangement

Math Center

This activity spotlights measurement skills, fine-motor skills, and counting skills! Label plastic vases with different numbers. Provide artificial flowers, measuring cups, and a tub of uncooked rice. A youngster uses a measuring cup to partially fill a vase with rice. Then he inserts the appropriate number of flower stems into the rice to create a beautiful flower arrangement. He continues with each remaining vase.

Petal Touch

Sensory Center

Remove the petals from a few flowers and place them in a tray. Then place the tray at the center along with magnifying glasses. If desired, provide translucent color paddles. A youngster touches the petals, exploring the soft texture. Then he uses a magnifying glass and color paddles to explore the petals visually.

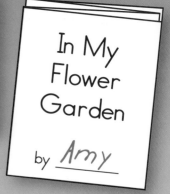

In My Flower Garden

Literacy Center

For each child, accordion-fold a 6" x 18" paper strip to make a four-page booklet. Title each booklet "In My Flower Garden." Also provide flower catalogs and crayons. A child writes her name on the cover. Then she cuts out pictures from the flower catalogs and glues them to the pages. Finally, she adds details and writing to the pages. 🖥

What Will You Grow?

Dramatic-Play Area

On the floor, place brown bulletin board paper with soil details drawn on it. Put plastic tubs partially filled with clean potting soil atop the paper. Provide garden props, such as seed packets, small plastic shovels, toy watering cans, gardening gloves and aprons, foam kneeling cushions, and artificial flowers. Youngsters use the props to engage in pretend gardening play. 🖥

Suzanne Foote, East Ithaca Preschool, Ithaca, NY

Seed Sacks

Discovery Center

Obtain packets of several different types of seeds. For each type of seed, put a dampened paper towel in a resealable plastic bag, place several seeds atop the towel, and then seal the bag; reinforce the seal with tape. Place the bags at a center along with the empty seed packets and magnifying glasses. A youngster uses a magnifying glass to investigate similarities and differences in the seeds and observe any changes that might occur.

TEC41054
TEC41054
TEC41054
TEC41054
TEC41054
TEC41054
TEC41054
TEC41054
TEC41054
TEC41054
TEC41054
TEC41054

Watermelon Centers

Once little ones get a taste of these juicy centers, they're sure to want more!

ideas contributed by Tricia Kylene Brown, Bowling Green, KY

Melon Masterpiece

Art Center

This craft gives youngsters a fine-motor workout! Set out white construction paper watermelon slices, shallow pans of red and black paint, a crumpled lunch bag, and green tissue paper scraps. A child dips the bag in the red paint and makes prints on the slice. After the watermelon is painted, he glues crumpled tissue paper along the bottom of the slice so it resembles a rind. Then he dips his fingertip in the black paint and dabs it on the watermelon to make seeds.

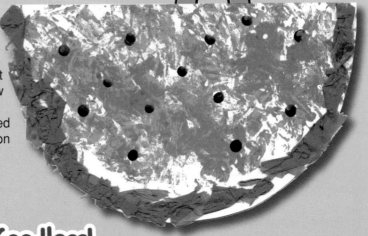

It's Seedless!

Math Center

Youngsters get rid of those pesky watermelon seeds with an activity on presubtraction skills! Place craft foam seeds on a watermelon slice cutout. Place a stack of number cards facedown. A youngster flips a card and identifies the number. He "picks" that many seeds off the watermelon and sets them aside. Then he continues with other number cards until all the seeds have been removed.

Sweet Sailboats

Water Table

Cut a small watermelon in half and scoop out the fruit for a future snack. Attach a tagboard triangle to each of two rulers (or dowels). Press each ruler into a separate watermelon half, as shown, so it resembles a sailboat. Float the sailboats in your water table and provide toy figures (passengers) and plastic ocean critters. A child uses the sailboats and props to engage in pretend ocean play.

Red and Green

Play Dough Center

Provide red and green play dough, a rolling pin, and plastic knives. A child molds red play dough into the shape of a watermelon. She flattens green play dough with the rolling pin to make the rind and wraps the rind around the watermelon. Then she uses a knife to slice her watermelon!

Load 'em Up!

Block Center

Use permanent markers to decorate green plastic eggs so they resemble tiny watermelons. Put the watermelons in the block area along with green Easter grass, watermelon seed packets, lengths of green yarn (vines), and a toy dump truck. A youngster uses blocks, the grass, the seed packets, and the vines to create a pretend watermelon patch. He acts out tending the patch and, when the watermelons are ready to harvest, loads them onto the truck!

Pairs of Seeds

Literacy Center

Color, cut out, and laminate several copies of page 206. Give each child at the center a watermelon slice and place the seed cutouts facedown in a pile. In turn, each child flips a seed. He scans his slice for the corresponding uppercase letter and then places the seed on the outline beside it. If the outline already has a seed, he returns the cutout facedown to the pile. Play continues until each child completes his board.

Watermelon and Seed Patterns

Use with "Pairs of Seeds" on page 205.

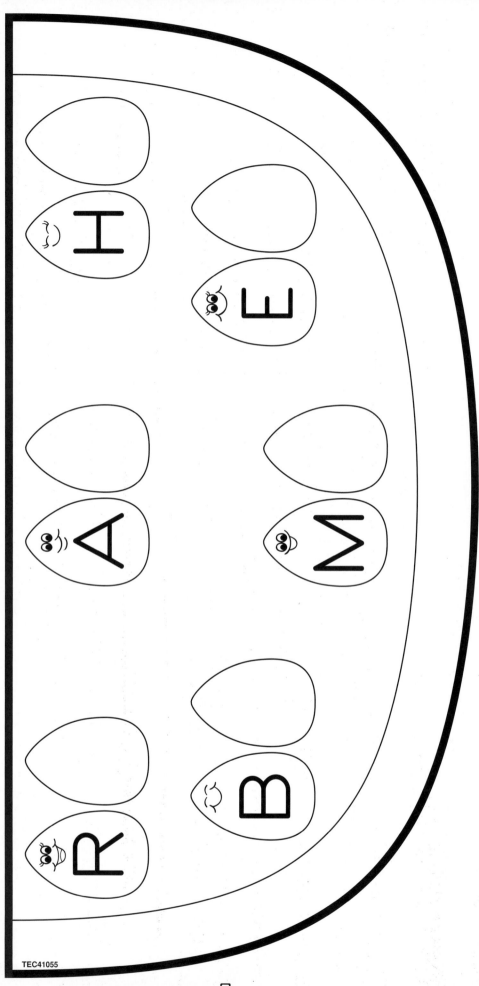

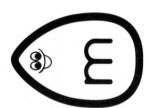

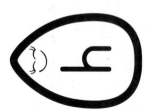

TEC41055

LITERACY UNITS

A Feast of Literacy Ideas!

No doubt your little ones have a craving for unique literacy activities. Look no further than this buffet of ideas just perfect for the Thanksgiving season!

Fabulous Feast

Beginning sounds

Your little ones are sure to enjoy this savory activity! Cut out a copy of the cards on page 210. Place the cards faceup and set a paper plate nearby. If desired, tie a napkin around your neck and carry a fork and spoon to use as dramatic props. Tell students that you are *really* hungry but need help deciding which food to put on your plate. Lead little ones in singing the song shown, inserting the beginning sound of one of the featured foods. Then ask youngsters to decide which food begins with that sound. When the correct food is determined, invite a child to put the card on the plate. Pretend to gobble up the food. Repeat the activity with each remaining card. 💻

(sung to the tune of "The Farmer in the Dell")

This food is looking great.
Oh, I can hardly wait.
Which food begins with [/m/]?
Let's put it on my plate.

adapted from an idea by Marie E. Cecchini, West Dundee, IL

Perfect Pies

Sorting uppercase and lowercase letters

Label white craft foam apple slices with either an uppercase *A* or a lowercase *a.* Store the slices in a bowl at a center along with a large and a small pie tin labeled as shown. Also provide two labeled piecrust cutouts. A child takes each apple slice from the bowl and puts it in the appropriate pie tin. After the bowl is empty, she tops off each tin with a piecrust.

Incredible Corn
Using descriptive language
Prepare a taste-testing area with different types of corn and corn-related products, such as whole-kernel corn, cream-style corn, corn bread, cornflakes, and corn chips. Invite small groups of students to sample the assorted products, encouraging each child to describe how they look, smell, feel, taste, and sound. Record youngsters' responses.

Thyme for Turkey
Developing phonological awareness
Give each child in a small group a copy of page 211. Explain that *turkey* begins with /t/. Prompt students to say "turkey" several times, listening for the /t/ sound. Next, encourage each child to smell a spice shaker filled with thyme. Explain that some people put thyme on their turkey when they bake it. Lead youngsters to notice that *thyme* and *turkey* both begin with /t/. Encourage youngsters to color the page. Then have little ones brush glue on their turkeys and sprinkle thyme on the glue.

Hot Potato
Manipulating phonemes
Try this giggle-inducing twist on a familiar game! Hold up a real or plastic potato and say its name followed by a rhyming nonsense word, such as "Potato, lotato." To play, have students sit or stand in a circle. Put on a recording of lively music and have students pass the potato around the circle. Periodically stop the music, signaling youngsters to stop. Encourage the child who is holding the potato to call out "potato" and a rhyming nonsense word.

Potato, dotato!

Beginning Sound Cards

Use with "Fabulous Feast" on page 208.

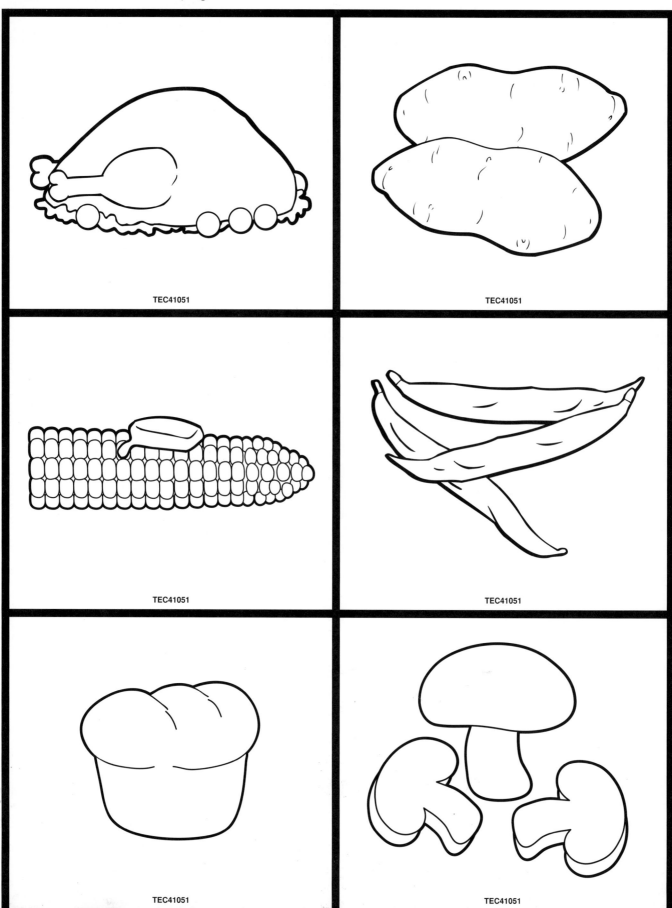

TEC41051

TEC41051

TEC41051

TEC41051

TEC41051

TEC41051

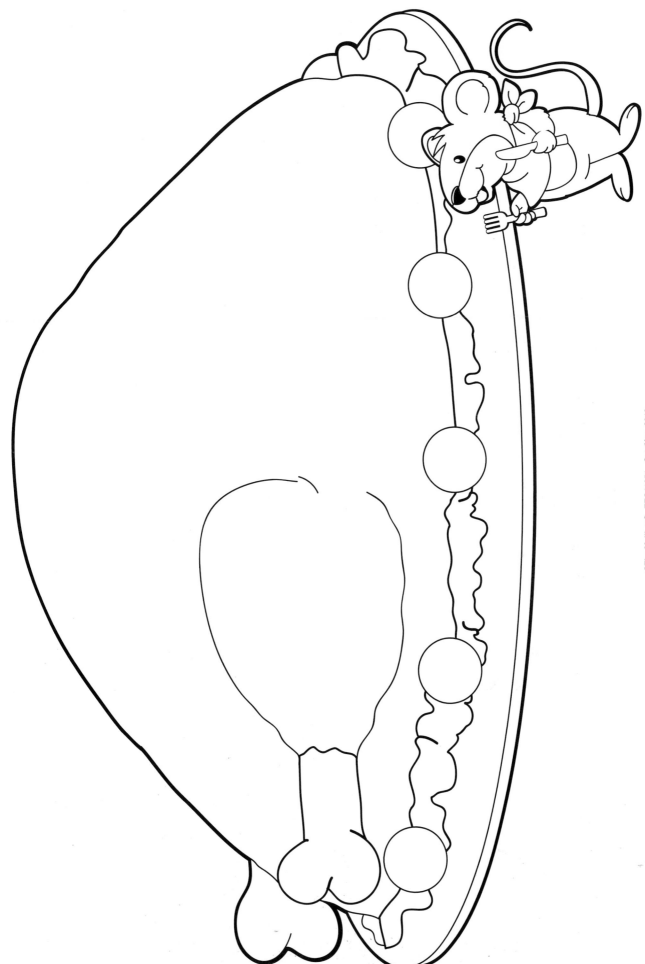

©The Mailbox® • TEC41051 • Oct./Nov. 2010

Note to the teacher: Use with "Thyme for Turkey" on page 209.

The engaging literacy ideas in this unit go along with three popular songs!

ideas contributed by Ada Goren, Winston-Salem, NC

Row, Row, Row Your Boat

Where Would You Go?

Speaking

Where would your little ones row? Find out with this no-prep activity! Seat youngsters in a circle and then sing the traditional song. Ask students where they think the person rowing the boat might be headed. After little ones share their thoughts, have a child sit in the middle of the circle. Lead students in singing the version of the song shown as the student pretends to row. Then have her announce her destination. 💻

Row, row, row your boat,
[Child's name], we want to know—
Tell us, tell us, tell us, tell us,
Just where will you go?

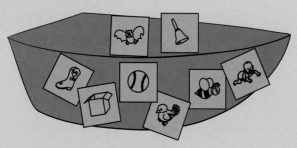

Beginning With *B*

Recognizing beginning sound /b/

Cut out a simple boat pattern and place it on your floor. Cut out a copy of the cards on page 215 and place the cards in a bag. Have a child pull a card from the bag and name the picture. If the picture name begins with /b/ as in *boat,* have students sing an enthusiastic round of "Row, Row, Row Your Boat" and then direct a child to place the picture on the boat. Continue with the remaining cards. 💻

Boat Float

Writing

Draw stream details on a strip of blue bulletin board paper and attach the stream to your wall. Have each child create a boat from construction paper and craft items. Then have her dictate information about her boat as you write her words on a large index card. Display the boats and cards on the stream with the version of the song shown.

Row, row, row your boats
On the stream so blue.
We made them with crafty stuff
And a lot of glue!

My boat is really big and purple.
I am on it with my dog.

Sara

The Muffin Man

Letter-Perfect Muffins

Sorting letters

Label a set of 12 muffin liners with one letter. Then label a second set with a different letter. Place the liners at a center along with two large muffin tins. A child sorts the liners into the tins. **For a more challenging version,** label one set of liners with uppercase letters and one set with lowercase letters!

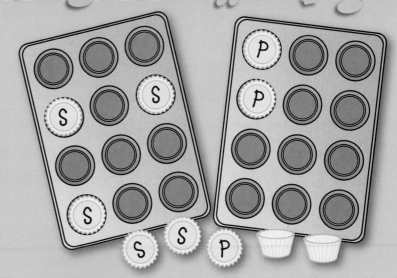

Mmmm!

Recognizing beginning sound /m/

Seat youngsters in a circle and then sing the traditional song. Prompt youngsters to say the words *muffin* and *man,* emphasizing the /m/ sound. Then hold a bowl and mixing spoon and say, "I'm making muffins and I'm mixing in macaroni!" Pretend to stir your ingredient. Then give the bowl and spoon to a child. Encourage her to repeat the sentence, adding her own ingredient that begins with /m/. (Accept both silly and real ingredients.) Then have her stir the bowl and pass it to her neighbor. Repeat the process with each youngster.

The Puffin Man?

Manipulating phonemes

You're sure to hear giggles with this fun phonological awareness activity! Write the first line of the song on sentence strips and place them in your pocket chart. Then gather several consonant letter cards. Read the line aloud. Then wonder aloud whether this song would sound different if you changed one of the letters. Have a child choose a letter card and then place it in front of the *M* in *Muffin.* Lead students in singing the resulting song. When the giggles die down, repeat the activity! 🖥

Do You Know the Puffin Man?

All Types of Teapots!
Participating in rhyming songs
Not all teapots are little! After singing the original song, prompt students to sing and act out different versions, including "I'm a Great Big Teapot," "I'm a Teeny Teapot," "I'm a Quiet Teapot," "I'm a Cranky Teapot," "I'm a Weepy Teapot," and "I'm a Happy Teapot." What fun!

Totally *T*s
Identifying letter T
Youngsters are sure to enjoy this terrific teapot center! Cut out an enlarged copy of the teapot pattern on page 215 and place it in a center along with letter manipulatives and cutouts, including many *T*s. A youngster visits the center and places only *T*s on the teapot! 🖥

What's in Your Teapot?
Writing one's name, dictating words
After a sing-along of the traditional song, have each child color a teapot cutout (enlarge the pattern on page 215) and attach it to a sheet of construction paper programmed as shown. Encourage a child to write her name where indicated and then dictate what would pour out of her teapot. Finally, have her glue paper strips to the spout so it resembles her drink of choice. 🖥

Emily's little teapot,
Short and stout.
When you tip it over,
What comes out?

Chocolate milk!

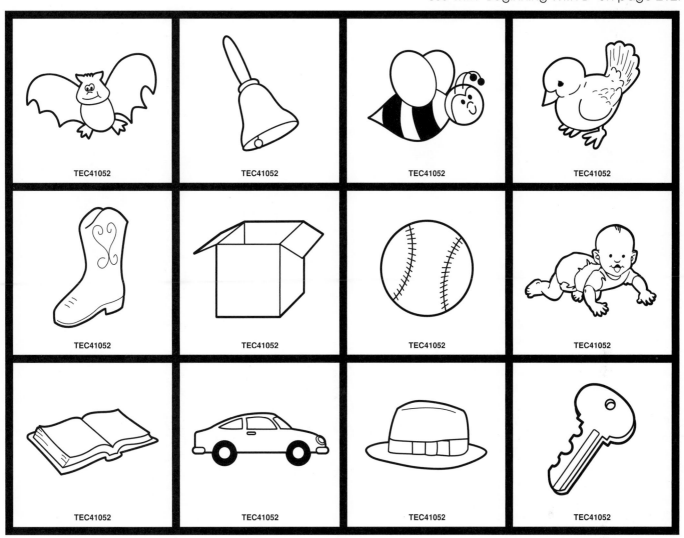

TEC41052 TEC41052 TEC41052 TEC41052

TEC41052 TEC41052 TEC41052 TEC41052

TEC41052 TEC41052 TEC41052 TEC41052

Teapot Pattern
Use with "Totally *T*s" and
"What's in Your Teapot?" on page 214.

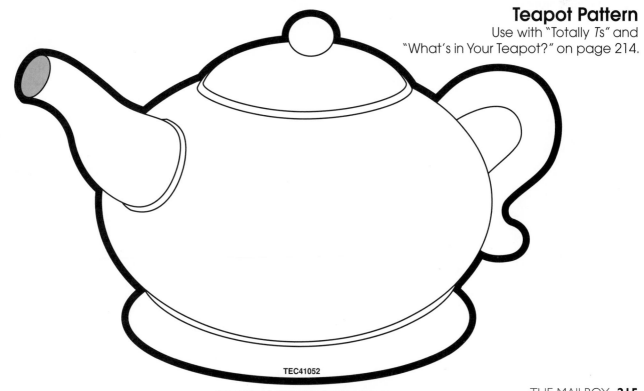

TEC41052

Excellent Anytime Literacy!

These breezy activities are sure to elevate youngsters' literacy skills!

Bingo Lingo!

Rhyming, initial sounds

Youngsters develop a sense of rhythm with this active idea! Gather five plastic containers and place them upside down so they resemble drums. Attach *B, I, N, G,* and *O* letter cards to the bottoms of the containers. Give one child a wooden spoon (mallet) and lead the whole class in singing the traditional song "Bingo," encouraging the youngster to hit each letter drum with his mallet when indicated. Next, help students decide on a real or nonsense word that rhymes with *bingo,* such as *tingo.* Replace the *B* card with the new initial consonant; then repeat the activity with a different volunteer and alter the song to match the new word. Continue with other rhyming words. 🖥

Tejaswini Duggaraju, Sunrise Co-op
Preschool, Renton, WA

Animal Lineup

Matching letters and sounds

Put your stuffed animal toys to use in this literacy center! Place two or three different stuffed toys in a row and place a container in front of each toy. Provide a stack of letter cards that correspond to the beginning sounds of the toys' names. A child chooses a card and decides which animal's name begins with that letter. She says the letter sound and animal name—such as "/d/, /d/, dog"—and then places the card in the appropriate container. She continues with the remaining cards.

Marie E. Cecchini
West Dundee, IL

Tasty Letters

Forming letters

Give each child in a small group a dark-colored disposable plate with a layer of whipped topping. Also give each child a cup of graham cracker sticks. Show the youngsters a letter card and prompt each child to use a graham cracker stick to write the letter in his whipped topping and say the letter's sound. Then each child smoothes the whipped topping with the side of the graham cracker stick and eats the stick. Continue with several letters. Yum!

Mandy Nihiser, Logan, OH

Which Is It?

Distinguishing real from make-believe

Place heading cards in your pocket chart, as shown. Cut out a copy of the cards on page 219 and place them facedown nearby. Encourage a child to choose a card and describe what she sees. Then discuss with students whether the picture shows something that is real or pretend. After students determine the correct category, have the child place the picture beneath the appropriate heading on the pocket chart. 🖥

adapted from an idea by Erin McGinness, The Learning Patch, Newark, DE

I Spy Letters!

Recognizing letters

Here's a unique letter-learning activity that youngsters will ask for again and again! Gather a small group of youngsters and scatter several letter cards faceup in front of the group. Place a supply of jumbo wiggle eyes in a container. Then say, "I spy with my little eye the letter [letter name]." Have a child pick an eye and place it on the corresponding letter card. Continue until all the letter cards have eyes!

Jennifer Gemar, Tripp-Delmont School District, Tripp, SD

Imagination Vacation

Speaking

Youngsters don't need to go anywhere to take this vacation! Give a student a toy camera or other vacation-related prop and say, "We're going on a trip! Where should we go?" Have him name a location for the trip. Then have him give the camera to a classmate. Ask, "What will we do there? What will we see?" Have the student share something she will see on the trip. Continue passing the camera, encouraging each student to share something she will see or do on the trip.

April Booker, Dickson Head Start, Kingsport, TN

Letter Hunt

Recognizing letters

Add interest to your reading center with the simple addition of letter cards! Place several identical copies of a letter card in your reading center. If desired, provide magnifying glasses. When youngsters visit the center, encourage them to take a card and a book and use the magnifying glass to search for the letter in the book text. Change the letter cards each day.

Christina Kasler, A Home Away From Home Childcare, Vacaville, CA

What Does It Say?

Matching letters and sounds

Give each child a letter card, making sure that more than one child has each letter you distribute. Place a basket in front of yourself and lead students in singing the song shown, inserting an appropriate letter sound and name. As you sing, prompt students with the corresponding letter cards to place the cards in the basket. Repeat the song with different letter sounds and names until all the children have participated. 🖥

(sung to the tune of "If You're Happy and You Know It")

If your letter says [/a/], bring it here.
If your letter says [/a/], bring it here.
If your letter says [/a/], then it must be an [A].
If your letter says [/a/], bring it here.

Susan Gresh, Northside Christian School, North Charleston, SC

TEC41053

TEC41053

TEC41053

TEC41053

TEC41053

TEC41053

TEC41053

TEC41053

Literacy Fun With Butterfly Friends!

These butterfly-themed literacy activities are just perfect for the spring season!

 /b/, /b/, Butterfly!

Recognizing matching sounds

Give each child a construction paper butterfly cutout (pattern on page 222). Provide items with names that begin with /b/, such as a small plastic bottle, blocks, a small ball, a plastic toy bear, a gift bow, and a banana. Place the objects near shallow pans of paint. A youngster chooses an item and says its name. Then she says the word *butterfly,* noticing that the two words begin with the same sound. She dips the object in the paint and then presses it on or drags it across the butterfly. She continues with the remaining objects until a desired effect is achieved.

Roxanne LaBell Dearman, Western NC Early Intervention Program for Children Who Are Deaf or Hard of Hearing, Charlotte, NC

Which Character?

Recalling book events

Read aloud the story *Bob and Otto* by Robert O. Bruel. In the story, Bob the caterpillar and Otto the earthworm are friends. But when Bob becomes a butterfly, Otto feels boring and useless. After the read-aloud, give each student a strip of pink paper (Otto) and a strip of orange paper (Bob). Have each child make blue stripes on the orange strip so it further resembles Bob. Name a story event. (See the suggestions below.) Then have youngsters hold up the critter that corresponds to the event. Continue with each remaining event.

Suggested events:
He climbs a tree.
He goes into the ground.
He digs under the tree.
He eats fresh, green leaves.
He eats rotten, old leaves.
He falls asleep on a branch.
He loves to dig.
He turns into a butterfly.
He says, "Why are you sad?"

Metamorphosis of Me
Writing

To make this adorable display, take a photo of each child wrapped in a green blanket so it appears as if she is a chrysalis. Help each child cut out her photo. Then display the photos upside down as shown. Prompt each child to say what she would be thinking if she were waiting to turn into a butterfly. Then write her words on a thought bubble and attach it near her photo. The next week, have her remove her chrysalis photo and attach it to a butterfly cutout (pattern on page 222). Have her decorate the wings as desired. Then display the butterflies with new dictation. 🖥

Danielle Rieth, The World Schools, Nashua, NH

When I'm a butterfly, I will be really pretty with big wings.

I can fly really high up in the air.

Bow Tie Butterflies
Identifying the letter *B*

Place bow tie pasta (farfalle) in a resealable plastic bag. Add a small amount of rubbing alcohol and food coloring. Then seal the bag and shake it to evenly distribute the coloring. (Add more coloring and alcohol, if needed.) Spread the pasta on a piece of waxed paper to dry overnight. Next, give each child a copy of page 223 and several pieces of pasta (butterflies). Have him glue a butterfly to each *B* on the page. *B* is for butterfly!

Editor's Tip:

These bow tie butterflies are also fabulous for arts and crafts. Have each student draw flowers on a sheet of paper. Then encourage him to glue bow tie butterflies around the flowers. Now that's a simple and cute craft!

Let's Fly!
Identifying letters, matching letters

Make a letter card for each letter in *butterfly*. Give each card to a child. Write the letter *b* on your board and help students identify the letter. Then prompt the child with the *b* card to "fly" to the front of the room. Continue with each remaining letter in the word until youngsters are lined up appropriately with their letter cards. Finally, have students hold up their cards as you read the word aloud. 🖥

Marie E. Cecchini, West Dundee, IL

Butterfly Pattern

Use with "/b/, /b/, Butterfly!" on page 220 and "Metamorphosis of Me" on page 221.

TEC41054

 # B Is for Butterfly

B   L   T   B

S   B   M   A

U   G   B   D

I   B   H   B

Bananas for Literacy!

There's no monkey business about this fun selection of literacy ideas!

Letters, Letters Everywhere!

Matching uppercase and lowercase letters

Youngsters will be eager to participate in this active game! Place a class supply of several different lowercase craft foam letters on a parachute (or a bedsheet). Instruct little ones to gently shake the parachute as you chant, "Letters, letters in the air. Letters, letters everywhere!" At the end of the chant, have students vigorously shake the parachute to toss the letters onto the floor. Then have each child pick up a letter. In turn, display corresponding uppercase letters, prompting each child with the matching lowercase letter to hold it in the air. Then have youngsters place the letters back on the parachute and repeat the activity.

James Butler, Laburnum Elementary, Richmond, VA

Can You?

Tracking print from left to right

Cut out two copies of page 227. Use one set of cutouts to make four pointers and use the remaining set to make rebus sentence strips as shown. Display the strips in a pocket chart. Use the appropriate pointer to track the print on each strip as you lead youngsters in reading the words aloud. After reading each strip, encourage little ones to make the specified sound. Then repeat the activity, guiding different volunteers in tracking the print. 🖥

Tracy Hora, Blessed Beginnings, Houston, TX

One, Two, or Three Scoops?

Counting syllables

Cut apart a copy of the cards on page 228. Attach the cards to separate ice cream cone cutouts. Store extra large pom-poms (or circle cutouts) in a clean ice cream container. A child chooses a cone and claps the picture word. After determining the correct number of syllables, he places that number of pom-poms (ice cream scoops) above the cone. 💻

Arleen Cummings, Holy Cross Head Start Akron, Akron, NY

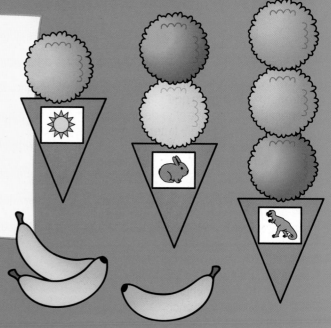

Sticky Letters!

Identifying and matching letters, letter sounds

Write letters on separate sticky notes and attach them to a clipboard. A child chooses a note and names the letter. She walks around the room, looking for the letter. When she finds it, she removes the note from her clipboard and attaches it to the match. She continues until the clipboard is empty. **For a more challenging option,** have the youngster identify the letter's sound and attach the note to an object in the room that begins with that sound.

Tricia Brown, Brown's Academy for Boys, Bowling Green, KY

Crafty Cookies

Matching simple words

Program pairs of craft foam cookie cutouts with matching words. Place one cookie from each pair on a baking tray and each remaining cookie on a serving plate. Display a cookie from the plate as you sing the song shown. Then invite a child to find a cookie on the tray that shows the matching word. After confirming he is correct, have him use the spatula to remove the cookie from the tray and place it on the plate. Continue until all the cookies are matched.

(sung to the tune of "Bingo")

I baked a cookie with a word.
The word it says is [*love*].
[*Love*], yes, that's the word!
[*Love*], yes, that's the word!
[*Love*], yes, that's the word!
The word it says is [*love*].

Anne Arceneaux, Ward Elementary
Jennings, LA

Letter Muncher

Identifying letters

Youngsters develop letter identification skills and hand strength with this unique idea! Cut a slit (mouth) in a tennis ball. Then hot-glue desired craft materials to the ball to make a friendly letter muncher like the one shown. Place several letter cards faceup. To begin, recite the first verse of the rhyme shown, inserting the name of a displayed letter in the last line. At the end of the verse, invite a volunteer to find the designated letter card. Then help her squeeze the letter muncher to open its mouth and slide the card in as you lead students in reciting the second verse. 🖥

Letter muncher, letter muncher,
Munch, munch, munch!
Would you like to munch
The letter [*A*] for lunch?

Letter muncher, letter muncher,
Munch, munch, munch!
The letter [*A*] is yummy
To munch for lunch!

Penny Ridgeway
Charlotte Valley Central School
Davenport, NY

Secret Whispers

Rhyming

Youngsters will need to turn up their listening ears and put on their thinking caps for this activity! Display several objects and have youngsters say each item's name. Next, whisper into a volunteer's ear a word that rhymes with one of the objects. Encourage her to find the rhyming object and hold it in the air (without revealing the rhyming word). Then ask the group to guess the rhyming word you whispered in the child's ear. The child who guesses the correct word takes the next turn. If the word is not guessed after several tries, reveal it to the group. Then invite a different volunteer to take a turn.

Marie E. Cecchini
West Dundee, IL

Syllable Picture Cards
Use with "One, Two, or Three Scoops?" on page 225.

TEC41055

TEC41055

TEC41055

TEC41055

TEC41055

TEC41055

TEC41055

TEC41055

TEC41055

TEC41055

TEC41055

TEC41055

MATH UNITS

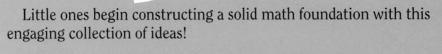

Building Math Skills

Little ones begin constructing a solid math foundation with this engaging collection of ideas!

ideas contributed by Margaret Aumen, York Springs, PA

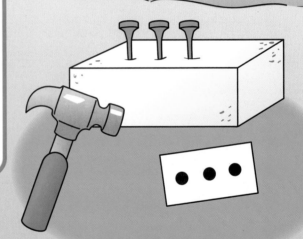

Hammer and Nails
Counting, making sets

Tap into number skills with this center activity. Draw dot sets on several different cards. Place at a center the cards, foam blocks, golf tees (nails), and a toy hammer. A child chooses a card and counts the dots. Then she taps a matching number of nails into the foam block. She removes the nails and repeats the activity using a different card. 💻

Building Skyscrapers
Sorting by color

Set out a tub of oversize linking blocks in three different colors. Tell little ones that they are going to help you build three skyscrapers. To begin the skyscrapers, take one block of each color from the tub and place it on the floor. In turn, invite a child to take a block from the tub and add it to the matching skyscraper. Continue until all the blocks are placed on the appropriate skyscrapers.

Brick by Brick
Matching numbers

For this small-group activity, divide a tagboard strip into five sections and label the sections with the numbers 1–5. Make a supply of corresponding number cards (bricks). Tape the strip to the table and place the bricks nearby. (For extra pizzazz, place the bricks in a toy dump truck!) In turn, each child takes a brick, reads the number, and places it above the matching number. Continue in this manner until all the bricks have been added to the wall. 🖥

		3		5
1		3	4	5
1	2	3	4	5
1	2	3	4	5

Picking Up Pipes
Making sets

Little ones load up on fun during this small-group activity. Gather a supply of short cardboard tubes (pipes), a large toy dump truck, and a large foam die. A child rolls the die and counts the number of dots. Then he and the group count aloud as he puts a matching number of pipes in the truck. He "dumps" his load, and the next child takes a turn.

Tinkering With Tools
Patterning

Make several copies of the tool cards on page 233. Hold up each card and have students identify the tool and pantomime using it. Next, have youngsters help you place tool cards in your pocket chart to make a simple pattern. Then prompt students to read the pattern while pantomiming the use of each tool. 🖥

The Wrecking Ball

Counting

Youngsters are sure to ask for repeated performances of this chant! Ready five building cutouts (pattern on page 233) for flannelboard use by attaching a piece of felt to the back of each one. Place the buildings in a row on the flannelboard. Then lead the youngsters in performing the rhyme shown, removing each building when appropriate. During the final verse, place the buildings back on the board. 🖥

Five old buildings stand in a row.
Which one will be the first to go?
The wrecking ball swings and hits one—bam!—
And knocks it down with a mighty slam!

Hold up five fingers.
Throw hands out to sides.
Clap hands loudly.
Hit floor with hands.

[Four] old buildings stand in a row.
Which one will be the next to go?
The wrecking ball swings and hits one—bam!—
And knocks it down with a mighty slam!

Hold up [four] fingers.
Throw hands out to sides.
Clap hands loudly.
Hit floor with hands.

Repeat this verse two more times, substituting the number as appropriate.

One old building, brick and stone,
Stands by itself. It's all alone.
The wrecking ball swings and hits it—bam!—
And knocks it down with a mighty slam!

Hold up one finger.
Stand very still.
Clap hands loudly.
Hit floor with hands.

No old buildings stand in a row.
The wrecking ball is done; now it can go.
The builders come with their tools in tow,
And five new buildings will stand in a row.

Shake head.
Wave goodbye.
March in place.
Hold up five fingers.

Tool Time

Number recognition, making sets

Enlarge the construction worker pattern on page 234 and make five copies. Label each construction worker's hat with a number from 1 to 5. Place at a center the construction workers and a set of the tool cards from page 233. A child chooses a construction worker, reads the number on his hat, and places a matching number of tools on his tool belt. She removes the tools and repeats the process with a different construction worker.

Building Pattern
Use with "The Wrecking Ball" on page 232.

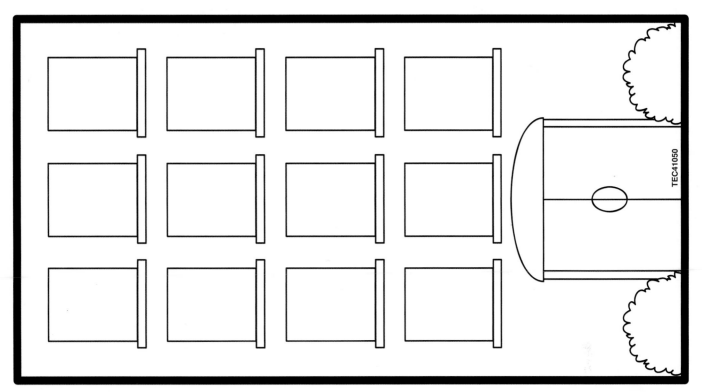

TEC41050

Tool Cards
Use with "Tinkering With Tools" on page 231 and "Tool Time" on page 232.

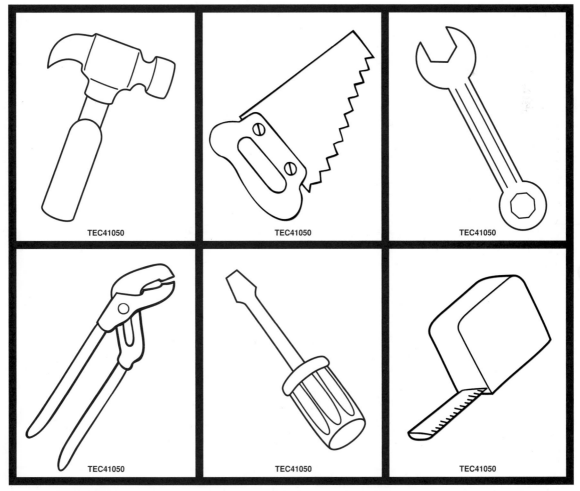

TEC41050

TEC41050

TEC41050

TEC41050

TEC41050

TEC41050

TEC41050

Fire-Safety Math

Spotlight National Fire Prevention Week with this selection of red-hot math ideas!

Moving All Around
Positional words

Your little firefighters will love using their gross-motor skills during this activity! To prepare, use classroom furniture and other items to set up an obstacle course that leads youngsters over, under, in, out, around, between, and through a variety of objects. Place a stuffed animal at the end of the course. Then invite students to pretend to be firefighters making their way through a burning building. Encourage each child to describe her position as she moves through the obstacle course. Then have her take the stuffed animal back through the obstacle course to rescue it!

Donna Olp, St. Gregory the Great Preschool, South Euclid, OH

Special Spots
Counting

Make a copy of the game mat on page 238 for each child. Provide pom-poms and a large foam die. A player rolls the die and counts aloud to determine the number of dots rolled. He then counts aloud that number of pom-poms and puts each one on a separate dot on his game mat. Players continue, in turn, until each spot on one player's dog is topped with a pom-pom.

adapted from an idea by Melissa Vandermark
Deposit Elementary, Deposit, NY

The Right Station
Color matching

Make a class supply of red, yellow, and green fire trucks (pattern on page 239). Display three corresponding colored sheets of paper (fire stations) in separate areas of the room. Give each child a fire truck and instruct him to look for a fire station that is the same color as his truck. Then ring a bell to signal each of your little firefighters to "drive" his fire truck to the matching-color station. Play several rounds of this fun game! 🖥

Marie E. Cecchini, West Dundee, IL

Badge Numbers
Number order

Label each of five badge cutouts (pattern on page 239) with a number from 1 to 5. (For a greater challenge, label more badges to a higher number.) Tape each badge to a different child's shirt; then have your little firefighters stand in a row, making sure the badge numbers are out of sequence. Lead the rest of the group in reading the badge numbers, guiding students to notice that the numbers are not in order. Then name volunteers as fire chiefs to help you arrange the firefighters so the badge numbers are in numerical order. 🖥

How Many Drops?
Making sets

Set out a construction paper flame cutout. Also provide a supply of craft foam water drops and number cards programmed with dot sets. A child takes a card, identifies the number, and places that many water drops on the flame. She says, "The fire's out!" Then she removes the drops from the flame and repeats the activity. 🖥

Floating Flames

Number recognition

Program each of several craft foam flames with a different number and float them in your water table. Provide a spray bottle filled with water along with a toy firefighter's hat, if desired. A youngster puts on the hat, reads the number on a flame, and then sprays it that number of times.

Tricia Brown
Bowling Green, KY

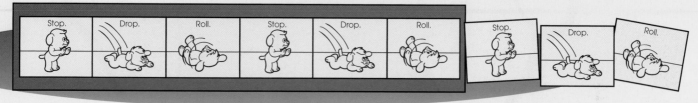

Stop, Drop, Roll

Patterning

Cut apart several copies of the fire-safety pattern cards on page 239 and attach two sets to a paper strip as shown. Place the remaining cards faceup nearby. A youngster studies the pattern and then uses the cards to extend it. When she is finished, she reads the pattern aloud and then acts out this important fire-safety tip. 💻

Zero!

No One Left

Understanding the concept of zero

Designate a few students as family members and ask them to go to the housekeeping area. Then invite two other children to be the firefighters. Pretend the family's house catches on fire and have the firefighters rush in and rescue the family. Lead the class in counting each person as they come out. After everyone has been rescued, ask the group to tell how many people are left in the house. Then explain that when there is nothing left to count, the number is zero.

©The Mailbox® • TEC41051 • Oct./Nov. 2010

238 THE MAILBOX   **Note to the teacher:** Use with "Special Spots" on page 235.

Firefighter Badge Pattern

Use with "Badge Numbers" on page 236.

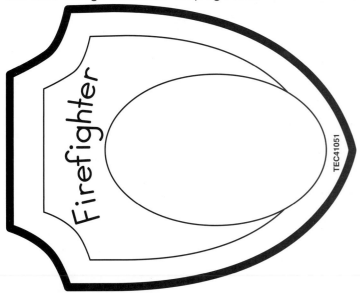

Fire Truck Pattern

Use with "The Right Station" on page 236.

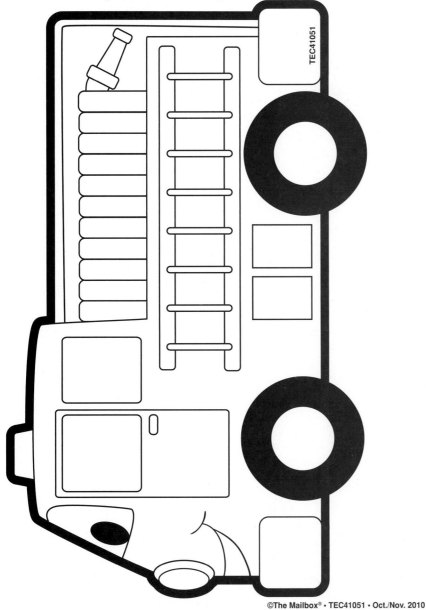

Fire-Safety Pattern Cards

Use with "Stop, Drop, Roll" on page 237.

Math With Jack and Jill

Jack and Jill of the well-known nursery rhyme are your youngsters' guides through this fabulous selection of math activities!

Jack and Jill went up the hill
To fetch a pail of water.
Jack fell down and broke his crown
And Jill came tumbling after.

Will They Fit?

Developing spatial concept

What besides water could fit in Jack and Jill's pail? Youngsters decide on appropriate answers to that question with this giggle-inducing activity! Cut out a copy of the cards on page 242 and place them in a bag. Present a pail to youngsters and have them recite the traditional rhyme. Then have a child choose a card from the bag and identify the pictures. Have students recite the rhyme again, substituting what's on the picture card for "water." When the giggles subside, ask youngsters whether Jack and Jill would be able to fit them in the pail. After a decision is made, continue with the remaining cards. 🖥

A Pail of Water

Estimation

How many cups of water will fit in a pail? Gather youngsters around a small, empty pail and a tub of water. Present a cup and have students estimate how many cups of water will fit in the pail. Write each student's estimate on a sticky note and have him attach it to the pail. Next, have youngsters place cups of water in the pail one at a time as you lead them in counting aloud. When the pail is full, compare the actual number of cups to the estimates.

Tricia Kylene Brown
Bowling Green, KY

Bumps and Bruises
Sorting by size

No doubt Jack and Jill had lots of bumps and bruises after they fell down the hill. Those bumps and bruises are going to need bandages! Get a box of multisize self-adhesive bandages. Enlarge page 243 and make a copy for each bandage size. Attach a different size of bandage to each page. Then place the pages at a center, along with the remaining bandages. A youngster chooses a bandage, removes the wrapping and backing, and then attaches it to the corresponding page. Encourage youngsters to keep visiting the center until all the bandages have been sorted and Jack and Jill have been patched up! 🖥

How Many on the Hill?
Presubtraction skills, concept of zero

Place a large green circle cutout (hill) on the floor. Then invite two youngsters to be Jack and Jill. If desired, give one of the youngsters a pail. Have students recite the first two lines of the rhyme, encouraging Jack and Jill to walk onto the hill. Stop and ask how many children are on the hill. After students answer, prompt them to recite the next line of the rhyme, encouraging Jack to pretend to fall down the hill. Ask how many children are standing on the hill now. Then lead youngsters in reciting the final line of the rhyme, encouraging Jill to pretend to fall down the hill. Once again, ask students how many children are standing on the hill, leading them to conclude that the number zero means none. If desired, place the hill and pail at a center for independent practice.

Tricia Kylene Brown, Bowling Green, KY

Tall Hills, Small Hills
Describing objects by size, making comparisons

Make several large and small copies of the Jack and Jill reproducible on page 243. Then transform them into stick puppets as shown. Place the puppets at a table along with green play dough. Have students visit the center and make small and large hills with the play dough. Then prompt them to stick the appropriate-size puppet in each hill. 🖥

Picture Cards

Use with "Will They Fit?" on page 240.

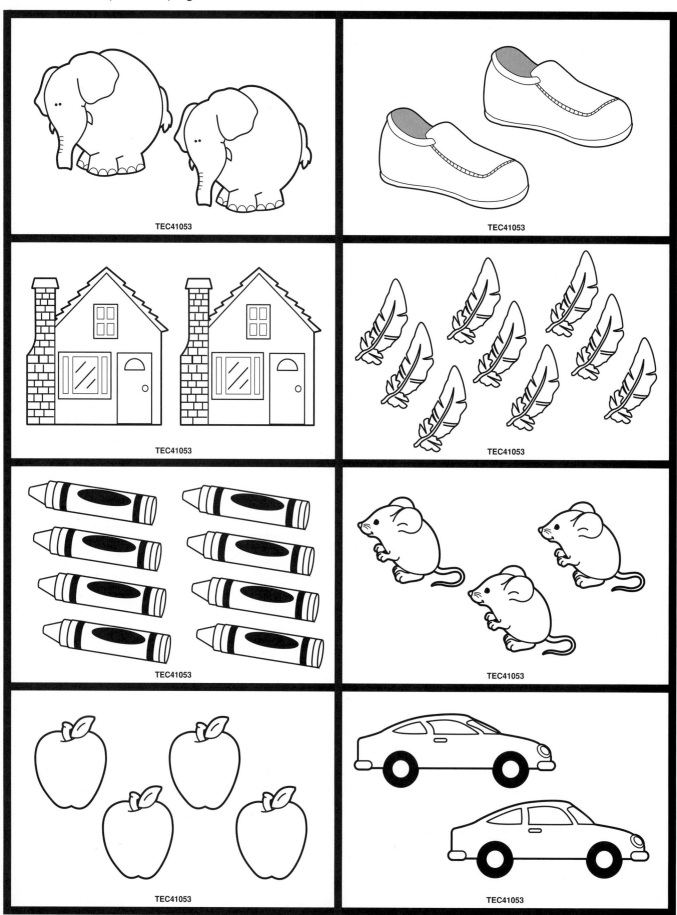

TEC41053

TEC41053

TEC41053

TEC41053

TEC41053

TEC41053

TEC41053

TEC41053

Note to the teacher: Use with "Bumps and Bruises" and "Tall Hills, Small Hills" on page 241.

THE MAILBOX **243**

A Big Batch of
Math Ideas

Stir in some math fun with this
marvelous collection of activities!

Shape Search

Identifying shapes, shapes in the environment

To prepare, place several shape cutouts in a bag. Invite a youngster to take a shape from the bag and display it for her classmates. Lead the group in singing the song shown, substituting the name of the shape where indicated. At the end of the song, ask volunteers to name objects in the room that have the same shape. Continue with the remaining shapes. 🖥

(sung to the tune of "Clementine")

Found a [circle], found a [circle].
There's a circle in [her] hand.
Right here, [she] found a [circle].
It's a shape that's pretty grand!

Mary Davis, Keokuk Christian Academy, Keokuk, IA

Found a circle...

Marlon's Fancy Footwork

Dad

Jacob

Mom

Sara

Marlon

Lucy

Fancy Footwork

Seriation

Little ones' families join in the fun with this activity. Send to each family a large sheet of construction paper, a resealable plastic bag, and a copy of a note from page 247. Each family helps the child trace family members' right feet, cut out the tracings, and place the cutouts in the bag to return to school. At school, each youngster orders the feet from largest to smallest. Then he glues them to a sheet of construction paper labeled as shown.

Rosemary Fraza, Alkek Elementary, Bandera, TX

Digging for Diamonds

Identifying the diamond shape, counting

Place a deck of cards in the center of a small group of children. Have youngsters take turns drawing cards. If a child draws a card with diamonds, he keeps it. If he draws a card with a different suit, he places it in a discard pile. When all the cards are gone, he counts his diamond cards. If desired, have students compare the different amounts. After each child has an opportunity to take part in the activity, place the deck of cards at a center for independent play.

Donna Olp, St. Gregory the Great Preschool, South Euclid, OH

Disappearing Numbers

Number recognition

For each child, use a white crayon to write numbers on a sheet of white paper. As you pass out the papers to little ones, explain that they are going to read the numbers on their papers to partners. Feign surprise when they tell you there aren't any numbers on their papers. Then encourage students to use watercolors to paint their papers since there are no numbers to read. When the numbers magically appear, invite little ones to read the numbers on their papers to partners.

Carolynn Sidlauskas, Covert Elementary Covert, MI

A Colorful Caterpillar

Number order

Enlist youngsters' help in getting this cute caterpillar in order. Make several numbered circle cutouts. On the floor, place another circle cutout decorated so it resembles a caterpillar head. Distribute the numbered circles. Ask the student with circle 1 to place it beside the caterpillar's head. Direct the child with the next circle to place it beside the first circle. Continue until the caterpillar's body is complete. Lead little ones in counting the numbers on the caterpillar's body to check the accuracy of the number order. 🖥

Sharon Berkley, Son Shine Christian Preschool Pasadena, TX

Here's the Scoop

Data collection and analysis

Introduce youngsters to glyphs with this fun activity! Prepare a supply of light- and dark-brown triangles (cones) and white circle cutouts (scoops of ice cream). Gather a group of youngsters and have each girl choose a light-brown cone and each boy a dark-brown cone. Instruct each child to take the number of scoops equal to her age and color them her favorite color. Direct her to glue her cone and scoops to a sheet of paper. Then invite her to share her finished glyph. Guide her classmates in gathering information from the glyph about the child's gender, age, and favorite color. If desired, display the glyphs and a key on a board titled "Getting the Scoop on Preschoolers."

Arleen Cummings
Holy Cross Head Start Akron
Akron, NY

Student Sticks

Counting, identifying numbers, comparing sets

To make student sticks, attach trimmed student photos to craft sticks. Set out the student sticks, a mound of play dough, and a set of number cards. Then invite a small group of youngsters to join you and choose one of the options below.

Counting: Give each youngster a few student sticks, varying the amounts. In turn, ask each child to count his sticks as he stands each one in the mound of play dough.

Identifying numbers: Give youngsters equal sets of student sticks and individual mounds of play dough. Display a number card and direct each child to put that many sticks in the dough.

Comparing sets: Pair students, giving each child his own mound of play dough and set of student sticks. Have each student put a few student sticks in his play dough. Then guide the partners to compare their sets using the words *more, less,* and *equal.*

Norinne Weeks, Carrillo Elementary, Houston, TX

Editor's Tip:
Feeling short on time? Simply have students complete the activity with plain craft sticks, bottle caps, or pieces of pipe cleaner!

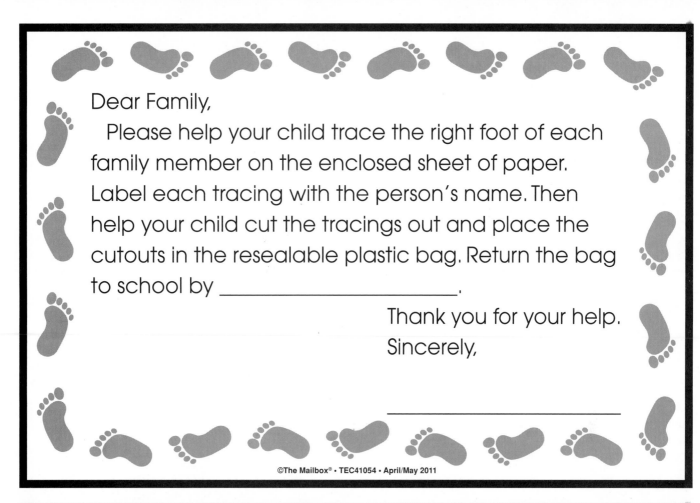

Dear Family,

Please help your child trace the right foot of each family member on the enclosed sheet of paper. Label each tracing with the person's name. Then help your child cut the tracings out and place the cutouts in the resealable plastic bag. Return the bag to school by _____.

Thank you for your help.
Sincerely,

_____

©The Mailbox® • TEC41054 • April/May 2011

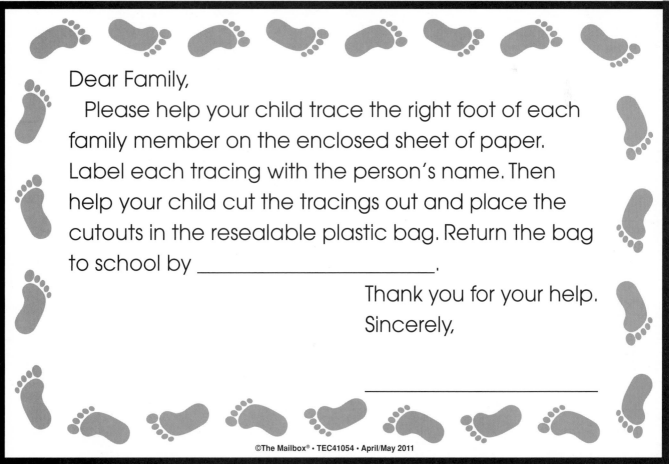

Dear Family,

Please help your child trace the right foot of each family member on the enclosed sheet of paper. Label each tracing with the person's name. Then help your child cut the tracings out and place the cutouts in the resealable plastic bag. Return the bag to school by _____.

Thank you for your help.
Sincerely,

_____

©The Mailbox® • TEC41054 • April/May 2011

Note to the teacher: Use with "Fancy Footwork" on page 244.

Pool-Time Math

Splash into math practice with these pool-themed activities just perfect for summertime!

ideas contributed by Ada Goren, Winston-Salem, NC

One Stroke, Two Strokes...

Counting

For an active approach to counting, engage your little ones in some pseudo-swimming! Place a length of blue yarn on the floor to make a large circle (pool). To begin, invite your little swimmers to jump into the pool. Then call out a number. Have youngsters pretend to swim overhand, counting aloud one number for each arm stroke. Challenge little ones by increasing the number of strokes each time. To conclude the activity, have youngsters pretend to splash their fellow swimmers!

Packing for the Pool

Estimating

To prepare for this activity, gather several folded beach towels and a pool bag. Display the items and ask students to guess how many beach towels will fit in the bag. Record youngsters' answers and then pack the bag with the folded towels. Encourage children to count each towel aloud as you add it to the bag. When the bag is packed, compare students' guesses to the actual number of towels that fit in the bag to see whether anyone estimated the exact amount.

A "Bear-y" Bad Pool Party

Developing presubtraction skills, making sets, concept of zero

Can one impossibly cute booklet target a variety of math skills? Why, yes it can! Copy pages 250 and 251 for each child. Have a child color the pages as desired. Then encourage her to make two fingerprint raindrops on the first booklet page, four on the second page, six on the third page, and eight on the final page. Next, read the text aloud, helping the child write the appropriate number in each blank to show the number of bears in the pool. Then help her cut out the pages and staple them between construction paper covers. Title the booklet as shown.

Towel Time

Sorting by attributes

Set out a container of beach or bath towels. (If desired, ask parents to send in towels.) Have youngsters sort the towels by various attributes. For example, you might have them sort the towels by color; by stripes and no stripes; or by characters and no characters. Once youngsters have the hang of it, invite them to sort the towels as desired, encouraging them to explain the reasoning behind their sorting process.

Dive Into Graphing!

Graphing

Seat youngsters in a circle. Display a two-column graph programmed with a pool-related question, such as "Do you wear a safety vest?" or "Do you have any pool toys?" To begin, play a musical recording and have youngsters pass a beach ball around the circle. After a few moments, stop the music and read the question aloud. Have the child holding the ball answer the question and then attach a sticky note to the appropriate column on the chart. After each child has had a turn, guide youngsters in comparing the results.

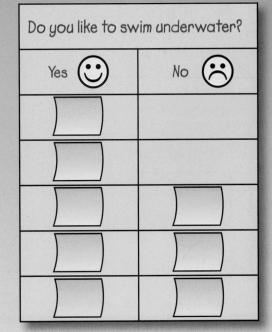

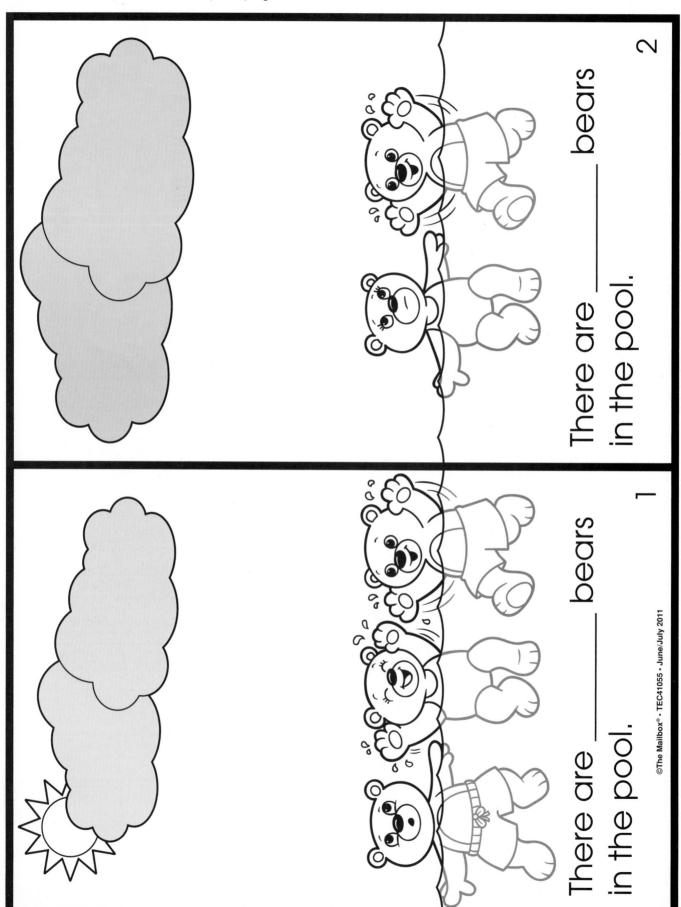

There are _____ bears
in the pool.

2

There are _____ bears
in the pool.

1

4

There are _____ bears
in the pool.

3

There is _____ bear in
the pool.

©The Mailbox® • TEC41054 • April/May 2011

Note to the teacher: Give each child a copy of this page. Hold up a number card and have her identify the number. Then encourage her to make that many blue fingerprints below the first cloud. Continue with the second and third clouds, choosing a different number card each time.

THEMATIC UNITS

A Farm-Fresh Preschool Welcome

Bring the farm to your youngsters with this fabulous welcome-to-preschool unit!

ideas contributed by Ada Goren, Winston-Salem, NC

Little Farmers

Cubby tags, nametags

Youngsters are sure to be able to find their cubbies and seats with these adorable tags. Encourage each child to wear a bandana and a floppy straw hat. Then take the child's photograph. Cut out the photo, as shown, and attach it to a personalized tag cutout (pattern on page 257). Then use the tags to label cubbies or attach them to youngsters' shirts as nametags.

Farmer Staci

Editor's Tip:
Try using diaper pins to attach youngsters' nametags. Diaper pins are easy to fasten and are available in fun colors!

So Busy!

Get-acquainted song

Youngsters get to know their classmates' names with this toe-tapping sing-along! Copy the barn pattern from page 258 onto red paper, masking out the poem. Then cut out the barn and give it to a child. Lead youngsters in singing the first verse of the song shown, inserting the child's name. Then prompt the child to give the barn to a classmate. Repeat the process with each remaining child using a different farm activity. 💻

(sung to the tune of "Mary Had a Little Lamb")

Farmer [child's name] mends the fence,
Mends the fence, mends the fence.
Farmer [child's name] mends the fence.
[She] takes care of [her] farm.

Continue with the following:
plows the field
feeds the hens
gathers eggs
rides the horse
shears the sheep
plants the seeds
picks the beans

Karen Eiben, The Learning House Preschool, LaSalle, IL

Who Is Here?

Attendance display

See at a glance who is present with these terrific little tractors! Make a personalized tractor cutout (pattern on page 257) for each child. Draw soil details on a length of bulletin board paper. Then attach a class supply of Velcro fastener buttons to the soil. Attach the corresponding Velcro fasteners to the tractors. If desired, add adorable farm animal details to the display. When youngsters arrive, have them find their tractors and attach them to the display. 🖥

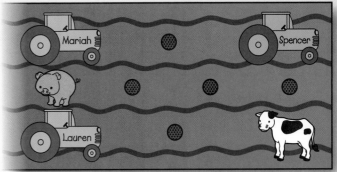

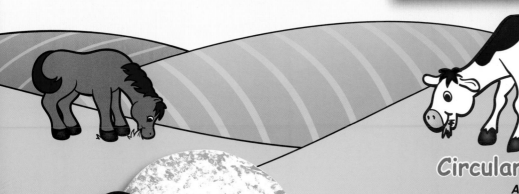

Circular Sheep

Art

Give each youngster a circle of light blue paper. Then prompt the child to make gift-bow prints on the paper with white paint. When he is finished, have him glue black paper strips (legs) to the painting. Next, place his hand on a sheet of paper with the thumb and pinkie finger arranged to make the head shape shown. Trace around his hand and cut out the tracing. Then have him add eye cutouts and attach the resulting head to the painting. Too cute!

A Disruptive Flea

Recalling story details

Read *The Flea's Sneeze* by Lynn Downey aloud to your youngsters. This adorable story describes the chaos that erupts when a flea sneezes in a barn full of sleepy farm animals. Next, have each child squeeze and crumple strips of yellow paper so they resemble straw. Encourage her to glue the straw and a mouse cutout (pattern on page 259) to a sheet of paper. Then have her glue a small black pom-pom (flea) to the mouse. Ask, "What happens in the story?" Then write the youngster's dictation on the page.

The flea sneezed and scared lots of animals. It was funny!

Amy

Lynn Downey
The Flea's Sneeze
Illustrated by
Karla Firehammer

Hens and Nests

Job chart

To make this adorable job chart, have each child color a personalized hen cutout (pattern on page 259). If desired, encourage him to glue craft feathers to the hen. Label simple nest cutouts with different jobs and display the nests. To assign jobs, simply attach a hen above each nest. 🖥

Grace
Line Leader

Tony
Plants

Raquel
Lights

Animals in the Classroom

Participating in a song

Your classroom will be filled with farm animals with this simple action song. Lead students in singing the song, encouraging them to move like cows as they sing. When the song is finished, lead students in enthusiastic mooing! Sing the song several times, substituting a new farm animal and sound each time. 🖥

(sung to the tune of "Old MacDonald")

[Teacher's name] has a class.
E-I-E-I-O!
And, in that class, she has some [cows].
E-I-E-I-O!
With a [moo, moo] here and a [moo, moo] there;
Here a [moo], there a [moo], everywhere a [moo, moo].
[Teacher's name] has a class.
E-I-E-I-O!

What's in the Barn?

Contributing to a class book

This adorable book is sure to be a favorite with your youngsters! Help each child cut out a copy of the barn pattern on page 258. Help her cut the doors so they open. Then have her glue the barn to a sheet of construction paper, as shown, leaving the doors unattached. Encourage each child to draw a farm animal on the paper and close the doors over her drawing. Write the name of the animal in the space provided. Bind students' work together to make a class book. Then read the book aloud to your youngsters.

Cock-a-doodle-do!
The night is done.
Who is awake
To see the sun?
Good morning, COW

Tag Pattern
Use with "Little Farmers" on page 254.

TEC41050

Tractor Pattern
Use with "Who Is Here?" on page 255.

TEC41050

Barn Pattern

Use with "So Busy!" on page 254 and "What's in the Barn?" on page 256.

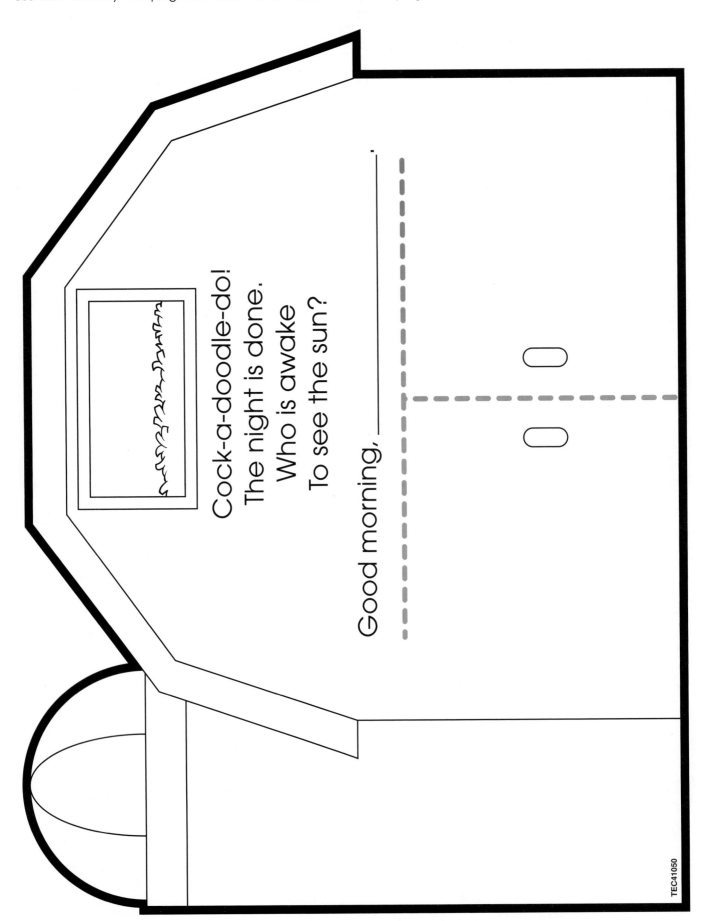

Cock-a-doodle-do!
The night is done.
Who is awake
To see the sun?

Good morning, _____

TEC41050

Mouse Pattern
Use with "A Disruptive Flea" on page 255.

Hen Pattern
Use with "Hens and Nests" on page 256.

TEC41050

TEC41050

Staying Clean and Healthy

Help little ones understand the importance of staying clean and healthy with this spiffy selection of ideas!

Clean Babies

Display a doll with brown paint smudges (dirt) on its face and body. Ask youngsters what would happen if they got dirty like the doll and did not bathe, leading them to understand that keeping our bodies clean helps us stay healthy. Next, put several dirty dolls in a clear plastic tub or water table. Provide soap and washcloths and invite little ones to give the babies a bath. After the dolls are clean, remove them from the tub and ask youngsters to describe the water, leading them to conclude that the water and soap washed off the dirt.

Danielle Lockwood, Colchester, CT

Yucky Mist

This demonstration helps little ones understand why it's important to cover their mouths when they cough or sneeze. Fill a spray bottle with tinted water. Place a sheet of white paper in front of you. Pretend to sneeze, spraying a mist of water onto the paper as you do. Draw students' attention to the mist that lands on the paper and explain that they spread germs in the same way if they do not cover their mouths when they cough or sneeze. Finally, demonstrate how to cough or sneeze into the bend of your arm; then lead little ones in singing the song shown. 💻

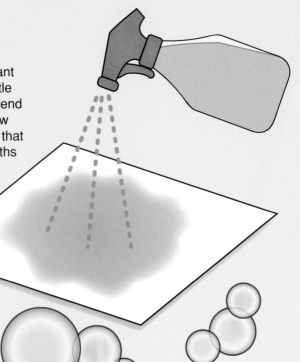

(sung to the tune of "Up on the Housetop")

Sneeze in your elbow, won't you please,
So you don't get germs on me.
Sneeze in your elbow, quick, quick, quick,
So nobody else gets sick!

Linda Larsen, St. Mark's Preschool, Evansville, IN
Marilyn Horsley, Valley View United Methodist, Overland Park, KS
Ruth Borrmann, Open Door Christian Academy, Washington, PA

Ugly Germs

This fun song reminds students that hand washing is important for getting rid of germs. Place five germ cutouts (pattern on page 263) in the pocket chart. Give a child a bar of soap. Then lead the group in chanting the first verse of the rhyme, prompting the child to touch one germ with the bar of soap during the fourth line and then to remove it from the pocket chart. Repeat the verse until there is one germ left; then lead the group in singing the remaining verse. 🖥

[Five] little germs were busy at play
On a child's hands one day.
They were playing side by side.
Then that child washed,
And one germ died!

One little germ was busy at play
On a child's hands one day.
Then that child washed away the ick,
Now the germs are gone
And he won't get sick.

Becky Bachman, Y Wee Care Early Learning Center, Virginia, MN

Use a Tissue, Please!

Invite each child to transform a paper plate into a self-portrait. Next, help her cut out a tracing of her hand and glue a tissue to the cutout. Finally, help her glue the hand to the plate, as shown. Display the projects as a reminder to youngsters to use a tissue when they need to wipe their noses.

Carissa Dwyer, Discovery Kids Preschool, Maple Plain, MN
Keely Saunders, Bonney Lake ECEAP, Bonney Lake, WA

Did You Brush?

Seat youngsters in a circle. Hand a child a simple two-sided tooth puppet like the one shown (pattern on page 263). Have students pass the puppet around the circle as you lead them in singing the song shown. At the end of the song, the child holding the puppet displays the happy, clean tooth. 🖥

(sung to the tune of "The Muffin Man")

Did you brush your teeth today,
Your teeth today, your teeth today?
Did you brush your teeth today
To keep them clean and strong?

Marie E. Cecchini, West Dundee, IL

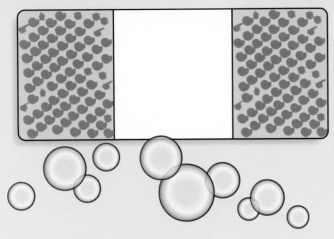

Big Bandage

To make this oversize bandage, a child paints a sheet of Bubble Wrap cushioning material with brown paint. Then he places a 6" x 18" sheet of light brown paper atop the painted surface and rubs his hand across it. He removes the paper and glues a white paper towel to the center of it as shown. When the paint is dry, trim any excess paper towel from the edges. Round the edges, if desired. Then display the projects and have students share experiences they have had with bandages. Also discuss with youngsters the importance of placing bandages on wounds.

Tammy Maijala, Kingdom Kids Christian Preschool, Rochester, MN

We Stay Healthy

Lead little ones in singing the song shown, encouraging each child to pretend to wash each body part mentioned in the song. Repeat the activity, replacing the underlined words with other body part words. 🖳

(sung to the tune of "The Ants Go Marching")

Oh, we stay healthy when we bathe each day, each day.
Oh, we stay healthy when we bathe each day, each day.
We wash our faces and necks and chests,
Our [arms] and [legs] and all the rest,
And we all use lots of soap to be clean,
To be clean, to be clean.
Scrub, scrub, scrub, scrub.

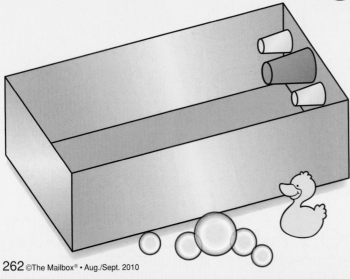

Bath Time!

This simple homemade bathtub will be popular in your dramatic-play area! To make one, obtain a large rectangular box. Hot-glue to the inside of the box two small disposable cups (faucet handles) and a large disposable cup (faucet). Place the tub in your dramatic-play area along with bath supplies, such as washcloths; empty shampoo, conditioner, body wash, and bubble bath bottles; a towel; and a rubber duck. Then let the scrubbing begin!

Rexann Roussel, Narrow Acres Preschool, Paulina, LA

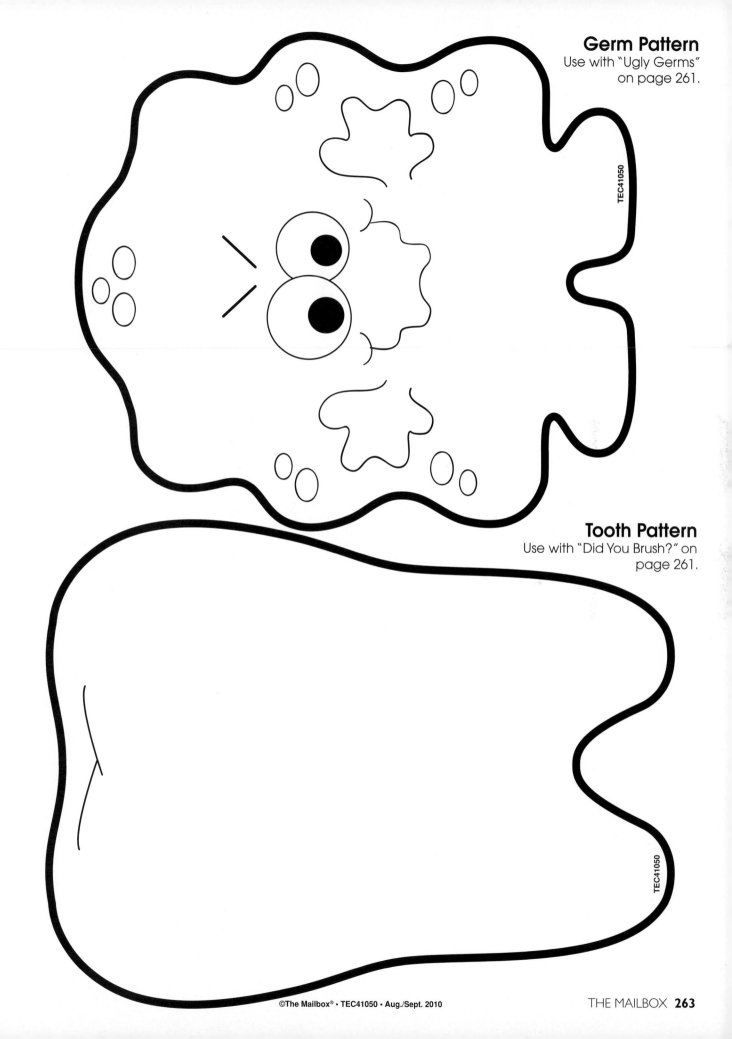

Germ Pattern
Use with "Ugly Germs"
on page 261.

TEC41050

Tooth Pattern
Use with "Did You Brush?" on
page 261.

TEC41050

Perfectly Pleasing Pumpkins!

This divine collection of ideas celebrates that famous fall fruit—the pumpkin!

Pumpkin Positions

Positional words

This little mouse needs a nice big pumpkin to hide in! Cut out a copy of the mouse pattern on page 267. Also cut the top off a pumpkin and remove the insides. (As an alternative, use a pumpkin cutout and alter the activity accordingly.) Give a child the mouse and lead students in reciting the rhyme shown, prompting the student to move the mouse as indicated. Continue with different volunteers and positional words.

A tiny little mouse (squeak, squeak, squeak, squeak)
Walks up to a pumpkin (sneak, sneak, sneak, sneak).
He hides [beside] the pumpkin, and he shivers in fright
Because it's dark and spooky on Halloween night.

Continue with the following: *in, on, behind, in front of, under*

Give Me a *P!*

Matching and naming letters

Make a class supply of pumpkin cutouts (patterns on page 268). Write a letter from the word *pumpkin* on each cutout. Then write the word *pumpkin* on the board. Scatter the pumpkins around your room. Invite students to find one pumpkin each and then return to their seats. Point to the first *P* on the board and say, "Give me a *P!*" Prompt all youngsters with the letter *P* on their pumpkins to stand, hold up their pumpkins, and say, *"P!"* Continue with each remaining letter. Then say, "What does that spell?" and prompt students to answer, "Pumpkin!" If desired, re-hide the pumpkins and play another round.

Marie E. Cecchini, West Dundee, IL

Plentiful *P*s
Recognizing letter **P**

Cut out several copies of the letter cards on page 267. Place the cards at a center along with a pumpkin and tape. Have children visit the center and find the *P*s. Then have them tape the *P*s to the pumpkin.

Keely Saunders, Bonney Lake ECEAP, Bonney Lake, WA

Did You Ever?
Participating in a song

This fun little action song highlights pumpkin variety!

(sung to the tune of "Did You Ever See a Lassie?")

Did you ever see the pumpkins,
The pumpkins, the pumpkins?
Did you ever see the pumpkins
That grow on the vine—

Hold arms in front as if holding a pumpkin and sway.

The fat ones and thin ones
And tall ones and small ones?
Did you ever see the pumpkins
That grow on the vine?

Hold hands wide apart and then close together.
Hold one hand above head and then close to floor.
Repeat first action.

Marie E. Cecchini, West Dundee, IL

Plumply, Dumply
Sorting, reinforcing rhyming words

Cut out several copies of the pumpkin patterns on page 268 and place them in a bag. Make the headings shown for your pocket chart. Read aloud *Plumply, Dumply Pumpkin* by Mary Serfozo. In this story, Peter the tiger bypasses lumpy, bumpy pumpkins to find a perfect plumply, dumply pumpkin. Have a child choose a pumpkin from the bag. Have him hold up the pumpkin. Then encourage students to label the pumpkin by saying "Plumply, dumply!" or "Lumpy, bumpy!" Prompt the student to place the pumpkin in the chart appropriately. Continue with the remaining pumpkins. After the activity, give each child a plumply, dumply pumpkin and have him decorate his cutout to make a showy, glowy jack-o'-lantern!

Jack-o'-Lantern of Mine

Participating in a song

If desired, have each student transform a pumpkin pattern (see page 268) into a jack-o'-lantern stick puppet. Then have students wave their puppets in the air during the first verse and blow a quick puff of air on their puppets when indicated during the second verse. What terrific pumpkin fun! 💻

(sung to the tune of "This Little Light of Mine")

Jack-o'-lantern of mine,
Watch you glow and shine.
Jack-o'-lantern of mine,
Watch you glow and shine.
Jack-o'-lantern of mine,
Watch you glow and shine,
Glow and shine, glow and shine, glow and shine!

Jack-o'-lantern of mine,
I'm going to blow you out. *(Puff!)*
Jack-o'-lantern of mine,
I'm going to blow you out. *(Puff!)*
Jack-o'-lantern of mine,
I'm going to blow you out,
Blow you out, blow you out, blow you out! *(Puff! Puff!)*

Roxanne LaBell Dearman, Western NC Early Intervention Program for Children Who Are Deaf or Hard of Hearing, Charlotte, NC

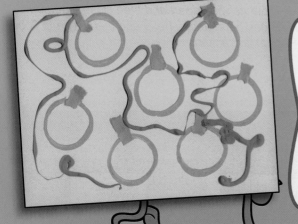

Print It!

Expressing oneself through art

To make this pumpkin project, dip the end of a cardboard tube into orange paint and then press the tube on a sheet of paper to make several prints (pumpkins). If desired, attach construction paper stems to the pumpkins. Then use a squeeze-style condiment container filled with diluted green paint to draw vines on the project.

Mary Ellen Moore, Miller Elementary, Canton, MI

Faux Pumpkin Fun!

Developing role-playing skills

With this activity, youngsters act out fun Halloween traditions! Cut a hole in the top of a faux pumpkin. Then cut a simple face in the pumpkin. Provide plastic knives, scoops, battery operated candles, newspapers, and white pieces of yarn mixed with craft foam seeds (pumpkin goop). Children can act out picking the pumpkin, placing it on newspapers, and carving it. They may even want to pick out the pumpkin seeds and pretend to roast them on a cookie sheet!

Donna Olp, St. Gregory the Great Preschool, South Euclid, OH

TEC41051

Letter Cards
Use with "Plentiful *P*s" on page 265.

P	S	P	D
TEC41051	TEC41051	TEC41051	TEC41051
B	P	Y	P
TEC41051	TEC41051	TEC41051	TEC41051

Pumpkin Patterns

Use with "Pumpkin Picking" on page 43, "Give Me a *P!*" on page 264, "Plumply, Dumply" on page 265, and "Jack-o'-Lantern of Mine" on page 266.

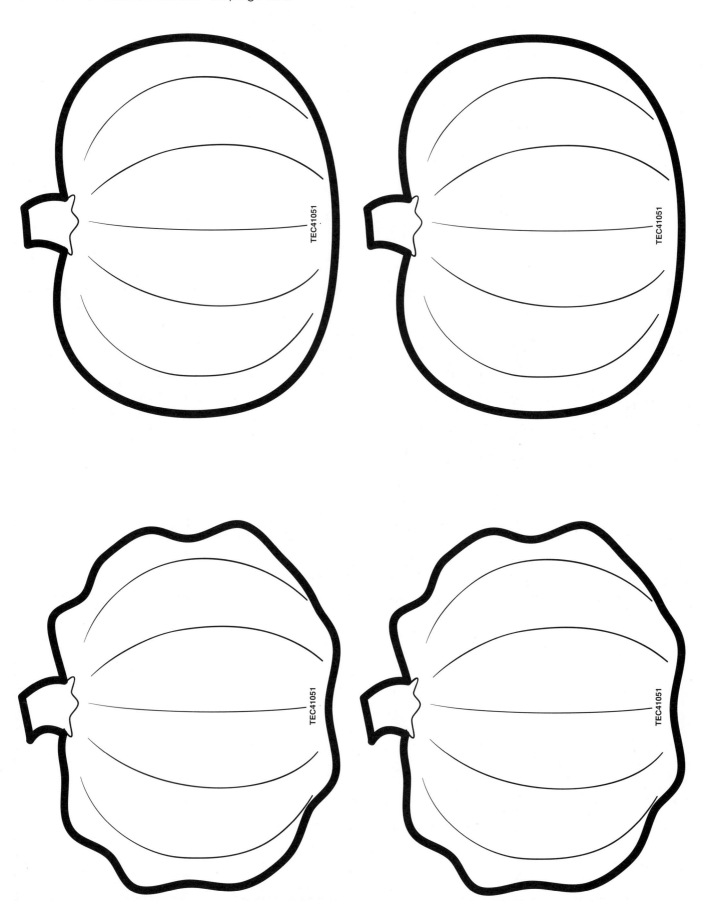

TEC41051

TEC41051

TEC41051

TEC41051

Prize Pumpkin

First Prize

©The Mailbox® • TEC41051 • Oct./Nov. 2010

Note to the teacher: Have each child color the page and cut out the prize ribbon. Prompt her to glue it to the pumpkin she believes should win the prize.

Fabulous Feelings!

You're sure to have happy little ones when they take part in these activities on emotions!

☺ How Do You Feel?

This adorable little booklet helps little ones track print as well as identify emotions! Make a copy of pages 272 and 273 for each child. Encourage him to color the cover and pages as desired. Then help him cut them out and bind them together. Read the booklet aloud with each child as you track the print with your finger. Prompt the child to mirror the mouse's emotion on each page.

How Do You Feel?

by John

©The Mailbox® • TEC41051 • Oct./Nov. 2010

I am frustrated.

1

Ms. Happy

Ms. Excited

Ms. Sad

Ms. Angry

☺ Name That Teacher

Make a simple poster like the one shown. During circle time, ring a bell and then assume one of the personalities. Teach for several minutes. Then ring the bell again and go back to your normal personality. Prompt students to look at the chart and choose the personality you were portraying. Repeat this activity several times throughout the day, using a different personality each time. 🖥

Donna Olp
St. Gregory the Great Preschool
South Euclid, OH

☺ Friends and Feelings

Happy

Your little ones practice their acting skills to create this display! Take a photo of each child demonstrating a specific emotion. Then ask her to name something that might make her feel this way. Write her words on an index card. Then display the cards and photos with the title "Our Preschool Friends Have Feelings."

adapted from an idea by Ann Davis, Gloria Dei Lutheran School and Childcare Center, Elizabethtown, KY

Emma feels happy when she has pizza for dinner.

☺ When I'm Glad

Lead youngsters in singing this catchy song about emotions! As they sing, prompt them to perform the appropriate motions when they say the action words. 💻

(sung to the tune of "London Bridge")

When I'm glad, I clap my hands,
Clap my hands, clap my hands.
When I'm glad, I clap my hands.
Clap, clap, clap, clap!

Continue with the following: *mad, stomp my feet; sad, wipe my tears*

Cherie Durbin, Hickory, NC

☺ Make a Match

Here's an emotion-matching activity that is sure to cause oodles of giggles! Prompt students to cover their eyes. Then say a silly sentence, such as "Bear ate the birthday cake," using an excited voice. Prompt students to open their eyes and have them pantomime the facial expression they imagine you used. Encourage students to identify the emotion. Then repeat the activity using a different emotion.

Amanda Boyarshinov, Boyarshinov Home School, Gainesville, FL

How Do You Feel?

by _____

©The Mailbox® • TEC41051 • Oct./Nov. 2010

I am frustrated.

1

I am glad!

2

I am surprised.

3

And now I am mad!

4

I am excited!

5

I'm sad and blue.

6

Do you have these
feelings too?

7

Gross-Motor Fun!

Jumping, throwing, balancing, and marching! Target a variety of gross-motor skills with these active anytime ideas!

Give Me a C!

Here's an activity that helps youngsters recognize letters and practice gross-motor skills! Collect a set of letter cards with a large quantity of Cs. Show youngsters a C card and tell students they need to clap each time they see the letter C. Next, quickly flip through the cards, prompting students to clap each time they see a C. Repeat the activity with the letters and actions below, modifying your cards as needed. 💻

Continue with the following:
B: bounce
H: hop
J: jump
M: march
W: walk (in place)
R: run (in place)

Shelley Hoster, Jack and Jill Early Learning Center, Norcross, GA

You're a Star!

Cut out a copy of the star cards on page 277 and place them in a decorated box (or bag). Have a child pull out a star and help her read it aloud. If desired, allow the child to wear special star-treatment sunglasses and to stand on a red carpet. Then encourage her to perform the action. When she's finished, prompt youngsters to give her an enthusiastic standing ovation. Continue with other youngsters and cards. 💻

Wanda Powers, Little Acorn, Lexington, TN

You're a star!

Hop on one foot.

Crawl on the floor.

Stretch up high.

Flap, Flap, Flap!

Have students name different animals that can fly. Write their suggestions on chart paper. Name one of the creatures on the list. Then lead them in singing a corresponding verse of the song shown as they flap their arms and move about the room. For added fun, occasionally name an animal that can't fly. Youngsters are sure to correct you before they take flight! 💻

(sung to the tune of "This Old Man")

[Bats] can fly. [Bats] can fly.
They can fly up in the sky!
Oh a [bat] has wings—
I often wonder why.
Did you know that [bats] can fly?

Two of Each!

Youngsters focus on pairs of body parts with this engaging action song! Lead students in singing the song as they swing their arms. Then repeat the song for each suggestion given. 💻

(sung to the tune of "Bingo")

Oh, I have [arms]—I need my [arms].
I use my [arms] all day-oh!
[Arms, arms, swing those arms].
[Arms, arms, swing those arms].
[Arms, arms, swing those arms].
I use my [arms] all day-oh!

Continue with the following:
Hands, hands, clap those hands;
Eyes, eyes, blink those eyes;
Legs, legs, wiggle those legs;
Feet, feet, stomp those feet;
Ears, ears, touch those ears

Shape-o-Saurus

Here's an activity that transforms little ones into shape-stomping dinosaurs! Cut oversize basic shapes from craft foam and scatter them on the floor. (You may wish to have two or three of each shape.) Lead youngsters in chanting the rhyme below as they march around the room. When the chant is finished, encourage them to find the shape named and stomp on it. Give the signal to stop. Then play another round of this game, naming a different shape.

Stomp, stomp, stomp to a dinosaur beat.
Stomp on a [triangle] with your feet.

Michelle Freed, Peru, NE

Dance and Sit

Place a chair for each child in an open area. Then have each child sit on a chair. Play a musical recording and have each child dance to the beat in front of her chair. Then stop the music, prompting youngsters to immediately sit down on their chairs. Continue in the same way for several rounds, playing different types of music to encourage a variety of dancing.

Rhonda Parker
Pageland, SC

Bubble Fun!

This activity is sure to work out the wiggles! Cut craft foam circles in pastel colors so they resemble bubbles. Then place them on your floor. Encourage youngsters to visit the bubble area and "pop" the bubbles by stomping on them. **To make a math game from this activity,** have a child roll a large die and count the dots. Then have her pop that number of bubbles and place them in a separate pile. The game is finished when she has popped all the bubbles!

Jeanette Anderson, Jeanette's Tots, Otsego, MN

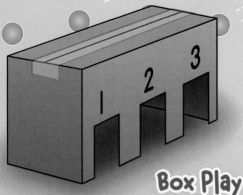

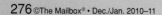

Box Play

Remove the flaps from a box and then cut doors in one edge of the box as shown. Place the box upside down and number the resulting doorways. Youngsters roll small balls through the doorways, identifying the number of the doorway each time they succeed. Instead of balls, they can also propel toy cars through the doorways.

Kimberly Kratochvil, Mountainland Headstart, Provo, UT

Jump up and down.

TEC41052

Wiggle your legs.

TEC41052

Pat your head.

TEC41052

Run in place.

TEC41052

Touch your toes.

TEC41052

Hop on one foot.

TEC41052

Twirl in a circle.

TEC41052

Wiggle your hips.

TEC41052

Flap your arms.

TEC41052

Crawl on the floor.

TEC41052

Stretch up high.

TEC41052

Curl into a ball.

TEC41052

Excellent Evergreens!

Youngsters are sure to enjoy these excellent evergreen-themed activities!

Ornaments Aplenty

Counting syllables

Youngsters decorate evergreen trees with this simple phonological-awareness activity! Make three enlarged copies of the tree pattern on page 281 and label them as shown. Gather colorful sticky dots (ornaments). Then say one of the suggested words below and prompt youngsters to chant the word and clap the syllables. Help them determine the number of syllables in the word. Then have a child place an ornament on the appropriate tree. Continue with each remaining word. If desired, have children compare the number of ornaments on the trees. 💻

Suggested words: *evergreen, ornament, holiday, pinecone, trunk, needles, pine, spruce, decorate, branches, presents, lights, tinsel, bark, green*

Triangle Tree

Ordering by size

Little ones make a "tree-mendously" tall evergreen with this marvelous math activity! Cut green construction paper into different-size triangles and place them at a center. A youngster orders the triangles from large to small, as shown, to create an evergreen tree. **For a different option,** have each child order his own set of triangles on a sheet of construction paper. Then have him glue the triangles in place and decorate the resulting tree!

Needle Art

Expressing oneself through art

Gather a variety of long and short evergreen needles and place them in a container. Make a mixture of white glue and paint. A youngster paints a sheet of paper with the mixture. Then she sprinkles needles over the mixture.

Danielle Lockwood, Colchester, CT

Editor's Tip:
Encourage youngsters to smell the evergreen needles before they're sprinkled over the art! (We here at The Mailbox always pause in our lobby to sniff a wreath made from evergreen branches. Sure, we look a little goofy—but it smells lovely!)

O Christmas   ! O Christmas   !

How lovely are your branches!

O Christmas Tree!

Rhyming

Cut out two copies of the cards on page 281. Write the first two lines of the traditional carol "O Christmas Tree" on sentence strips, leaving a space in place of the word *tree* as shown. Place the strips in your pocket chart. Tell students that you really enjoy this Christmas carol but you need help remembering the words. Place the knee cards in the spaces on the strips. Then sing the two lines of the song. Youngsters will surely tell you that these are the wrong cards! Repeat the process with the bee, key, three, and pea cards. Finally, reveal the tree card and sing the song with the correct words. Youngsters are sure to agree that this is the best version! 🖳

Let's Decorate!

Developing fine-motor skills

Set up a small artificial holiday tree at a classroom center. Provide an assortment of nonbreakable holiday decorations, such as plastic ornaments, candy canes, and small strands of garland. A student visits the center and decorates the tree as desired. The next visitor removes the decorations and redecorates it to his liking.

Pamela Miller
Little Lambs Christian Preschool
Seminole, FL

How Many Pinecones?

Counting, making sets

Cut out several enlarged copies of the tree pattern on page 281. Gather pinecones and place them at a center along with a die. A child rolls the die and counts the dots. Then she places the appropriate number of pinecones on a tree. She continues until each tree has a set of pinecones. 🖥

Marie E. Cecchini, West Dundee, IL

Six Little Evergreens

Ordinal numbers

Make a copy of page 282 for each child and encourage him to color it as desired. Next, lead students in reciting the rhyme shown as they point to each appropriate tree on their pages. Repeat the rhyme several times. Then assess youngsters' ordinal number knowledge by having them respond to directions, such as "Point to the second tree" or "Point to the fifth tree." 🖥

Six little trees standing in a row,
Their prickly needles all covered with snow.
The first tree is short.
The second tree is tall.
The third tree looks like it just might fall.
The fourth tree is skinny.
The fifth tree is stumpy.
The sixth tree's bark is rough and bumpy!
Six little trees standing in a row,
Their prickly needles all covered with snow.

Editor's Tip:

For extra vocabulary building, focus youngsters' attention on the word *stumpy*. Have them look at the corresponding tree and guess what the word *stumpy* means. Can they name other things that might be labeled as stumpy?

Tasty Treat

Following directions

This special treat is just perfect for the holidays! To make one, spread green-tinted frosting (or whipped cream cheese) over an upside-down sugar cone. Then decorate the cone with sprinkles and cereal pieces. What a tasty tree!

Jodi and Linda Remington
Busy Day Childcare
Okemos, MI

Tree Pattern

Use with "Ornaments Aplenty" on page 278 and "How Many Pinecones?" on page 280.

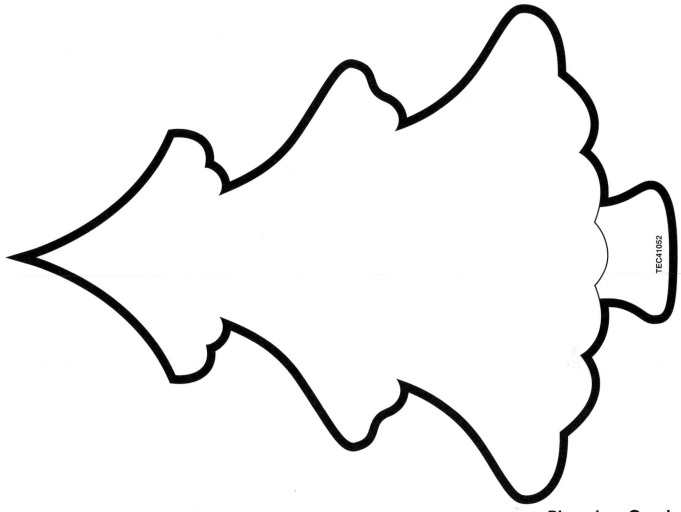

TEC41052

Rhyming Cards

Use with "O Christmas Tree!" on page 279.

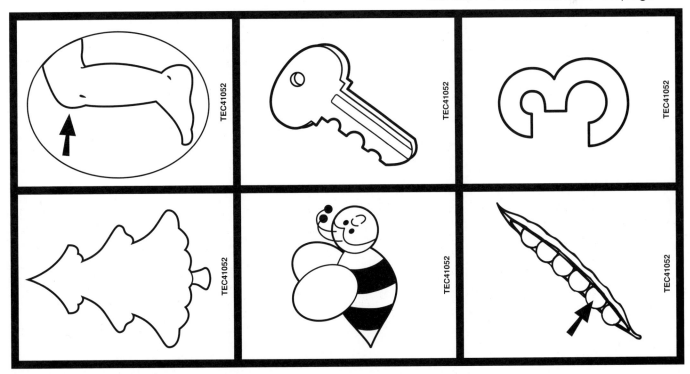

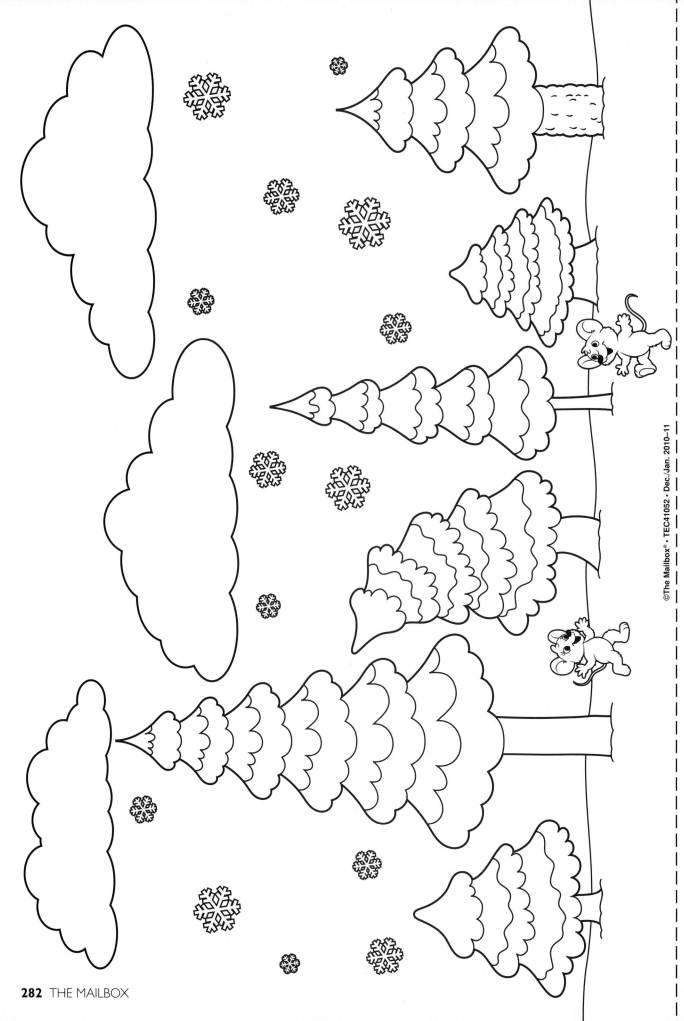

©The Mailbox® • TEC41052 • Dec./Jan. 2010–11

Note to the teacher: Use with "Six Little Evergreens" on page 280.

February and March Celebrations!

The months of February and March are full of fabulous celebrations, so engage youngsters in this sweet selection of timely activities.

☘ Run, Little Leprechaun! ☘

Gross-motor skills, playing a group game

Your little leprechauns practice social skills and following directions as they take part in this group activity! Have youngsters sit in a circle. Then give a child a yellow circle cutout (gold coin). Play a recording of upbeat music as youngsters pass the coin around the circle. After several passes, stop the music and say, "Run, little leprechaun!" Prompt the child with the coin to run around the circle and sit back down in his previous location. Next, have him give the coin to his neighbor. Then play another round of this engaging game!

Keely Saunders
Bonney Lake Early Childhood Education
    and Assistance Program
Bonney Lake, WA

Dear Family,
    We're doing a graphing activity! Please have your youngster color each heart a different color. Help your child cut out the hearts. Then return the hearts to school by February 10.

    Thank you very much!
    Ms. Verdonck

| red | blue | yellow | orange | green | purple |

♡ Lovely Colors ♡

Graphing

Send a copy of page 286 home with each child along with a note similar to the one shown. On the designated date, place basic color labels on a floor graph, as shown, and help students graph their hearts. When all the hearts are on the graph, prompt students to compare the columns using words such as *more, fewer,* and *equal.* If desired, remove the color labels and replace them with labels showing the different heart facial expressions. Then have students re-sort their hearts. 🖥

Ashley Verdonck
Early Childhood Center
Westminster, CO

Listening, following directions

Here's a fun and simple circle-time activity that's just perfect for Presidents' Day! Cut out a copy of the penny pattern on page 287. Explain that the person on the penny is Abraham Lincoln, who was president of the United States many years ago. Have the children cover their eyes as you place the penny somewhere in the room. Have students open their eyes. Then encourage them to walk around the room without talking as they look for the penny. As each child sees the penny, encourage him to quietly take his seat. When all the youngsters are seated, choose a child to reveal the penny's location! 🖥

adapted from an idea by Keely Saunders
Bonney Lake Early Childhood Education and Assistance Program
Bonney Lake, WA

♥ Groundhog Song ♥

Participating in a group song

Spotlight Groundhog Day with this song and role-play idea! Ask a volunteer to pretend to be a groundhog. Have him curl up in a ball and pretend to be asleep in his burrow as you lead youngsters in singing the song shown. Encourage him to "wake up" and then decide whether spring is coming. Repeat the process with different volunteers. 🖥

(sung to the tune of "Are You Sleeping?")

[Mr.] Groundhog, [Mr.] Groundhog,
Please come out, please come out.
Tell us winter's leaving.
Tell us spring is coming.
Bring good news, bring good news!

Marie E. Cecchini, West Dundee, IL

♣ Handy Things ♣

Developing fine-motor skills

Which well-known author has a birthday in March? Why, Dr. Seuss, of course! Read aloud *The Cat in the Hat.* Then have students celebrate Dr. Seuss's birthday with this adorable project! Paint the fingers of a youngsters' right hand blue and her palm white. Have her press her hand on a sheet of paper. Then paint her left hand red, omitting the ring finger, and have her press her hand below the right handprint, as shown. When the paint is dry, encourage her to add a face and a white circle cutout labeled either "Thing 1" or "Thing 2." Cut out the projects and display them on a wall around a cake cutout decorated by your youngsters. Then add the title "Happy Birthday, Dr. Seuss!" 🖥

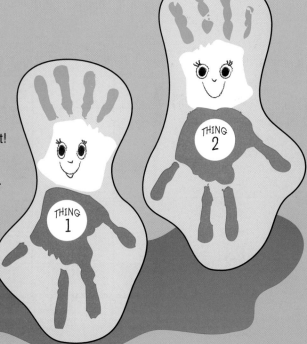

Carey Simone, Giggles & Grins Child Care Center
Plantsville, CT

🍀 A Leprechaun Trap 🍀

Speaking in a play situation

Gather a variety of items such as a box, craft sticks, shamrock cutouts, pom-poms, a spatula, a wooden board, crayons, and tape. Place the items at a center and encourage youngsters to use the items to build a trap for a leprechaun. Encourage students to communicate and work together as they build. When students are gone for the day, place class treats at the center along with a note from a leprechaun, such as the one shown. The next day, read the note aloud and share the treats. 🖥

Barb Samoray, Dodson Chapel Childcare
Hermitage, TN

Dear Preschoolers,
You have built a very fine trap indeed, but I am too tricky. You didn't catch me this time! I have left you a special leprechaun treat because you are excellent workers.

Yours truly,
Fergus O'Sullivan, Leprechaun

Editor's Tip:
To keep this center fresh and inviting, remove and add different materials each day! This will challenge youngsters' problem-solving and fine-motor skills. Who knows—it may even increase their chances of catching a leprechaun!

💜 Splendid Sweets! 💜

Identifying letters

Make a supersize heart cutout so it resembles a box of chocolates. Label the heart with a variety of letters and place it on the floor. Cut out several brown construction paper copies of the chocolate patterns on page 287 and place them near the heart. Encourage a child to point to and name a letter. Then have him place a chocolate on the letter and prompt youngsters to say, "Yum, yum!" Continue until all the letters are covered. 🖥

Heart Patterns
Use with "Lovely Colors" on page 283.

TEC41053

TEC41053

TEC41053

TEC41053

Penny Pattern
Use with "Find the Penny" on page 284.

TEC41053

Chocolate Patterns
Use with "Splendid Sweets!" on page 285.

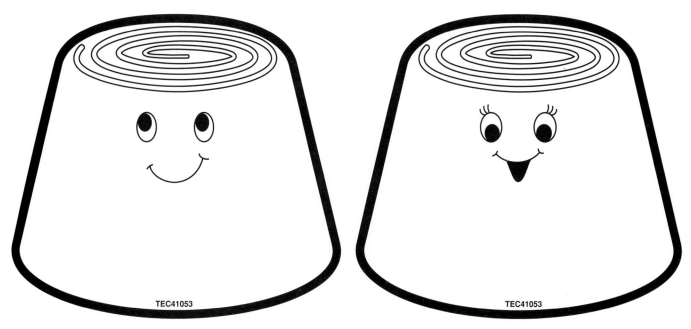

TEC41053

TEC41053

The Splendid Five Senses!

Youngsters will be all ears for this collection of activities on the five senses!

A Song of Senses

This toe-tapping ditty is perfect for introducing little ones to the five senses. Name each of the five senses and invite youngsters to name the body part used to experience that sense. Then lead youngsters in singing the song shown, changing the body part and sense for each verse. 🖳

(sung to the tune of "The Farmer in the Dell")

We use our [ears] to [hear].
We use our [ears] to [hear].
Heigh-ho, what do you know?
We use our [ears] to [hear].

Debbie Bartsch, Gloria Dei Preschool, Crestview Hills, KY

Tootsy Touches

Place a variety of textured items—such as pieces of Bubble Wrap cushioning material, corrugated cardboard, linoleum, tile, sandpaper, faux fur, and carpet—in a center. Invite each child to visit the center and remove his shoes and socks. Then encourage him to walk on the different materials, noticing the different textures.

Marie E. Cecchini
West Dundee, IL

Sweet, Sour, or Salty?

Tickle little ones' taste buds with this fun taste test. Collect a lemon wedge, an M&M's Minis candy, and a potato chip for each child. Display three tongue cutouts labeled as shown. Encourage each child to taste the lemon. Then have the students determine whether a lemon is salty, sour, or sweet. Write *lemon* on the appropriate tongue cutout. Then have students name other foods that are sour. Write their ideas on the tongue. Continue with each remaining food sample. 🖳

Deborah Garmon
Groton, CT

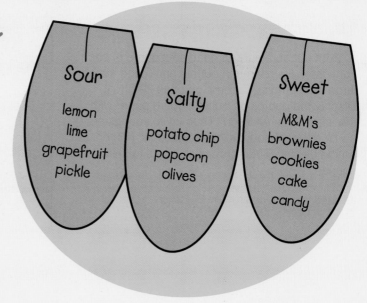

Sour
lemon
lime
grapefruit
pickle

Salty
potato chip
popcorn
olives

Sweet
M&M's
brownies
cookies
cake
candy

Squeeze a Scent

Gather scented liquids, such as baking extracts, scented oils, and vinegar. Place a few drops of each liquid on a separate cotton ball. Then place each cotton ball in a separate empty squeeze-style water bottle. Sit in a circle with youngsters. Demonstrate how to squeeze a bottle and smell the scent inside it. Pass the bottle to a child and invite him to squeeze the bottle and sniff before he passes it to the child beside him. When everyone has had a turn, ask youngsters to describe the scent and discuss whether or not they like it. Repeat the process with other bottles.

Leigh Ann Panorelli
Merrimack Valley YMCA Childcare and Enrichment Center
Lawrence, MA

It's a Tie

In advance, gather several ties of varying patterns and colors. Display the ties and invite volunteers to describe each one. Ask students to close their eyes. Remove and conceal one of the ties. Have little ones open their eyes and name the missing tie. After the correct tie is named, return it to its place and play another round. If desired, make the game more challenging by removing two ties.

Marie E. Cecchini
West Dundee, IL

We're All Ears

Print out an enlarged head shot photo of each youngster. Help him cut out his photo and attach large ear cutouts (patterns on page 291) to it. Display the photos on bulletin board paper with the title "We're All Ears!" Then invite youngsters to name different sounds. Write students' responses on the display. Then prompt students to imitate the sounds.

adapted from an idea by Ann E. Fisher
Toledo, OH

We're All Ears!

television

dog barking

doorbell ringing

fingers snapping

kitchen mixer

Pudding

Sweet Observations

Pudding is the perfect snack to encourage little ones to use a variety of senses. Give each child an unopened pudding cup and a spoon and guide students in following the steps below.
1. Shake the cup. Discuss the sound it makes.
2. Open the cup and look at the pudding. Discuss how the pudding looks, being sure to notice the color and texture.
3. Smell the pudding. Discuss the scent of the pudding and what flavor it might be.
4. Taste the pudding. Discuss the flavor of the pudding and whether it matches the flavor predicted during Step 3.

Alyson Flanagan
Riverton School
Riverton, NJ

Body Part Collage

Give students a fine-motor workout with this activity! Label a sheet of chart paper as shown. Provide a supply of magazines, scissors, and glue sticks. A child searches through a magazine for pictures of body parts used to experience the senses. He cuts them out and then glues the hands, eyes, noses, ears, and mouths to the paper. Youngsters continue until the paper is filled.

adapted from an idea by Toni-Ann Maisano and Desiree Magnani
Babes in Toyland Preschool
Staten Island, NY

The Five Senses

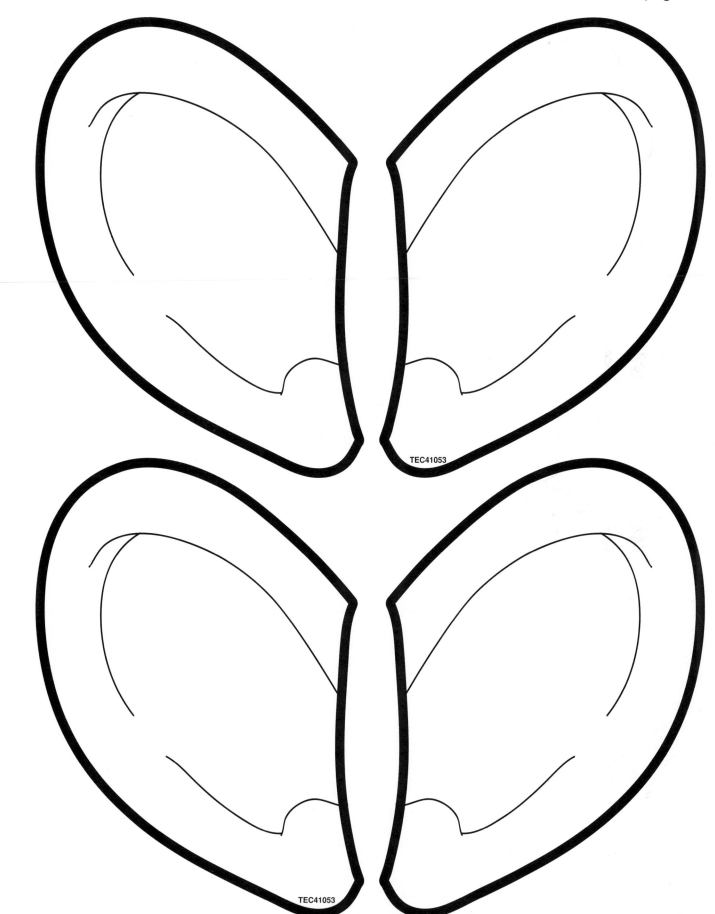

TEC41053

TEC41053

Excellent Eggs!

Spotlight the incredible egg with this selection of "egg-citing" ideas!

What's Hatching?

Investigating living things

What could be hatching from these eggs? Your youngsters find out with this fun circle-time activity! Cut out a copy of the cards on page 294 and place them on the floor. Cover each card with an egg cutout. Lead students in singing the song shown. Then invite a child to remove an egg and identify the animal beneath it. Reinforce that this animal hatches from an egg. Then sing another round of the song and encourage a different child to uncover an egg. 🖥

(sung to the tune of "London Bridge")

Eggs are breaking all around,
All around, all around.
Hear their crunching, cracking sound.
What is hatching?

chicken

For an "egg-stra" activity option, place a combination of cards from page 294 and page 302 on the floor. Have little ones place egg cutouts on the animals that hatch from eggs.

Sunny-Side Up, Please!

Developing role-playing skills

You're sure to see a lot of sunny smiles at this breakfast diner dramatic-play area! Provide the props listed below. Then explain that there are many ways to cook eggs. Have students share their knowledge of cooked eggs. Further explain the ways to cook eggs, such as hard-boiling them, deviling them, frying them sunny-side up or once over, scrambling them, and making them into omelets. Encourage youngsters to visit the center and order or cook their favorite eggs. 🖥

Props

plastic eggs
fried eggs fashioned from craft foam
yellow and white play dough (for making egg creations)
plastic deviled egg plate
sanitized egg cartons
frying pans
pots
aprons
notepads and crayons
plates
silverware
play cash register

Nest Builders

Developing fine-motor skills

Place a shallow box at a table and provide a variety of nest-building materials, such as branches, twigs, cotton balls, ribbon, yarn, cotton batting, and leaves. Also provide plastic eggs. If desired, post pictures of nests around the area. A youngster visits the center and practices her nest-building skills by making a nest in the box!

Erin Hedstrom, Bright Beginnings Childcare, Princeton, MN

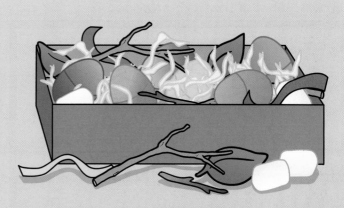

Egg Stands

Patterning

Cut cardboard tubes into several rings, as shown, to make egg stands. Provide a basket of plastic eggs. A child places several egg stands in a row. Then she sits eggs in the stands to make a pattern and reads her pattern aloud. **For an option that targets counting**, use a permanent marker to write numbers on the eggs. Then prompt her to place the eggs in the stands in numerical order. **For an option that targets ordinal numbers**, place four stands in a row and place a different-color egg on each stand. Then ask youngsters questions such as "Which egg is third?" or "In which position is the blue egg?"

Marie E. Cecchini, West Dundee, IL
Carrie Froman, Gypsum View Preschool, Gypsum, CO

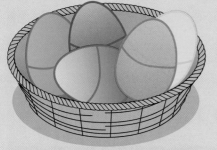

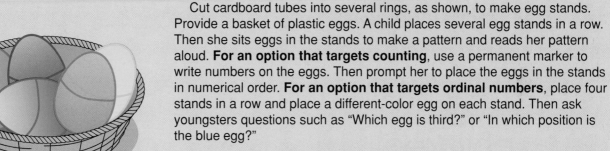

What's Inside?

Listening, developing new vocabulary

Help youngsters understand the interior of an egg with this listen-and-do activity! Gather a small group of students and give each child a copy of page 295. Have each child point to the shell of the egg. Encourage him to run his finger beneath the word *shell* as he says the word. Next, instruct him to repeat the process with the egg white and the yolk. Encourage him to color the yolk yellow. Then explain that a baby bird (or other animal) is in the yolk. In fact, the yolk is its food while it's in the egg. Have him glue a small pink pom-pom to the yolk so it represents a baby bird.

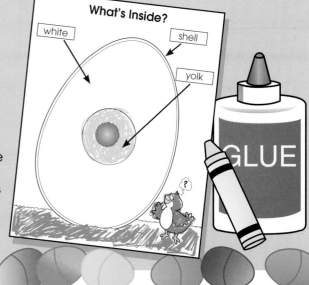

What's Inside?

white

shell

yolk

snake
TEC41054

turtle
TEC41054

chicken
TEC41054

duck
TEC41054

lizard
TEC41054

crocodile
TEC41054

owl
TEC41054

platypus
TEC41054

What's Inside?

white

shell

yolk

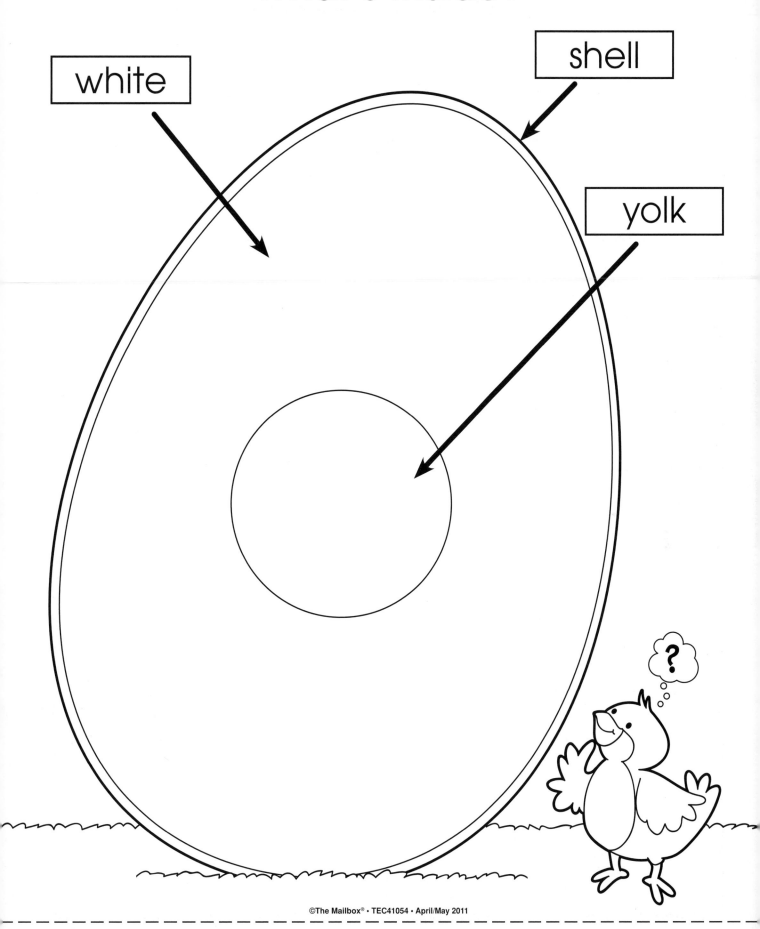

Note to the teacher: Use with "What's Inside?" on page 293.

THE MAILBOX **295**

Awesome Animal Babies

Puppies, calves, chicks, and cubs! Spotlight baby animals with these cute-as-can-be activities.

Wandering Chicks

Making sets, counting

These chicks are on the loose! Have little ones bring some order to the chaos with this marvelous math activity! Gather a supply of large yellow pom-poms (chicks) and scatter them around your circle-time area. Say, "Oh my goodness, all the chicks have gotten loose!" Give each child a hen cutout (enlarged copy of the pattern on page 299) labeled with a number. Have each child name his number. Then encourage him to find the appropriate number of chicks and place them on his hen so that the chicks are back with their mothers. Check each hen for accuracy. If desired, collect and redistribute the hens for another round. 🖥

Growing Up

Ordering by size, sorting

Make copies of the cards on page 302 in three different sizes, reducing and enlarging as needed. Cut out the cards and place them at a table. A child sorts the cards by animal. Then she orders each set of cards by size to show the animal growing bigger as it ages. 🖥

Roxanne LaBell Dearman, Western NC Early Intervention Program for Children Who Are Deaf or Hard of Hearing, Charlotte, NC

Searching Mamas
Participating in a song

Cut out the animal mother cards from pages 300 and 301 and place them in a bag. Have a child choose a card, identify the animal, and name its baby. Then lead youngsters in singing the song shown, inserting the appropriate names and then making the animal's sound at the end of the song. Continue with each remaining animal card. 💻

(sung to the tune of "Mary Had a Little Lamb")

Mama [bear] can't find her [cubs],
Find her [cubs], find her [cubs].
Mama [bear] can't find her [cubs]
Until she hears them call.

Baby Bunny Burrow
Investigating living things

Youngsters peek in a bunny burrow with this simple project! In advance, gather a large disposable cup for each child. Also make a class supply of brown circle cutouts that fit the opening of the cups. To begin, explain that baby bunnies are called kits and many kits live in burrows, which are holes or tunnels dug in the ground. Have each child attach bunny stickers to the circle (or draw bunnies on the circle). Then help her attach the circle to the cup opening so the bunnies are facing inward and poke a hole in the bottom of the cup. The child can peek through the hole and view the bunnies in their burrow!

Charlotte Merchlewicz, Merchlewicz Family Daycare, Saint Cloud, MN

Pass the Kitten
Rhyming

Obtain a stuffed toy kitten and toy puppy. Tell students that you brought a baby cat to school. Have youngsters identify the name of a baby cat. Then reveal the kitten toy and give it to a child. Prompt the child to say the word *kitten* and then a real or nonsense rhyming word. Encourage him to pat the kitten on the head and then give it to a classmate. Prompt the new youngster to come up with another real of nonsense rhyming word. After several rounds, repeat the activity with the puppy.

Baby Names

Developing new vocabulary

Little ones learn the names of animal babies with this toe-tapping song! Cut out the cards from pages 300 and 301. Order the baby animal cards in your pocket chart to correspond with the song. Then give a youngster a pointer. Prompt the child to point to the appropriate cards as you lead students in singing the song. 💻

(sung to the tune of "Go in and out the Window")

A baby cat's a kitten.
A baby dog's a puppy.
A baby duck's a duckling,
A baby bear's a cub.

A baby pig's a piglet
A baby owl's an owlet.
A baby swan's a cygnet.
A baby seal's a pup.

Jacquiline Schiff, Moline, IL

Piglet Play

Developing fine-motor skills

Cut out several copies of the piglet patterns on page 299 and attach each one to a craft stick. Place a supply of brown play dough at a table. A youngster molds and shapes the play dough to make big mud puddles. Then she stands the little piglets in the mud. What messy fun! 💻

Who Lives There?

Extending a story

Read aloud *Growing Like Me* by Anne Rockwell. In this story, a little boy identifies animal babies and the adult animals they will grow into. At the end of the story, ask youngsters what other animal babies could be found in a setting similar to the story's. (If needed, prompt them with the suggestions shown.) Write their ideas on a sheet of chart paper. Then encourage each child to draw a picture of an animal baby not in the book. Have him cut out his picture and slide it into the book. Place the book in your reading center and encourage youngsters to look at their classmates additions.

ANNE ROCKWELL
Growing Like Me
Illustrated by
HOLLY KELLER

Suggested animal babies:
turtle (hatchling)
bear (cub)
dear (fawn)
beaver (kit)
fox (pup)
raccoon (kit)
squirrel (kit)
snake (neonate)

TEC41054

Piglet Pattern
Use with "Piglet Play" on page 298.

TEC41054

TEC41054

Animal Cards

Use with "Searching Mamas" on page 297 and "Baby Names" on page 298.
Also use the cards for mother and baby matching activities and naming activities.

dog
TEC41054

puppy
TEC41054

cat
TEC41054

kitten
TEC41054

duck
TEC41054

duckling
TEC41054

bear
TEC41054

cub
TEC41054

Animal Cards

Use with "Searching Mamas" on page 297 and "Baby Names" on page 298.
Also use the cards for mother and baby matching activities and naming activities.

pig TEC41054

piglet TEC41054

owl TEC41054

owlet TEC41054

swan TEC41054

cygnet TEC41054

seal TEC41054

pup TEC41054

Animal Cards

Use with "What's Hatching?" on page 292 and "Growing Up" on page 296.

TEC41054

TEC41054

TEC41054

TEC41054

TEC41054

TEC41054

TEC41054

TEC41054

Let's Explore the Ocean!

Fish and crabs and coral, oh my! Get ready for a wave of excitement to wash over your classroom when little ones investigate the ocean with these activities.

Preschool Pincers

Investigating living things, developing fine-motor skills

Preschoolers get plenty of pincer-grip practice when they pretend to be crabs! Place pieces of green craft foam (water plants) in your water table. Then place an empty container nearby. Show youngsters a picture of a crab, leading them to notice its claws. Then encourage students to move their thumbs and pointer fingers to imitate crab claws. Tell students that some crabs eat seaweed and algae. Then encourage little ones to visit the center and pretend to be crabs, using their pincer grasp to pick up water plants and place them in the container.

Roxanne LaBell Dearman
Western NC Early Intervention Program for Children Who
    Are Deaf or Hard of Hearing
Charlotte, NC

My squid is bigger than this crayon.

That's Big!

Measurement

Read aloud *I'm the Biggest Thing in the Ocean* by Kevin Sherry. In this hilarious story, a giant squid brags about being bigger than shrimp, a crab, and other ocean animals. But will a whale stop its bragging? Not likely! After the read-aloud, have each child make a simple squid that resembles the main character of the story. (Don't forget the bulbous eyes!) Have a child "swim" his squid around the room, looking for an object smaller than the squid. When he finds such an object, encourage him to say, "My squid is bigger than this [object's name]." Continue with each remaining child.

adapted from a idea by Roxanne LaBell Dearman

Fishnet Treasures

Expressing oneself through art

Place a piece of a fishnet (or plastic canvas or mesh produce bag) over a sheet of green paper. Sponge-paint the net and paper blue. Then remove the net. Next, glue fish cutouts, crab cutouts, and dyed seashell pasta to the paper. What a fabulous catch! 🖥

Marie E. Cecchini, West Dundee, IL

Splendid Ocean Song

Participating in a song

Lead little ones in several rounds of this fun action song! 🖥

(sung to the tune of "The Wheels on the Bus")

The [waves] in the ocean go [in and out],   *[Sweep arms back and forth.]*
[In and out, in and out].
The [waves] in the ocean go [in and out]
All through the day.   *Shake pointer finger to beat.*

Continue with the following:
turtles; snap, snap, snap   *Move hands like snapping jaws.*
fish; swim, swim, swim   *Shake hips.*
sharks; chomp, chomp, chomp   *Move arms like chomping jaws.*
swimmers; splash, splash, splash   *Pretend to swim.*
coral; (silence), (silence), (silence)   *Strike a pose to resemble coral branches.*
lobsters; click, click, click   *Move hands like snapping pincers.*

Diana Visser, Castle Academy, Castle Rock, CO

The Daily Vote!

Graphing, using comparison words

Youngsters share their preferred sea creatures with this idea! Cut out a copy of the cards on pages 307 and 308, discarding the squirrel, cow, and dog cards. Place a simple graph on your floor and place two sea creature cards on the graph. Give each child a seashell (or a sticky note) and have him place it on the graph to show his preferred sea creature. Then count the seashells in each column and compare the amounts using the words *more, less,* and *equal.* Repeat the process the next day with two new sea creatures! 🖥

Loree Boyd
Downingtown Educational Center
Downingtown, PA

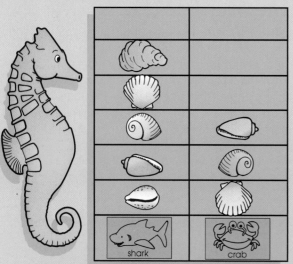

Dive Beneath the Ocean

Developing vocabulary, sorting

What creatures live in the ocean? Youngsters find out with this easy idea! Cut out a copy of the picture cards on pages 307 and 308. Place them on the floor and cover them with a blue blanket (water). A child "dives" under the water and retrieves a card. He holds up the card and youngsters name the creature. Then they decide whether the animal lives in the ocean. If it does, the child places the card in a designated area. If it doesn't, youngsters say, "That doesn't belong there!" and then the child sets the card aside. Continue with each remaining card.

Trudi Wagner, Cherub's Haven, Linwood, MA

Sharks and Minnows

Developing gross-motor skills

You're sure to get repeated requests for this whole-group game! Have little ones (minnows) line up on one side of a spacious room. Stand in the middle of the room with other adult helpers and pretend to be sharks. Encourage the minnows to cross the room using a specific gross-motor movement. Use the same type of movement as you attempt to tag the youngsters. When a child is tagged, she kneels on the floor and pretends to be a sea anemone, using her arms to tag other minnows. Continue having minnows cross the area until there are only a few left!

Aletha Scheck, Crown of Life Lutheran School, Colleyville, TX

A Stellar Craft

Investigating living things, developing fine-motor skills

Trace a sea star shape on a piece of waxed paper for each student. Mix yellow cornmeal and white glue. Have each child observe a sea star tracing and notice that it has five arms. Tell students that most sea stars have five arms but some can have as many as 40! Give each child a dollop of the mixture on his tracing and encourage him to form it into the sea star shape. Allow the project to dry for several days. Then peel it from the waxed paper.

Cathy Calder, Roswell, NM

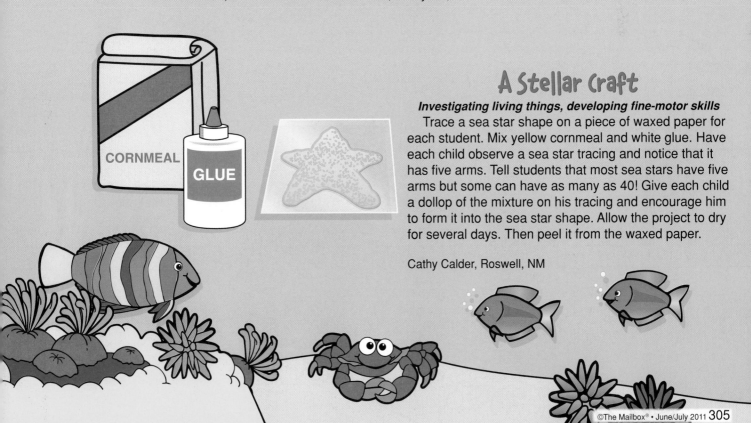

Alphabet Chomp
Identifying letters

This hungry shark is looking for some letters! Have each child color a sealed business-size envelope gray. Cut a triangle from the envelope to make a mouth. Then encourage her to attach the triangle cutout to the envelope to make a fin. Have her attach yarn gills and rickrack teeth. Next, gather a small group of youngsters with their sharks. Give each youngster an identical set of letter cards. Then say, "Mr. Shark is hungry for the letter [letter name]!" Prompt each child to find the corresponding letter card and place it in her shark's mouth. Continue with each remaining card. 💻

Angie Kutzer, Burlington, NC

Five Little Fishies
Developing presubtraction skills

It's bedtime for these tired little fish! Lead students in performing this action rhyme four times, changing the number in the first line as appropriate. Then have them perform the final verse shown. 💻

[Five] little fishies swimming in the sea,
Jumping, diving, happy as can be.
One little fishy got tired and said,
"See you fish later. I'm off to bed!"

Hold up [five] fingers.
Put hands together and make small diving motions.
Hold up one finger.
Wave goodbye.

Final verse:
One little fishy swimming in the sea,
Jumping, diving, happy as can be.
That little fishy got tired and said,
"Now it's my turn to go to bed!"

Hold up one finger.
Put hands together and make small diving motions.
Hold up one finger.
Throw arms out to sides.

Sarah Berkey, Growing Tree Preschool, Chambersburg, PA

Picture Cards

Use with "The Daily Vote!" on page 304 and "Dive Beneath the Ocean" on page 305.

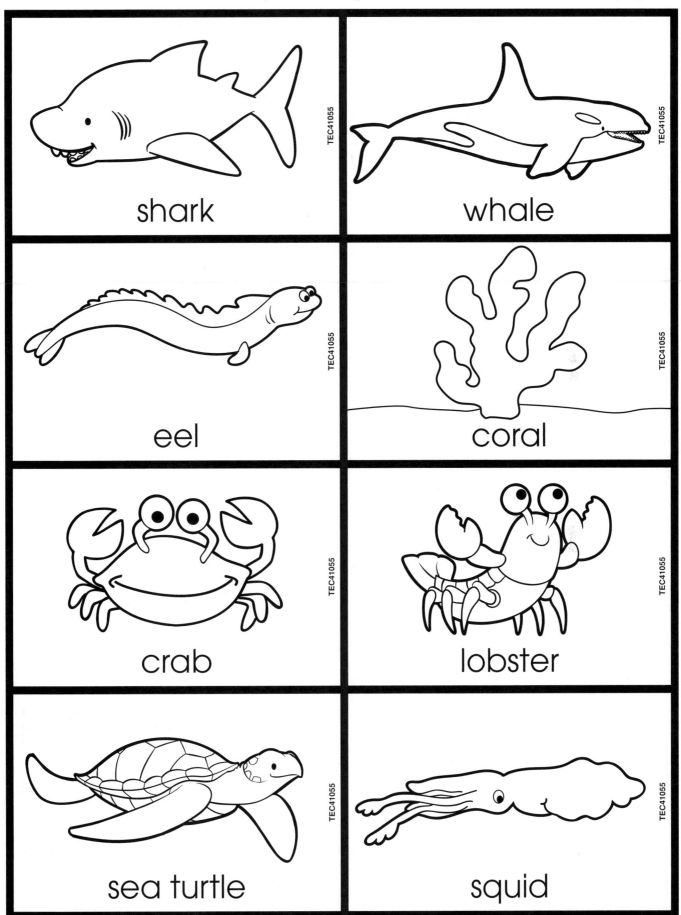

shark

whale

eel

coral

crab

lobster

sea turtle

squid

Picture Cards

Use with "The Daily Vote!" on page 304 and "Dive Beneath the Ocean" on page 305.

dolphin

octopus

jellyfish

seahorse

sea anemone

squirrel

cow

dog

Cool Tools

Combine preschoolers and an engaging unit on tools, and what to you get? Why, you get busy youngsters developing new vocabulary and fine-motor skills, that's what!

Where Does It Belong?

Developing vocabulary, sorting

Youngsters will be eager to rearrange this sorting disaster! Cut out a copy of the people patterns on page 311 and place the people in separate plastic hoops. Also place kitchen and construction tools in the hoops at random. Point to the chef and have students identify her occupation. Then indicate the tools in the hoop and explain that you believe a chef would use these in her kitchen. Have students identify the tools. No doubt they will explain that many of these tools aren't appropriate for a chef! Repeat the process with the construction worker tools. Then have students help you sort the tools correctly. 🖥

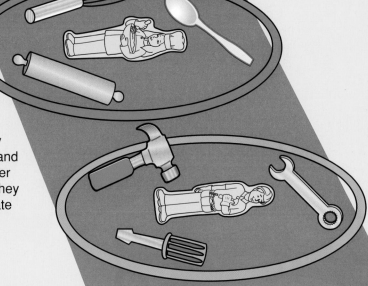

Open-Ended Exploring

Creative thinking

Wonderful things happen when you provide tools and a variety of unrelated items! Place at a table several tools, such as a whisk, a toy screwdriver, a garden trowel, a rolling pin, and a toy wrench. Also provide random classroom items, such as play dough, bear counters, and pipe cleaners. Invite students to the center to explore, investigate, and create!

Go to page 312 for a tool-themed **reproducible literacy activity**!

How Long?

Measurement

Youngsters explore measurement tools with this open-ended center. Gather fabric measuring tapes, rulers, and yardsticks. Give youngsters a basic demonstration of how to measure with the items. Then place them in a center. Youngsters visit the center and explore the tools, using them to pretend to measure items in the classroom.

Anastacia Zahl, Noodle Noggin Learning House, Eagan, MN

Make a Copy

Developing new vocabulary, speaking

Place several tools on your copy machine and make a copy. Repeat the process with another set of tools. Then place the tools in a bag and gather students around the copies. Have a child choose a tool from the bag. Help her identify the tool and name what it might be used for. Then encourage her to place it on top of the matching picture. Continue with each remaining tool.

Robin Russell
Tiny Tech Child Development Center
Fond du Lac, WI

Hammer and Pop!

Developing fine-motor skills

This outdoor activity is perfect for summer! During outdoor playtime, provide pieces of Bubble Wrap cushioning material and toy hammers. Encourage youngsters to place the cushioning material on a sidewalk or cemented area. Then prompt him to hit the cushioning material with the hammer. Pop, pop, pop!

Suzanne Foote, East Ithaca Preschool
Ithaca, NY

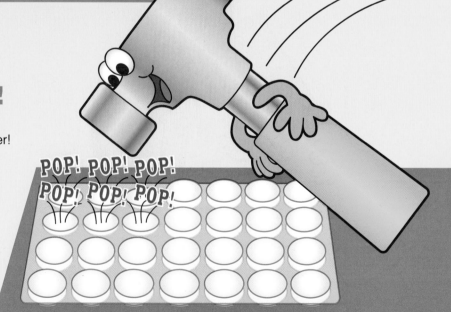

POP! POP! POP!
POP! POP! POP!

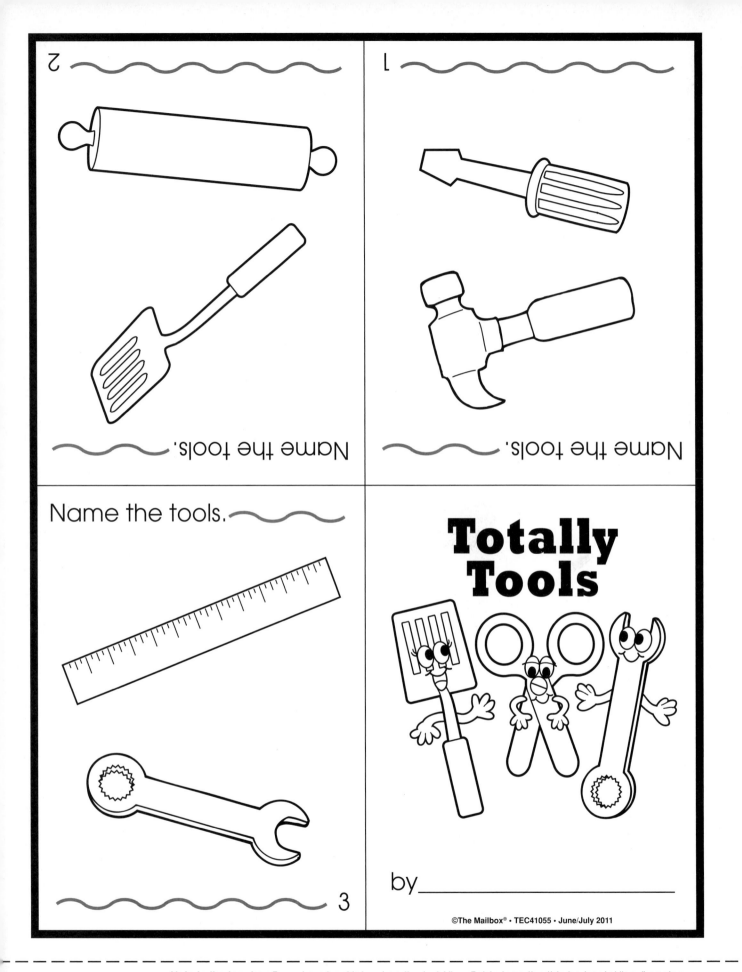

Totally Tools

by_____

©The Mailbox® • TEC41055 • June/July 2011

Name the tools.

2

Name the tools.

1

Name the tools.

3

Note to the teacher: To make a booklet, cut on the bold line. Fold along the thin horizontal line (keeping the programming to the outside) and then fold along the thin vertical line (keeping the cover to the outside). Read each booklet page aloud and help the student name the tools.

INDEX